THE LETTERS OF
OLIVE SCHREINER
1876—1920

OLIVE SCHREINER, 1897.

Frontispiece.

THE LETTERS OF OLIVE SCHREINER

1876–1920 · *Edited by*

S. C. CRONWRIGHT-SCHREINER

ILLUSTRATED

T. FISHER UNWIN LTD
LONDON: ADELPHI TERRACE

First published . . . . . *October* 1924
Second Impression . . *November* 1924

PREFACE

I<small>N</small> the Preface to *The Life of Olive Schreiner*, I stated that book would soon be followed by a volume to be called *The Letters of Olive Schreiner*, adding "Though the *Life* is complete without the *Letters*, they may be regarded as a necessary complement to the *Life*. Largely if not wholly autobiographical and often constituting a kind of intimate diary from day to day, they are essential to the understanding of her inner life."

This volume has been unavoidably delayed by several causes, one of them being the unexpected receipt from several sources, almost at the last moment, of some four hundred or more letters, making in all, I should say, a total of nearly six thousand from which selections have been made. Not many have been published in full ; it has seemed best to give only such parts as may be considered illuminatingly autobiographical or otherwise of general interest. I do not think there can be many more letters extant that would add much of interest to what is contained in this volume.

A few words as to her manner of writing letters may serve to explain certain obvious peculiarities, for I have refrained as far as possible from touching them, especially the punctuation, the unusual use at times of the personal pronouns and the construction of some of her sentences. My first comment is that letter-writing was a form of her imperative impulse to express herself to others, and constituted also a mild form of physical exercise. She once said to me of herself that, just as walking or other muscular exertion was essential to the bodily health of some people, so talking was to others, that talking was not merely a mental relief and stimulus, but was, in its other effect, a physical and renovating exercise. This was true. Even when far from well, several hours of keen, animated, strenuous talk revived her, as a long, swinging walk did others. So, when she had read enough, and had no adequate opportunity for talk, and, from weariness or other cause, was unable or disinclined to tackle her literary work, she would fly to letter-writing ; indeed, it almost seemed at times that she resorted to letter-writing as a justification for postponing her more arduous literary work. Apart from thinking, she did not like, she was averse to, any form, of close, continuous, systematic work, mental or physical ; and letter-writing was easy and was not so lonely. Usually such writing was done rapidly, impetuously, carelessly, and almost invariably without any revision or re-reading. It is noteworthy too that her letters, even to public persons on important public questions, such as those to W. T. Stead, are as careless, undated, often written on odd, unmatched scraps of paper, hard to piece together, as those to her intimate friends. She wrote with absorption, and at times, as it were, with a kind of unconsciousness ; she might begin a letter with name of place (omitting the date and putting merely the day of the week), " My dear So-and-So," and perhaps a few lines, then lay it aside and so leave it ; she might do the same with a half-written letter ; sometimes with a complete letter, forgetting all about it. These habits will explain some obvious defects which could hardly have escaped correction if the letters had been re-read, however hurriedly ; they no doubt account, too, for the curious fact that she wrote so many commonplace letters (nearly all omitted in this volume) about commonplace things, and at times as though she were expressing herself warily or " writing down " to her correspondent in matter and form, at others as though her mind at the moment were in a state akin to Wordsworth's when he was in merely a rhyming mood, and not in a state of " inspiration " ; though, even then, she would at times, as he used to, flash into a commonplace utterance something brief but glorious.

Letters and extracts from letters to Havelock Ellis are most numerous in this volume, notwithstanding that the greater number were addressed to myself. This is

due mainly to the purposeful inclusion of a copious selec-
tion from her letters to him from 1884, when she first met
him, to the end of 1889, when she first returned to South
Africa, and then on to the end of 1892, when she first met
me.   It was, it seemed to me, especially of interest to do
this, as these letters are almost the only continuous detailed
record of importance throughout the time she was a young
woman in a new and strange environment.   Ellis married
late in 1891 and Olive early in 1894.   With the new
conditions and with six thousand miles of the " unplumbed,
salt, estranging sea " between them, it was natural, perhaps
inevitable, that the intervals between the letters should
be longer ; but they never ceased, and were continued
until her death.   Nor did their great friendship cease ;
the man whom she once described as her " oldest and best
friend " remained such, and in addition became the friend
of her husband.

Her letters to me from 1892 to 1901, and of 1920 are
dealt with in the *Life* ; so that only a very few of them
appear here.

In addition to the letters, this volume contains also
certain appendixes, thus completing all I purpose publishing
from her pen in permanent form, except " The Dawn of
Civilization," which is to be added to all further reprints
and editions of *Stories, Dreams, and Allegories,* and her two
novels, *Perhaps only——* (*From Man to Man*) and *Undine.*

And so I complete my contribution to a study of genius
by one who loved, and lived in long, close and continuous
contact with, a woman of genius, having thus had the rare
opportunity of watching, not only with loving interest and
tender devotion, but also with reverential scientific ardour,
a quality of mind strange and wonderful in its manifestations
and in some of its physical reactions.

S. C. CRONWRIGHT-SCHREINER.

LONDON,
August 1924

*With deep gratitude I thank those who so kindly placed
letters at my disposal for use in this volume : Mrs. John Brown,
Edward Carpenter, Mrs. C. A. F. Rhys Davids, Havelock*

Ellis (and for a letter to his wife, Edith), Miss Louie Ellis, Miss Emily Hobhouse, F. W. Pethick Lawrence, Mrs. F. W. (Emilene) Pethick Lawrence, J. T. Lloyd, Mrs. Haldane Murray, Mrs. J. H. (Isalene) Philpot, Mrs. W. F. (Anna) Purcell, Mrs. Francis (Adela Villiers) Smith, Mrs. E. J. (Clifford Cawood) Stanley (for letters to herself, and to Mrs. R. Cawood, Willie and Dora Cawood, now dead), W. T. Stead (his representatives), Dr. King Roberts, Mrs. Tenney (formerly Mrs. Mary King Roberts), and T. Fisher Unwin.

CONTENTS

CONTENTS

CHAPTER XIII

PAGE

ILLUSTRATIONS

THE LETTERS OF
OLIVE SCHREINER

The Letters of Olive Schreiner

CHAPTER I

FROM SOUTH AFRICA 1876 TO 1881, FROM ENGLAND 1881 TO 1883

1876

To Mrs. R. Cawood. Victoria Hotel, Cradock, *5th May.*
(*On her way to Ratel Hoek from Klein Ganna Hoek.*)

I don't know when I felt more lonely in my life. I wish you were here my dear old friend. I don't think you can understand how much you have brightened and gladdened the year I have past at Ganna Hoek. Give my love to the dear little people.

To Mrs. Cawood.   Ratel Hoek, *8th Sept.*

I have thought so much of you, and you would hardly believe how I wish to see you. You must get strong, very strong. I could not spare you out of the world. . . . I am very well and comfortable. Ratel Hoek is as much better than Ganna Hoek as Ganna Hoek was better than Colesberg and for both these good changes I have to thank you.

1877

To Willie Cawood (*the second son*).
    Ratel Hoek, *4th April.*

I suppose by this time you've quite forgotten me and when you get this letter you have to sit for half an hour and rub your head before you can remember who Olive

2

Schreiner was. I'm afraid so, but hope not, for I don't like big people or little people to forget me if I love them.

We are having very great storms here. One night, just in the middle of the night, I thought the house was struck by the lightning and in the morning we found four sheep dead in the kraal close by the house. You can't think what a place for snakes this is, Will. This morning Mrs. Aurett heard a funny hissing noise in the parlour, and Mr. Aurett went in and killed a big yellow snake just by the piano. And the other day when we went into the school-room we saw a great fellow lying asleep in one corner of the room. He was too lazy to run away. He just looked up at us, as much as to say, "What do you mean by making such a noise and waking me up?" and then he went to sleep again, so we soon killed him. Now when we go to school we always peep in the corners to see if his brother has not come to look for him. There's a nice little schoolmaster here to-day, but I don't think you would like him to be your schoolmaster. Guess what he does when the boys are naughty ! He has a stick with the end all split, and he sticks it into their hair, and twists, and twists, till he gets a little bunch of hair out. If I was one of his boys I would cut my hair so short that there was not any left for him to pull.

To Mrs. Cawood.   Ratel Hoek, 8*th Sept.*

. . . I don't know how it is, I seem to have met more likeable people in the course of the last year than in all the rest of my life. Perhaps I am growing less critical, perhaps more stupid and less able to see their faults. . . .

To Mrs. Cawood.   Kat Kop, 4*th Nov.*

[She had just heard " the joyful news " that Mr. Martin was sending for the wagon almost at once to take them back to Ratel Hoek ; the van Heerdens had been very kind but the house so full. When in Cradock she saw the Fouches] : " Mother Fouche says that Stoffel [her husband] is determined that, when Annie [Fouche] has been a year in Cradock, I shall come back to them. . . . Ratel Hoek does not suit my chest but I could not be more comfortable anywhere."

To Mrs. Cawood.   Tarkastad, *9th Dec.*

I wish you were here to talk matters over with me. I know you always make my affairs your own. The Tarkastad people want me to come and open a school here. The Dr, the Magistrate, Mr. Barker, Mr. Souter (all big guns here) would support me, and it would pay splendidly ; but there are some poor girls who have a school here, and my coming would knock it on the head at once. I can't face that. It would[n't] be right, and yet, if I don't come, they will only send for someone to England. As the boy said, "If I don't eat the apples somebody else will." Mr. Martin would I know send his little girls in as boarders, and a great many other country people would do the same. I might, after ten years or so, save enough to go home [England] and study. It's all very well to say one can teach and study at the same time, but after five hours of school keeping the spring is out of you. Every evening when school comes out I go to my room and don't leave my books till ten or eleven, except for supper, and yet it's very little I am able to do. Of course before breakfast I have to go for a little walk and do my needle-work and the days pass and I seem to stay just where I am.

[In a footnote she adds] : " I have made up my mind not to come here."

1878

To Mrs. Cawood.   Seymour, *17th Jan.*

. . . My year at Ratel Hoek is up on the 10th May, and if I wished I could leave, and I have such a great wish to come and teach your children, that I would offer myself to you if it were not for one thing. As far as the mere teaching goes, I don't think you would be at all disappointed in me but I'm getting to live so much in my books and my scribbling, that I'm not a bit a bright, pleasant person to have in a house. I can't bear to think of your being disappointed in me in any way. Can you understand the feeling ? It's just because I love you so much that I have it. A stranger would think me unsociable and disagreeable, and I would not care, if they only thought I did my work well ; but with you it is quite different. . . . Will [her brother] is now with us. I don't know what he would seem to other eyes, to mine he is satisfying and joy-giving. This meeting with him has been one of the most unmixed joys that has ever been given me.

To KATIE, HER SISTER.   SEYMOUR, 4*th Feb*.

. . . I am as you see still at Seymour but I think I shall be leaving next week. . . . The [Kaffir] war is still on, and is nearer to us now than ever, but I don't think we are in any real danger just yet. All the men in the district are armed. We got 300 fresh guns from Fort Beaufort last week.

To KATIE, HER SISTER.   TARKASTAD, 10*th March*.

[She tells of her brother's Will's engagement to Miss Fanny Reitz, and continues] : I am now in Tarkastad, waiting for Mr. Martin to come and fetch me. I am much better, only a little weak and shall be quite strong when I get out to the farm and drink lots of milk. I can't tell you how kind everyone was to me in Queenstown. In spite of all the pain and weakness the time spent there will always stand out like a sunny dream.

[In a letter from Ratel Hoek, early in 1878 but undated, she says she strums a good deal at the piano] : I am always thirsting for beautiful, beautiful, beautiful music. I wish I could make it. Perhaps there isn't any music on earth like what I picture to myself.

To MRS. CAWOOD.   RATEL HOEK, 24*th April*.

[She writes apropos of Will's engagement which was to have been kept secret but which has leaked out] : Love, smoke and a cough cannot long be hid ! You say you wish it had been my own engagement that I wrote to tell you of. You will never hear of that. The power of loving has burnt itself out in me ; not in the widest sense, for I don't think I ever cared for so many people as I do now. But no one will ever absorb me and make me lose myself utterly, and unless someone did I should never marry. In fact I am married now, to my books ! I love them better every day, and find them more satisfying. I would not change lots with anyone in the world, and my old sorrows look very foolish to me now.

To Mrs. CAWOOD.   RATEL HOEK, 4*th* Aug.

And now I'm going to quarrel with you. What do you mean by going to Cradock and staying there all that time and never having your likeness taken, when I've asked you so often and when you knew how much I wanted it ? I had a beautiful nice large likeness taken when I was in Queenstown last, but I won't send you one, and there now Madam ! And I'll never do anything that would please you ; and there now Madam ! And I nearly did die the other day ; I woke up in the morning and felt as if I were dying, and I went to call someone, and fell against the door and cut my face all open, and it was half an hour before I got warm and could speak, and there now Madam ! And I'm going to " spook " you about that likeness one of these days, and there now Madam !

To Mrs. CAWOOD.   RATEL HOEK, 10*th Sept.*

I am beginning to understand for the first time your wish to live to be an old woman. However hard one has to work, however much one has to suffer, it is better to live than to die. At least I feel so now.

[This is consequent upon her illness ; in a letter a few weeks before she was very despondent about her health, the doctor having taken a grave view of it apparently.]

To Mrs. CAWOOD.   RATEL HOEK, 27*th Dec.*

I am going to leave this in May, and if I haven't got a situation by that time perhaps I might come and spend a few weeks with you. But I'm trying very hard to get one. I am almost sorry now that I gave notice but I have a feeling (it may be foolish but I can't help having it) that I'll never get well while I stay here and that I would soon be strong if I went to another place. I really don't see why I shouldn't get quite strong, but something always seems to keep me back here. It'll be very hard to leave this place, my dear old room and the folks ; they've always been so kind to me. In all these three years I've not had an unkind word or look from anyone, and I feel I won't be so well liked anywhere else. Do you know I get so tired sometimes I wish it were all over and yet at others there is such a clinging to life. I wish when I was two hours old the nurse had tied a garter round my neck, then I would never have known the pain of living, never have known the pain of dying. . . . I saw Annie Fouche in Cradock. She is wonderfully improved. She is quite a lady ! Her manners are so refined and gentle I hardly knew her. I think a teacher's feeling is something like a parent's ; you can't help seeing things as better than they are, so perhaps she is really not so very nice.

1879

To Mrs. Cawood.   Ratel Hoek, 9*th Jan.*

I wish I could see you. Perhaps it would give you a little happiness, and it would do *me* so much much good. I mean mentally and spiritually. I am getting to be such a selfish miserable creature. I wish I were as good as you. Perhaps if I saw you I would get like you. I would like to be so good that everything that I loved and that loved me was better and nobler and stronger for that love, but now it isn't so. I am so selfish. I'm not content to love. I want to be loved back again. We talk so much of intellect and of knowledge, but what are they ! After all, the heart can't live on them. One would barter all one's knowledge for one kiss and all one's intellect for one tender touch—just one. . . .

To Mrs. Cawood.   Ratel Hoek, 24*th Jan.*

[Her mother was with her.] Now as to my coming to you. It is as though someone held out a very nice ripe apple to very thirsty lips that were afraid to taste. Mamma says, " If you want to go so much, why don't you ? " She doesn't know how much I would lose if I lost you, and I'm sure you wouldn't keep on loving me as much if you saw what a poor weak miserable creature I am really. My heart is very bitter lately. I sometimes wish I could die ; it seems as though love was all selfishness and trust almost thrown away and nothing left. But you *are* one of the things that are left to me and I am so afraid of anything that would take you from me. If I can at all manage it I want to come and spend two or three weeks with you when I leave this ; you won't be able to get tired of me in such a little time. I know that your children would love me because I am getting to understand children better, and I am sure they would get on, and I don't think you would quite leave off caring for me if I live with you, but you might get to like me less than you do now, and that's what I don't want.

To Mrs. Cawood.   Ratel Hoek, 4*th Feb.*

Who do you think was here to-day, Mr. Stoffel Fouche ! He came to get me he said, and he would not go away unless I came with him, but of course I told him I couldn't do anything of the kind. . . . He offers me £55 per annum and I will only have to teach Peter and Christina for three hours in the morning, and he will get a piano at once and build on two nice rooms for school-room and bedroom for me. If he does all he says, it will be very nice. Of course there will be troubles and draw-backs, but heaven is not on this side of the river of death, and I fear not on the other. One reason why I would rather go there than to the Bonteboks is that I would be nearer you, and *perhaps* some day I might see you. . . . I have such a splendid little book of anatomy. I never read any work more clear and just what I wanted. I am going to try and get some dead baboons to experiment upon.

To Mrs. Cawood.   Ratel Hoek, 24*th Feb.*

From seven years to eleven or twelve they [children] should not study too hard, but after that let them work, even at some slight physical cost. If we are willing to give up nothing, we must expect nothing. I suppose no intellectual work is ever done without a certain price having to be paid for it. No great book was ever written that did not cost many a sleepless night and many hours of weariness and lassitude ; and with the lesser mental exercises it is the same. *Nothing for nothing ;* the longer I live the more I feel that to be nature's inexorable law. We get nothing in this poor old world but the cash has to be laid down first.

To Mrs. Cawood.   Ratel Hoek, 26*th Feb.*

. . . Now that the time for leaving begins to come near I begin to feel a great pain at my heart ; but I would have had to leave in a few months' time, and it would not have been easier then than now, but rather harder. I really do not think there are in the world two such sweet little girls as mine. I never mean to stay at a place so long again ; you get to care too much for everything and then you must just leave it. Even this dear old quiet parlour that has been my study so long, I feel as if it wasn't right that I should leave it. I think with all its physical suffering the time I have passed here has been the quietest and best of my life. . . . If I had my way in educating children they would have a great deal less to do with dead language and a great deal more to do with nature. How interesting and eager the little creatures are if you try to explain to them the structure and uses of the parts of a flower, but if you have to press an irregular verb into their heads what labour it is.   I am wonderfully stronger.

1880

To Katie, her Sister.   Lelie Kloof, 29*th May.*

I am very glad dear Mamma seems so happy in Grahamstown. . . . Already we have had two heavy falls of snow about the house, but the cold suits me well and I am much better than I was all the summer. The Fouches are very kind to me and I grow more and more fond of the children who are very warm-hearted and loving, and not at all more stupid than English children. . . .

P.S.—I send you a likeness of myself.

To KATIE, HER SISTER.   LELIE KLOOF, 14*th Oct*.

I am very well, better than I have been for years. The cold mountain climate suits me splendidly. Mrs. Fouche's little baby was baptised when we went into Cradock and I am its godmother. It is a very pretty little thing and I am very fond of it. The two girls I teach are nice loving children and give me no trouble at all. It is certainly much pleasanter to teach among the Dutch than among the English. . . .

1881

To KATIE, HER SISTER.   LELIE KLOOF, 5*th Jan*.

I don't think I shall ever return to this country unless my health gives way again. I shall spend about a month with Fred before I go to Edinburgh. I am not going to become a doctor ; that costs money of which I have none, but can become a nurse without paying anything, and after all, if they cannot be of so much use as the doctors, they can still relieve a great deal of suffering.

To CLIFFORD CAWOOD (now MRS. STANLEY).
                                    EASTBOURNE, 7*th May*.

I came with the intention of becoming a nurse, but since I have been here I have made up my mind to study medicine. My generous old brother Fred has promised to let me have as much money as I wish, and I hope to begin my studies very soon. Isn't it jolly to be able to realise an old day dream at last ?

I have spent since I came to England the happiest time of my life. . . . From Burnley I went to Scotland and spent six or seven days in Edinburgh, which I think to be the prettiest, grandest place in the world.

To MRS. CAWOOD.   EASTBOURNE, 15*th Aug*.

I don't think when we human beings really love one another we can ever leave off doing so, and I never seemed so to long for love, or feel as though I had so much to give out as I have done since I came to England. . . .

I am not yet beginning my medical studies as both my brothers think I had better get my books ready for publica-

tion before I begin. They think I ought to stick to
literature, but I can't quite see it. I am a man with two
loves and don't know which to choose. . . .

I had such a delightful voyage. Lord Colin Campbell,
the brother of the Marquis of Lorne, was one of the
passengers. He was very kind to me and we became
great friends. He gave me letters of introduction to a
sister of the Duke of Argyll and several other of his friends,
but I have not used them. . . .

To Mrs. Cawood.   Eastbourne, *3rd Oct.*

I leave on Saturday for London to enter the Endell
Street Hospital for three months to study midwifery. . . .
It is a great lying-in hospital in one of the lowest parts of
London, so that I shall be able to do that which I so much
wish, and learn to know our poor. My chest is very bad
again, I am worse than when I came to you to Ganna Hoek
that time to be made well, but I am as likely to stand the
winter in London as anywhere else. This ill-health makes
it very hard for me to study.

1882

To Mrs. Cawood. 81, Guilford Street, Russell Square,
London, *14th May.*

Dear old friend, so you won't write to me, won't you?
Well then I'll write to you. How are you? Don't you
think a body wants to hear from you sometimes, especially
when you must have such interesting news to give? . . .
I like the life here and am in much better health. . . .
Is Annie [Clifford] at home now? Where is Willie?
Is Ossy at Lovedale? How does your baby fare? Why
have you got so many? I'm sure you don't need them
all. And I would give just anything for one. I'm going
to adopt a child as soon as ever I'm rich enough. . . .

To Mrs. Cawood.

11, Porchester Gardens, London, *11th July.*

Will came to say goodbye to me on Thursday. [He
was returning to South Africa.] We had a very happy

time together. In the afternoon we went for a walk in Kensington Gardens ; then he took me to dinner at the Anglo-Indian dining rooms, and after that we went to Drury Lane Theatre, and saw Madame Ristori, the greatest actress now living, act Lady Macbeth. It was glorious. Her moan of remorseful agony in the sleep-walk scene made one quiver. . . . As far as material things go, I have everything a heart could wish for, my old brother takes such care of me. . . . I have had a touch of inflammation of the lungs, since last I wrote, and am not so very strong. . . . I am doing a great deal of reading and writing, but not attending lectures.

To Mrs. CAWOOD.　　ST. LEONARDS-ON-SEA, 19*th Oct.*

You see I have left my dear old London, ordered away by the doctors, and have been sent here for the winter. . . . There are a hundred and fifty-three boys in the school [New College, Eastbourne.] He [Fred] has many more applicants than he has room for this term. . . . A few days ago I went to see George Macdonald [the author of *David Elginbrod*, etc.] lecture. Have you ever read any of his books ? I think they are just the style you would like. He is a short broad-built man with grey hair and beard.

1883

To Mrs. CAWOOD.　　ROSE COTTAGE, BEXHILL, 15*th Nov.*

I am having to go back to St. Leonard's on account of my chest. . . .

I hope you will like the enclosed [a photo of herself, in corsets, on the corner of a table ; the only photo of her in corsets]. The man made me jump up on the table and then said when I was only half up, " Now, steady," and took me ; that is why I am in such a funny position. . . . Almost every week I get letters from people I have never seen, telling me how much my little book has helped and gladdened them. I feel often as if too much of the good and joy of life were put into my cup. One must but try to give back what one gets.

CHAPTER II

FROM ENGLAND, 1884

To HAVELOCK ELLIS.   ST. LEONARDS-ON-SEA, 2 5th Feb.

My dear Sir, on my return from a visit to London I found your letter which my publisher had forwarded here. Had I received it sooner I should earlier have written to tell you of the pleasure your expression of sympathy with the little book *An African Farm* gave me. Thank you for having written.

The book was written on an up-country farm in the Karroo, and it gives me much pleasure to think that other hearts find it real. I have been now almost three years in England but I long always for that old life.

I agree with you in objecting to Bonaparte ; he is drawn closely after life, but in hard straight lines without shading, and is not artistic, nor idealised enough. I had no definite idea when I wrote the story that I should ever come to England to publish it. It was just one of the many stories I had been writing ever since I was five years old, and its kind reception at the hands of the critics here surprised me much, and a letter such as yours I value much indeed.

There is too much moralising in the story, but when one is leading an absolutely solitary life one is apt to use one's work as Gregory used his letters, as an outlet for all one's superfluous feelings, without asking too closely whether they can or cannot be artistically expressed there.

I intend bringing out another book towards the close of the year.

Thanking you again for your letter which has given me much pleasure.

> I am, dear Sir,
> Yours sincerely,
> OLIVE SCHREINER.

To HAVELOCK ELLIS.   ST. LEONARDS-ON-SEA, 16*th March.*

Yes, it would be impossible to return to the old life ; the outward circumstances might be recalled, but the hope that made it beautiful would never come back when once the outside world had been known, and found empty.

I have not read any of Hardy's novels, but am sending for the *Westminster Review* to read your article. What you say in your letter about " the melodramatic and farcical element " is very true. When I said that Bonaparte was not " idealised " enough, perhaps I was using the word in a sense of my own ; what I meant was, that he was painted roughly from the *outside* (just as I might offhand describe the people who sat at dinner with me this evening), not sympathetically from the inside showing the how and the why of his being the manner of sinner he was. I should have entered into him and showed his many sides, not only the one superficial side that was ridiculous ; then he would have been a real human creature to love or to hate, and not farcical at all.

Is it very long since you left Australia ? Do not you miss the starlight nights when one can be out all night ? I miss them so. It is so hard to think shut up in a room.

To MRS. CAWOOD.
          EDINBURGH HOUSE, ST. LEONARDS, 20*th March.*

[After saying how happy her mother is at the Convent, Grahamstown, and telling of having met " a blind poet, Philip Marston," she continues] : The great pleasure to me however has been the meeting of some, I may say many, fine women. The outcome of my experience of the world and of things is greatly to increase my faith in women. . . . Ralph Iron, Esq., gets so many letters, and then I have to answer them for him !

To Havelock Ellis.   Edinburgh Hotel, 28*th March*.
My dear Mr. Ellis.

I have just finished reading your article in the *Westminster Review*, and I have read *A Pair of Blue Eyes*. I think your criticism very adequate and just. I shall read *Far From the Madding Crowd* and then I shall better be able to make up my mind as to whether I like Hardy much or not. Now I hardly know——there seems to me a certain shallowness and unrealness about his work——no, that's putting it too strongly ; it seems to me as though he was only fingering his characters with his hands, not pressing them up against him till he felt their hearts beat.

Thank you for your letter. I liked the last sheet about your Australian life. Yes, our African sky gives one the same sense of perfect freedom and wild exhilaration ; sometimes one feels as though, for no reason that could be given, one were almost in an ecstasy of happiness when one goes out alone. Here one never is alone.

[Paragraph about Waldo's Stranger, quoted in *Life*.]

Have you read a little play called *Nora* ? [*The Doll's House*] by Ibsen, translated from the Swedish [*sic*] by Frances Lord. It is a most wonderful little work. I should like it to be reviewed by some able reviewer that it might be more widely read, but perhaps you would not like it. It shows some sides of woman's nature that are not often spoken of, and that some people do not believe exist——but they do, I think.

It is very funny that in the book that I am revising now [*From Man to Man*] there is one character who reminds me somewhat of Knight in his relation to Elfride [*A Pair of Blue Eyes*]. The likeness is not strong, still it is there. He is a man who, when the woman he loves confesses to him, turns away from her ; but my woman tells him that which he could never have known if she had not told him, and he yet turns away from her.

To Havelock Ellis.   Edinburgh Hotel, 8*th April*.

It happens that the book I have been reading the last few days has been *James Hinton's Life and Letters*. I have loved the man himself. I like to know that saying of his that you tell me of [" Jesus was the Saviour of men, but I am the Saviour of women, and I don't envy him a bit "]. In his feeling for women he *is* like Jesus but like few other men. I have had a feeling while I have been reading the book, that the writer, without meaning to be untrue, is not quite showing the real man : your letter of this evening tells me that I was right. I look forward to seeing the book you talk of : will it be ready soon ? . . . I am glad you feel sympathy with socialism.

[Paragraph about her feeling towards Herbert Spencer, quoted in *Life*.]

I have read Strauss's *Old Faiths and New*, but that was lately. I suppose you have read his life of Jesus ? It had rather a strange effect upon me ; it made me love Jesus so much. I never cried over the crucifixion till I read Strauss's cold dispassionate criticism of that poor loving human soul that had been so tender to others, left there to face death alone. I am glad those women went after him. I believe Mary Magdalene stood close to the cross where the blood of his feet dropped down on her.

With regard to *Nora*, I think Ibsen *does* see the other side of the question, but in a book which is a work of art, and not a mere philosophical dissertation, it is not always possible to show all the sides. I have a sense of something wanting in the book, but I do not see how he could have supplied it. In the ideal condition for which we look men and women will walk close, hand in hand, but now the fight has oftenest to be fought out alone by both. I think men suffer as much as women from the falseness of the relations. Helmer's life lost as much as Nora's did through the fact that they never lived really together.

To HAVELOCK ELLIS.   EDINBURGH HOTEL, 21*st April*.

That extract from Mr. Hinton's letter I liked very much ; though I could not quite understand it I could fill in. James Hinton's life has been a help to me. Sometimes I get an almost despairing feeling, that women will have to save women alone—*and yet I feel that to be impossible*. Strength comes when I see one man's heart that has seen these things, and burnt over them. He has chimed in with the thoughts and feelings that are just now dominant in my life. I shall like to read that article of yours upon him.

The book I am revising now [*From Man to Man*] is the story of a woman, a simple, childlike woman, that goes down, down. I wish, I wish I had more power ; I would put it all into this book ; I would write so that no one who read it shall ever forget it. You will find many artistic faults, but I think you will sympathise with it.

Thank you for telling me about " Arabella." Your sonnet is much more beautiful to me now. When I first came to England I was nursing in a hospital for a little time, and I had such a beautiful girl. She was almost dying of inflammation of the lungs. A little thrill of pleasure used to run through me every time I had to touch her or do anything for her, and she used to open her sweet eyes, just like two stars, and look at me. I don't know if I should have liked your sonnet quite so much but for that. That is the best of writing what is true ; other lives are sure to answer back to it. I wonder if your girl looked like mine.

Strauss's *Life of Jesus* is very different from Renan's, I think better ; though I like Renan. I shall be glad when his life of his sister is published. It will be the record of a true relation between a man and a woman.

I love Shelley, and there is another man I love in that same personal way, Heinrich Heine. I personify myself with him. I know how and why he wrote every line that he did write. There is more depth and passion in one of his sneers, more quivering tenderness veiled under it, than in the outcries of half the world. I feel that I owe a debt of personal gratitude to the girl who comforted him in his " mattress grave."

I have not the same personal feeling for Hinton that you have, who know so much more of him than I can from that *Life* ; but one thing that draws me to him very much is his *fear of feeling* ; that comes out so clearly in the extract you sent me. Some people *dare* not feel fully—all life must be a long self-repression.

If you know of any very good book, will you please tell me of it ? I got down ten last time, and of them all only Hinton's *Life* was a real book. I want scientific reading : my mind needs it just now.

To HAVELOCK ELLIS.   EDINBURGH HOTEL, *2nd May*.

Heine is not understood, and I almost doubt whether anything one could do would cause him to be better understood. He belongs to his own, like Emerson. One might cause him to be more read (and that would be something) but the real man, the infinitely burning, tender, passionate heart, will be known only to a few—it must be heart to heart.

I have been reading that little book you lent me [Edward Carpenter's *Towards Democracy*] all the afternoon. I like it, and I like it more the more I read it, and when I re-read a page or two I like it better than at first. It is true, and it expresses what is in our hearts, ours of to-day. I must get Whitman and read him. I have read nothing of his yet. One evening a friend began to read him aloud to me, but I was in a wicked mood and began to laugh. I made fun of him and made them all laugh so that there was no more reading. I have sent for him to-day.

[Account of stay at Edinburgh Royal Infirmary already quoted in *Life*.] Yes, my little glimpse of nursing life was very sweet to me ; I am glad I had it though it was so short. The dream of my life was to be a doctor : I can't remember a time when I was so small that it was not there in my heart. I used to dissect ostriches, and sheeps' hearts and livers, and almost the first book I ever bought myself was an elementary physiology. I don't like to talk of my old dream even now, my heart is still tender over it. It seems to me that a doctor's is the most perfect of all lives ; it satisfies the craving to know, and also the craving to serve. A nurse's life is sweet, but not so perfect.

Thank you for those papers you sent me. I think I should like to join that Society [the Progressive Association] though, like you, I have not much faith in societies. An old woman sitting in her bedroom alone, reading her Bible alone, is sincere, but six old women at a " class meeting " make humbugs—very often. Ideally, nothing can be more perfect than the aims of that Progressive Association. I like the New Life, especially the clause on the necessity of combining physical with mental labour. My feeling about Socialism is exactly yours. I sympathise with it, but when I see the works and aims of the men who are working for it in London my heart sinks. What will it benefit us to seize away the money from the rich? At the same moment that the greedy hands are seizing it there will pass over with it the disease of which the rich are dying, the selfishness, the hardness of heart, the greed for the material good. What we want is more love, and more sympathy. Does it ever strike you, it often does me, how within the sixteen miles that make London lie all the materials for heaven on earth, if only something could come suddenly and touch our hearts one night; there would be nobody sad and nobody lonely: every aching head with a hand on it, every miserable old maid let out of her drawing-room and her old life-blood flowing; every wailing little child hushed in somebody's arms and making them warm: nobody hungry and nobody untaught, the prisons emptied and the back slums cleaned, everybody looking with loving eyes at the world about them. That would be heaven, and it only wants a little change of heart. I haven't faith in anything that promises to raise us by purely material means.

I am glad you are so busy, you must be happy. Thank you for telling me about that new book of Romanes. I think you are wrong in saying that scientific *reading* is not of much use. It is. To touch and handle would be far better, but it is better than nothing. You don't know what a gap would be left in my life if all the good I have had from scientific books were taken out of it (making the word " scientific " cover everything from Darwin and Carl Vogt to little primers on Heat and Light). I think that even the mere reading helps one to the feeling that truth is before all things, and to have a kind of love for things in their naked simplicity. I think that the tendency of science is always to awaken these two feelings: don't you?

I want to tell you what my feeling is about woman, but I can't to-night because I would have too much to say. I have just got a letter I should like to show you. It is from a woman whose heart is being broken; and the man who is doing it doesn't know and doesn't *realise* what he is doing. Why can't we men and women come near each other, and help each other, and not kill each other's souls and blight each other's lives? There is no need why it should be so.

I am coming up to live in London next week. My address will be 5, Harrington Road, South Kensington, after next Thursday. I shall like to know more of what Hinton thought, and of what you think. The question of woman's having the vote, and independence and education, is only part of the question, there lies something deeper.

To HAVELOCK ELLIS.

  7, PELHAM STREET, SOUTH KENSINGTON, 12*th May*.
MY DEAR Mr. ELLIS.

  I have not got your letter. I found the house at 5, Harrington Road, in a terrible condition and all the people drunk. The woman seized hold of me and would not let me have my luggage removed till I had paid her 30s. though I had only been five minutes in the house. I am quite sure they will have torn up any letters that came for me. I am very much troubled about it. I hope there was nothing in Hinton's handwriting in your letter. I don't know in which part of London I shall settle. Until Friday this will be my address, and I will let you know the new one.

What a splendid fellow Carpenter must be. I have just been reading his article in *To-day*. It expresses what I feel so exactly that I seem to feel as if I had written it myself. What kind of a man is he?

      14*th May*.

. . . Don't you think there must *always* be some sense of pain in learning to know more of people whom you have known only through their books? I think so.

I went to St. James's Hall last night. Every fibre in my being revolted against Old Bradlaugh, and I wanted to like him.

To HAVELOCK ELLIS. 7, PELHAM STREET, 17*th May*.

Yes, isn't it beautiful how grateful those women are for little acts of tenderness? Ach, if you only handle their babies kindly how grateful and bright they look! Some of

those hospital nurses are so unkind and rough with them.
I wish I was back at my hospital work ; the brain works
better if the hands work too. I have been to the Brompton
Oratory this evening and enjoyed the quiet and the music.
I got a dark corner where I could kneel down.

To HAVELOCK ELLIS.   7, PELHAM STREET, 20*th May*.
MY DEAR Mr. Ellis,
              I enjoyed going with you to that lecture so
much.   Thank you for coming for me.   If you are not
too busy and do not feel it would be a waste of time I should
be glad if you could sometimes come and see me.   It
would be a help to me.
      I have made up my mind not to leave town just yet.
I shall remain here till Friday, then my address will be
32, Fitzroy Street.
                          Goodnight,
                          OLIVE SCHREINER.

To HAVELOCK ELLIS.   7, PELHAM STREET, 21*st May*.
MY DEAR Mr. Ellis,
              I have so much to say about Hinton and Hinton's
views (I have some questions to ask too) that I shan't try
to say it to-day.   Thank you very much for your letter
and for the proofs. . . .   Hinton says much in these proofs
that I have thought and felt but *never* seen expressed before
but, I think, I see what he does not see, and where his
theory utterly breaks down.   Did he apply the same
measures to man and to woman?   Would he have been
satisfied if his wife had had six " spiritual husbands "?
I mean this really as a question.
      I am going to see Herbert Spencer on Sunday week.

To HAVELOCK ELLIS.   32, FITZROY STREET, 26*th May*.
I enclose my subscription for the Progressive Association.   Last night, after you went, I read Miss Jones'
description of Hinton.   I think I should like her.   But
Mrs. Hinton is the woman I *love*.   Will you some day
show me Hinton's likeness ?

You must come to see me whenever you care to. If you tell me what time you are coming I will stay in.

I wish I was really your sister ; it would be very nice.

To HAVELOCK ELLIS.   32, FITZROY STREET, 28*th May*.

Come to-morrow afternoon, if you can, because on Friday I may have other visitors and then we can't talk so well, and I have much I want to say and you to hear.

Don't think of, and dwell upon, Hinton *too much*. I think it is not well for any of us to allow another personality to submerge in any way our own. Do you ?

I have been walking about in the quiet part of Regent's Park all the morning.

To HAVELOCK ELLIS.   32, FITZROY STREET, 30*th May*.

I think that when Mrs. Hinton says that we can " cure licence not by restriction but by greater freedom " she is giving expression to one of Hinton's quite truest ideas. The very fact of freedom takes away the morbid desire which restriction has created.

I only say what I do about Hinton because I see you take the other side. It's my nature to be " koppig." [1] (That's a Cape Dutch word which means that when you turn a horse's head to one side of the road it's bound to go and see what's on the other). I don't think it's quite a bad quality, at least it always makes one stick up for the absent. I love Hinton and I feel sympathy with him ; when he's most wrong I feel it most. But why must I say I love him when you love him ?

What you say about jealousy is exactly what I feel. When we rise to the last highest, white-heat of love, all selfishness dies away. " And if I love thee, what is that to thee ? " and, " What do I ask of thee ? "

Yes, but you *do* let Hinton submerge you ; and you mustn't. It's not good for you. It's just because I know and feel you are so unlike Hinton in many ways that I don't want you to be drawn out of your natural line of growth by him. Can you understand what I mean ?

I like Whitman very much.

[1] Koppig, literally " heady," means headstrong, perverse. She mis-spelt it " kopach."

To HAVELOCK ELLIS.　　32, FITZROY STREET, 11*th June.*

You aren't angry with me because of what I said on Monday, are you? You mustn't be. I have much to say but I am too stupid to say it. I have been lying down since yesterday afternoon with a heavy chest cold. You aren't angry with me are you?—O.S.

To HAVELOCK ELLIS.　　32, FITZROY STREET, 12*th June.*

I will like to come on Monday if I am well enough. I am glad you are not angry. I hope you will enjoy going to Oxford. I am still in bed and so stupid. Please let Miss Jones know I can't come just now.—OLIVE.

To HAVELOCK ELLIS.　　32, FITZROY STREET, 16*th June.*

I am so sorry you have been ill. You and I seem to have had the same thing. It's very funny. On Thursday night my head got so bad I thought it was going to burst. I thought Eleanor Marx was my sister Ettie. I hope you are quite better and that to-day's journey will do you good. If my head is better I shall like to go to-morrow evening ; If we don't feel well enough we can just stay with each other. My chest and throat are better now ; it is only my head that is so bad. Dr. Donkin says it is nervous prostration.

To HAVELOCK ELLIS.

HOLLY COTTAGE, ASPLEY GUISE, WOBURN, 28*th June.*

I got here this afternoon at half-past six. I think the place will suit me. It is very quiet. Thank you for your letter.

I am glad your mother and sister did not dislike me. I am very glad I went to see them. I can picture your life so much better.

I feel a bit sad this evening, but that is only because the rain is beating on the trees outside and the place is strange to me. I think it is rather a sad place but I shall work here.

I have much I could say but nothing I could write about. Write to me when you have nothing better to do and it doesn't interfere with work. You have an exam, haven't you ?

I feel very grateful to you ; you are very good and very tender and very true. To-morrow I shall begin my reading and writing and have something rational to write about to you.

To HAVELOCK ELLIS.   ASPLEY GUISE, 29*th June.*

Did you tell Louie [the sister previously mentioned] all about me ? Please do. I hope you feel happy, and are able to work well. You mustn't tell her or anyone things that I tell you about other people, but things that are about myself alone are in your hands ; you can do what you like with them, and I shall think it right. I have such a strong feeling for Louie. When she put her arm round me on the sofa I wanted to cuddle close up to her, but I was ashamed. I liked it. I have such an odd feeling for her. You know when I tell you people have loved me or anything of that kind you must not tell anyone. Love that has been given you is too sacred a thing to be talked of to anyone (don't you think so ?) except just to the person who is like part of you and who will feel it as you do. . . . Will you please tell me little things about yourself, about your work and everything like that.

I am so bad I can't write better than this to-day, my head goes round and round. I want to do so much work. You don't know how I am mentally much better since I knew you. I *ought* to work now.

To HAVELOCK ELLIS.   ASPLEY GUISE, 30*th June.*

I am a bit better this evening. Have been reading Heine. Isn't it odd how when you sympathise with any-one in the main you sympathise with them in the little tiny things too ? Now Heine's hatred to Wellington is so delicious to me. I never found anyone who could quite sympathise with my loathing for that man.

I have read almost the whole volume of Galton [*Inquiries into Human Faculty*], like it very much, because it is suggestive, but he generalises from quite insufficient data, it is ludicrous sometimes (didn't it strike you so ?).

back into the past without blaming those that are dearest to one, and it is better to let the past bury its dead, eh ? I have not been able to go for any walks. Twice I have been for a little way and yesterday I walked up and down before the door. You wouldn't know me if you were to see me, I look so funny, my face is such a dark red with the blood in my head. There is no need to be anxious about me ; I shall be better when I get to a fresher, breezier place.

You will perhaps like to see some of the reviews of *An African Farm,* so I send you some. Send them back because they are my Dadda's [brother Fred's]. I'm sorry I didn't keep any. It would be rather amusing after many years—if I live so long—to look at them.

You say I must tell you what I am doing. But I don't do anything except walk about my room and try to breathe, and lie down on my bed and try to breathe. I feel as though if I stayed here long I should stay here altogether.

To HAVELOCK ELLIS.   ASPLEY GUISE, 4*th July.*

Henry, you are spoiling me by being so good to me. I can't write because my head is so bad ; I have neuralgia which contracts one eye. Will you tell me the name of a good head doctor, a specialist ?

I have been lying all the afternoon talking to you jn my mind. I hope you will go in for the exam ; I should like it. I do not see that writing to me will take much out of you, if you say what comes first. Yes, it will be good for me that you write as much as you can. Your letters cool and strengthen me. Some day, when you are in need of help, I will help you. Send me that diary, please. I don't think you are good in the common way. When I say " good " I mean good to me. And by " good " generally I mean *unselfish.* I don't know if I care for you much. . . .

I shall prize being allowed to see the diary. I will show you my journal when I am with you some day. You wouldn't be able to understand it alone. When I come to something wrong, I put it into such words that one can't understand. . . .

I would like to have your critical judgment of my mind,

or rather of my work, which is really me. What did you think of " New Rush ? " You haven't told me, and I won't tell you what I think of it till you have. Do you think it would be right for me to publish it ? I think not.

[Paragraph quoted in the *Life*, regarding her descent from the Olivers, Ellis being also descended from a family of the same name.]

To HAVELOCK ELLIS.   ASPLEY GUISE, 7*th July*.

Yes, you must write to me every day when you want, and then let a week or ten days go without writing when you want not. If I feel wanting a letter very badly I will write and ask you for one. And when I want a little love, expressed love, I will write and ask for that too. Sometimes I can do without it, but sometimes I need it.

I am so glad I am going to-morrow, but I feel weak to pack.

Yes, I have the feeling as if you and I were so young together. The dream, the faith, that I should find someone just like myself was with me all through my childhood. I think one would hardly believe how young it was there.

To HAVELOCK ELLIS.   BOLE HILL, 8*th July*.

. . . But you are wanting to know about me. I got here last evening in the rain. This is a beautiful place and a delightful clean little cottage of four rooms on the side of a hill overlooking the little tiny town of Wirksworth. It is perhaps not so pretty as some parts of Derbyshire may be, but to me who have longed so for my old hill life, it is so delightful. One feels nearer God here. My chest is still so very bad. I hope I will be able to stop here, I like it so.

To HAVELOCK ELLIS.   BOLE HILL, 10*th July*.

You are right in all you say about Marston. That is just it : you have no right to describe him in exactly the same words I described him the other day though !

I feel somewhat ashamed after what I said the other day. Fancy being ashamed of you ! Now I'm not.

was first a woman) and she said that from the day she married she never knew she had a chest again.

The food is very good here. We shall have such nice little dinners and teas together.

OLIVE.

To HAVELOCK ELLIS.   BOLE HILL, 13*th July*.

[She had now received Ellis's diary.]   I must have a long talk with you some day (perhaps in a letter) on your use of the word " God " and the old symbols generally. The use of them by people like you and me is never quite true.   (That is what makes Hinton's writings so false.) We *cannot* always stop to *define* what *we* mean by " God," etc., so the best way is not to use the terms at all.   I have taken care that the word " God " does not occur in this last book of mine, hateful damned name that it is.   A word may become so defiled by bad use that it will take a century before it can be purified, and brought into use again. I'm not explaining what I mean but I think you will understand.

Goethe has been for you just what he has been to me, and I think it was at the same time.

Mid-day.

I have just got your letter.   Yes, I have felt afraid that in my feeling that Hinton had too much power over you I might affect you too strongly on the other side.   But I think that in after years when we look back we " will " see [Ellis had criticised her use of " will " and " shall "] that I have been to some extent right.   Hinton is a great man ; the world will be better for hearing what he has to say ; you are doing good work in helping the world to hear it.   In truth I do not think it was so much dear old Hinton himself as the effect of Hinton's admirers that has not been good for you.   I can quite imagine that if I were among people who were always telling me I was a second George Sand I might in the end fancy I was and lose some of my own virtues in trying to imitate hers.   And yet I never would be George Sand, and I should lose Olive Schreiner, who might be every bit as good.

If you heard me defending Hinton to other people you would say I "must like him a little." I *love* Hinton because he had a great free-loving soul. I hate his clinging to the old symbols when he didn't cling to the thing meant, and his fear of saying the things he meant in naked black and white. Darling, you mustn't let me trouble you on this point. If you feel that I am not good for you in this way you must tell me not to write about it any more. Perhaps if all Hinton wrote were nakedly published, that kind of holding back I complain of would be found not to be in the man. Yes, my boy, we are only children together, to help each other to grow.

To HAVELOCK ELLIS.   BOLE HILL, 15th *July*.

When will you be coming if you do come? You will have your meals here. My chest is bad, to-day particularly bad. I sometimes feel almost hopeless. It seems to me like asthma more than anything else for it comes in fierce paroxysms of suffocation, and it leaves me so weak that I can only lie before the fire till the next one comes.

Henry, I will have been here a week to-morrow and I haven't been able to do *anything*. I haven't been able to read, only a little bit of Emerson. It's been such a comfort to me, I keep the book close to me when I can't read it. I am so glad you are going to write that article on Bebel's *Woman*. I haven't read him yet. Yes, we must talk of it, of so many things.

To HAVELOCK ELLIS.   16th *July*.

Speaking of the effects sexual feeling has on the mind, it is very clearly proved in the case of women. I must make more inquiries among other women, my friends, who will have noticed and been able to analyse their feelings. With myself, *while* I am unwell every month my feelings are particularly sensitive and strong. A little word that would not pain me at another time causes me acute agony I can't help feeling, and a little word of tenderness is so precious to me (especially the man who loves you ought to be tender with you then). The time of greatest and most wonderful mental activity is just after, and perhaps the last two days of the time too.   I was unwell last week, and now, though my chest is so troublesome, I can lie on the sofa half asleep and the thoughts are continually crowding in on me.   Last night it suddenly flashed into me, the solution of all my difficulties with *From Man to Man*.   It has been brooding in the background of my mind these many days, and now it has suddenly come.   I shall have no more difficulty with it, it is as clear as daylight.   I have got what I wanted.   It is so splendid, I mean the feeling is, I get so excited I don't know what to do.

But to go back to the sexual feeling.   Of course one may very easily exaggerate what I have been talking about, but there is no doubt there is some truth in it.   Eleanor Marx, the only woman I have spoken to on the subject, feels much the same.   My acquisitive power, my power of learning, is not *at all* weak just at the time, but my feelings are so strong.   I am going to write and ask Mrs. Walters and some of my intimate friends.   This subject is interesting because *as far as the power of the purely physical-sexual extends, so far must the power of the mental-sexual extend*.   If the physical feelings extend their power over a certain portion of the soul, then the relationship between man and woman will be able to work upon the same portion.   Do you carefully observe (I mean unconsciously, I always look at myself unconsciously, don't you ?) the interaction of your manly upon your mental nature.   I should like to know the man's side of the question.   I should think the relationship must be almost as close.   Look at the effect of celibacy on monks and hermits, etc. !

Yes, you never look anyone in the face, eh ?   I couldn't understand it at first.   I think what I called that glorious look in your eyes was just the *once* or *twice* when you looked really into mine.   They were godlike.   What is rather funny is that some years ago I never looked at anyone in the eyes.   I couldn't.   I had a cousin who used to hate me and she used to say that that was why she couldn't bear me.   I wonder if you will change like I have and look people full in the face like I do now.   And I used to be reserved and secretive without any reason for it ; I'm not like that now.　I'm glad you too turn away your face and look down.　I don't think you will always.

To HAVELOCK ELLIS.　　　　　　　　BOLE HILL, 18*th July*.

Did you ever read the passage in Shelley's letters when he talks about genius (I think he repeats it from another book) : *Genius does not invent, it perceives !*　I think that this is so wonderfully true, and more true the more one looks at it.　It agrees with the true fact that you noticed the other day, that men of genius are always childlike. A child sees everything, looks straight at it, examines it, without any preconceived idea ;　most people, after they are about eleven or twelve, quite lose this power, they see everything through a few preconceived ideas which hang like a veil between them and the outer world.　By the bye (this doesn't bear directly on that) did you ever do what I was very fond of doing when I was a child (I used to call it looking at things really) look at your hand for instance, make an effort of mind, and dissociate from it every preconceived idea.　*Look at it simply as an object which strikes the eye.*　You will be surprised how new and strange and funny it looks as though you had never seen it before.　I used to do it often in Church to pass away the time.　It can be done with the other senses.　Listen to people talking just as a mere noise striking the ear.　It is utterly different from what one fancies. . . .　I know you can criticise my work as if it were anyone else's, as I could yours ;　in fact I think I am more keen to see a fault in you than in anyone else.

I am going to subscribe to the London Library next year.　I can get fifteen books there and never need more than four or five at once, so if the other self cares he can have the rest.　Tell me any good books you think of.

I am suffering from such depression of spirits to-day, and I don't know why.

To HAVELOCK ELLIS.　　　　　　　　BOLE HILL, 21*st July*.

I am so tired.　I did not go to sleep till the dawn light was shining strong in my windows.　I have done a little good work to-day and yesterday ;　worked with such

4

grow bigger and bigger and go—he knows not where. Yet, when I get a letter, even like your little matter-of-fact note this morning, I feel : " But this thing is yourself." In that you are myself I love you and am near to you ; in that you are a man I am afraid of you and shrink from you.

Do you know that butterfly that the artist of the beautiful makes in Hawthorn's story ?

Yesterday I heard part of Ibsen's play, *Ghosts*, still in MS. [Read to her by Aveling.] It is one of the most wonderful and great things that has long, long been written. I wanted you so, too, to be sitting there by me, to hear it. There was one line. . . . It made me almost mad. I cried out aloud. I couldn't help it.

How is our exam going ? It's this dry-as-dust part of the work that must be so horrible, especially, you see, if you don't think in your future life of making the practice and study of medicine the central point (and I feel most distinctly that your " call " is to literature, just as mine was, in spite of my medical longing).

Mrs. Walters says that I seem years gladder and younger than when she saw me this time last year, just as if I was only fifteen. Do you know it is you who have made me feel so young ? Almost altogether you. I feel younger, much, than when I was a child of ten.

I think of you like a tall angel, as you looked at the Progressive meeting.

To HAVELOCK ELLIS.   BOLE HILL, *2nd Aug*.

I am beginning to have such a *horror* of Dr. A. [Aveling], other-self. To say I dislike him doesn't express it at all ; I have a fear and a horror of him when I am near. Every time I see him this shrinking grows stronger. Now, you see, when I am at Bole Hill they come every day to see me. We shouldn't be much alone ; and we have so many things to talk about. . . . It may be the last time we are together (certainly for months), perhaps for years. I have to stick to my book till the winter (and I don't know that I shall have it ready by November), then I shall have to go to the South of France or at nearest to Ventnor. . . . And if we are at Wirksworth the Avelings will be always with us. I love her, but *he* makes me so unhappy. He is so selfish, but that doesn't account for the feeling of dread. Mrs. Walters has just the same feeling. I had it when I first saw him. I fought it down for Eleanor's sake, but here it is, stronger than ever.

I wish I could read Bebel's book before you come, but now until my little boy [Fred's son Wilfrid] goes I shan't be able to look at a book or a newspaper. When he is with me I only play and amuse him and tell him stories and walk about with him from the time he gets up till the time he goes to bed. Then I am too tired to read or write. We must read all we can on the woman question. Just now it is our question. In after years it may be something else. I will tell you about *Ghosts* when you come. It deals with the question of equal moral laws for both sexes, and of physical relationship even between a half-brother and sister " when good "—and with what wonderful *art !* It is a translation by Frances Lord. The book is considered too strong even on the Continent. What will they think of it in England !

Do you know that Wirksworth is the scene of *Adam Bede* and that George Eliot's aunt lies buried there ? Ach, I want you to see Wirksworth, ugly as it is, we will arrange everything when you come.

To HAVELOCK ELLIS.   BUXTON, 4*th Aug.*

No letter from you this morning. . . . Bring something interesting for us to read when you come ; though with all we have to say, our walks, and our French reading, we shall not have much time over. . . . This is a very short note, but you would rather have it than nothing. It does us such good to get letters from each other.

To HAVELOCK ELLIS.   BUXTON, 5*th Aug.*

I like Seeley. Now he is a man to whom I feel akin. That is something different from merely admiring a writer. I always feel (I did from the first moment I opened his book) akin to Emerson. I never read now, never touch a book. You can't think in what a completely stupefied state of mind I am. I can't even make stories to myself after I go to

bed. Good-night, my brother. How nicely I will rest
when I know you are sleeping in a room not far off.

Your little comrade.

To HAVELOCK ELLIS.   BUXTON, *6th Aug.*

We went for a drive this morning to a place called " The
Cat and Fiddle." I *must* go to it with you. It is the
first and only place that I have seen in England that gives
one the feeling we both miss so here. It is a bare wild
mountain top 2,000 feet above the sea. You have the
sense of solitude even though there are many people near
you. This afternoon we went for a walk to Miller's Dale.
That, too, is beautiful, but it is the English beautiful, not
ours.

To HAVELOCK ELLIS.   BUXTON, *7th Aug.*

I will explain to you about my style when I see you. I
never know *why* I write things in a certain way when I
write them, but I can generally find out if I think afterwards.
What you mean is what I call " writing ribbed." I don't
know when I invented that term for a certain style of writing.
I am changing a whole chapter of *From Man to Man* from
what I call the plain into the " ribbed " style. Sometimes
the plain is right, sometimes the ribbed. I *think* I generally
write descriptions in the plain and philosophise or paint
thought in the ribbed. (You know in knitting there are
two stitches, one makes a plain surface and the other makes
ribs. Ribbed knitting goes up and down, up and down.)

Goodbye till to-morrow, my own friend. What a
difference you make in my life ! . . . Your sister OLIVE.

To HAVELOCK ELLIS.   BOLE HILL, *9th Aug.*

So glad my brother [i.e. *Ellis*] has passed [his medical
exam.]. I had set my heart on it. . . .

[The almost daily letters were at this time much taken
up with Ellis's approaching visit, which was to be after
Wilfrid—Fred Schreiner's son—had gone and after Ellis
had passed a medical examination. It was to be to
Wirksworth. They did not go to Buxton. Many of the

letters about this period were re-read and more or less
destroyed in 1917 when Olive was much disturbed about
the existence of letters.]

To Miss Louie Ellis.   Bole Hill.

I don't know if Ellis is writing to you. I want to write
to you. I'm glad you have been having such a fine time.
What was the gown you planned for me ? I want to wear
boy's clothes and *will* as soon as I can get other women to
join me. Boy's knickerbockers, but not coats, I think they
are ugly. A kind of blouse reaching to the knee. Ellis
will tell you about the long walks we have been, our going to
Miller's Dale, etc., etc. He is sitting at the other side of the
room now writing away to someone or other [Mackay]. We
have had a very jolly time, and I think he is looking much
better than when he came. I fancy working for that exam
tired him.

We are going to have lunch now. I just wanted to
write a word to you.

To Havelock Ellis.   Bole Hill, 27*th Aug.*

I am going to begin work now. I miss you more than
I thought I should. . . . I feel happy, though not well.
Your little comrade.

Bole Hill, 28*th Aug.*

I have been working since nine o'clock this morning.
Have not left off even to eat, eat walking up and down.
Have not laid down to-day ! ! ! Can you believe that ?
I *have* to keep on working or I would miss you.

Bole Hill, 29*th Aug.*

You seem to have had such a good effect on my mind.
I am working better than I ever have since I came to
England.

Bole Hill, 30*th Aug.*

I have been working all day though I have not written
much. I have been tearing up. I did a splendid bit
this evening, though ; or rather it's come to me, I haven't
written it yet.

To HAVELOCK ELLIS.   BLACKWELL FARM, *3rd Sept.*
(About a mile or two away.)

I got here this afternoon.   The woman is so horrible.
They want me to take and pay for the room I didn't take.
I don't know what to do or where to go.   [She asks through
several pages for addresses of rooms, or likely places near
London, etc.].   When the woman was talking to me I
began to cry and I've been crying ever since.   I feel so
weak and I feel so tired, love.   Put your arms round me.
Yes, I know you do and it helps me so.   I feel I want someone to stroke my hair.   Oh, I haven't anywhere to go to.
I must have a place somewhere, if it is only one tiny little
room, and no one shall turn me out.   Above all things,
any rooms you get must be *quiet*, *quiet*, *quiet*.   I only
want to rest.

To HAVELOCK ELLIS.   BLACKWELL FARM, *5th Sept.*

Thank you for that prescription.   My stomach is so
weak that I can take nothing.   I think that is partly why
I am so bad.   You know how splendidly I could eat when
you were with me.   I have such sudden wild outbreaks
of crying that weaken me so.
[Refers, as she often does, to reading Emerson for
consolation.]
[Some destroyed letters and then others asking Ellis
to find rooms for her in London at once.]   I can't stay
here any more.   I shall go mad.   I never felt like this
before.   It's so awful.   Harry, what does make me feel
like this?   It's as much my mind as my body that is ill.

To HAVELOCK ELLIS.   BLACKWELL FARM, *9th Sept.*

That medicine has done me much good already.   I
feel that I could eat.   [In reply to former questions of
Ellis's.]   I landed in England on the 30th of March, 1881.
I have looked the date up and think it is right.
I went to the Crystal Palace Concerts once or twice in
1882.   In the summer or spring it was that I heard the
Choral Symphony of Beethoven that seemed so splendid
to me and helped me so, and *I think* it was the Saturday
before that I heard the Italian Symphony (Mendelssohn)

that helped me so too.   No music will ever seem like that to me.   How much better and sweeter life is to me now, how much I have to be thankful for.   It seems to me such a wonderful and sweet thing that you should have come into my life. . . .   I shall always be more sympathetic now to all kinds of human suffering.   That's weakness in one way, but a kind of strength too.   Only, physically, I shall never be what I was when I landed in England.

To Mrs. CAWOOD.

39, BELGRADE ROAD, LONDON, 13*th Sept.*

[She had written from Bole Hill in July.]   I haven't changed a bit in the way you fancy, though I have changed.   When dear old John Pursglove was in England [Mr. Cawood knew him at the Diamond Fields] all he could say about me the first few days he was here was, " Well, Miss Olive, you *have* changed," and when I asked him how—" Why, you've grown so soft."   I couldn't get any further information out of him.   I should love you ten times more than ever if I knew you now. . . . We have often talked about good and noble men.   I wish you knew my friend Henry [Havelock] Ellis.   He is so tender to others' weaknesses and so unselfish. . . .   On my way back from Regent's Park I went through a large graveyard and found a very old woman trying to find her mother's grave.   She must have been eighty I think.   I found it for her at last and she was in such a state of delight.

To HAVELOCK ELLIS.   ST. LEONARDS, 12*th Oct.*

The doctor says it is not asthma, it is bronchitis.

13*th Oct.*

I am getting better but I think the morphia makes me stupid.   I feel happy when I think of you.   You are the first human being who has been perfect rest to me.

16*th Oct.*

Send me some books from the London Library about the woman question and social questions, ethics, and some novels, *Mehalah,* etc.   I must have something that will make me forget.

17th Oct.

Can you get me any books at the London on prostitution. And what is the cost of the Blue Book on the Contagious Diseases ? If not too expensive I mean to buy it. There is a place in Endell St. . . . Don't love me too much. . . . Of course we can share the Library books. You *are* my family. What other family have I got ?

To HAVELOCK ELLIS.   ST. LEONARDS, *19th Oct.*

I am much better in mind and body and am going to work to-day. . . . I haven't seen any human creature since I came here except Wilfrid.

To HAVELOCK ELLIS.   *20th Oct.*

Yes, it wasn't really me. But you know I am tired and feel bitter sometimes. I do fight so hard against the feeling. I shall conquer it soon. . . . I am having to make myself a bit hard and tough. I should break down altogether if I didn't. It's not because I feel so. So you understand.

To HAVELOCK ELLIS.   ST. LEONARDS, *21st Oct.*

I won't write to you unless I can write you real letters. My heart is always real to you though. I wish I could tell you *everything* in my life, *everything*. I can tell you about myself, but the parts about other people I can't and that makes me sad. . . . I feel happy now and calm. I wrote a little last night. I am getting well and strong. I wish I could feel as well in London. I like my rooms. . . . My best way with French will be to get a good French novel and an English translation. I am doing French exercises now, but that isn't the quickest way for me.

To HAVELOCK ELLIS.   ST. LEONARDS, *22nd Oct.*

I had most terrible asthma last night. The doctor says I must never hope to be well, relief is all I must look for, from narcotics. I have worked to-day, though, very well.

This morning I got another letter from " H. Rider Haggard." [She had mentioned previously a man called Haggard who had sent her a novel, *Dawn*, and written.] Do you know I half believe it is Lady Florence Dixie.

To HAVELOCK ELLIS.   ST. LEONARDS, 24*th Oct.*

[Been reading the Blue Book and writes ferociously about prostitution.]

I am working. I have written all the " Remembrances " I mean to write and will send you to-morrow.

I read a good deal of Madame Roland yesterday with the dictionary. I keep my French Grammar by my bedside for as soon as my eyes are open. I am going to work this winter like I used to at the Cape.

To HAVELOCK ELLIS.   ST. LEONARDS, 26*th Oct.*

We had the greatest storm I have ever known in England last night. This morning I had one of the worst times I have ever had. In a few minutes I was bathed in perspiration. It is such wild terrible agony. I have been lying down all day, but I will work to-morrow.

To HAVELOCK ELLIS.   ST. LEONARDS, 27*th Oct.*

I went this afternoon to the doctor to have the morphia injected, but he said when he felt my pulse that he couldn't do it. He said it was " a sad case, a very sad case " . . . Hasn't your heart ever been like iron ? Mine was for five years. Then for the three years I first spent in England I cried every night for hours.

To HAVELOCK ELLIS.   ST. LEONARDS, 29*th Oct.*

I am going to write an article on prostitution as soon as my book has got on a bit. It's *good* for me to think and study about the woman question, especially prostitution, while I'm working at my book. It's the only thing that doesn't take me away from my book or that I can really study at the same time. Of course the subject of my book [*From Man to Man*] is prostitution and marriage. It is the story of a prostitute and of a married woman who loves

...her man, and whose husband is sensual and unfaithful.
...hen I've got this work off my soul I shall look round at
other sides of life.

To HAVELOCK ELLIS.   ST. LEONARDS, *3rd Nov.*

Revising *Reminiscences* [see Chapter I of the *Life*].
You know it isn't meant to be carefully written. It's
just anyhow.

I like Ben Jonson's *Bartholomew Fair*. You know the
sixteenth and nineteenth centuries have the same spirit
in them. They answer back to each other in everything.

To HAVELOCK ELLIS.   ST. LEONARDS *5th Nov.*

You know I've wanted for so many years to die but
I don't any more. . . . When I first knew you I thought
here is one person into whose relationship with me no pain
will ever enter because we are so near each other and
understand each other so. Now it seems as if I was going
to make you sad. If you could see deep into my soul you
would see that the feeling that is yours [my feeling towards
you] is the most pure and perfect feeling that I have ever
had for anyone—I mean the kind of feeling that can't go
away. If I had passion for you perhaps I couldn't have
this feeling (I think it's like Montaigne felt for his friend)
and this is something much more rare and I think higher.
It is no figure of speech when I say you are my other self.
You have taken a place in my life which no marriage or
passionate love of mine could ever take from you. My
boy, my own, for so many years I have longed to meet a
mind that should understand me, that should take away
from the loneliness of my life. Now I have found it.
Sweet one, you will feel how you are coming to help and
rejoice another human being, and that will make you glad.

To HAVELOCK ELLIS.   ST. LEONARDS, *7th Nov.*

I think my brother liked your article on the Woman
Question. He likes me to like you, he thinks you are
so good and noble. He liked those first letters you wrote
me, and he hasn't liked Alfred St. Johnston or anyone.

To HAVELOCK ELLIS.   ST. LEONARDS, 16*th Nov.*

[Weather getting bad. Much pain in chest.] Oh, I would give all the rest of my life if for one year I might be able to breathe like other people.

It was because I was so perfectly well in my chest at Lelie Kloof that I thought of coming home to nurse.

To HAVELOCK ELLIS.   ST. LEONARDS, 17*th Nov.*

You know, one thing that troubles me so is that I see that if I am to live I *must* leave England for ever. You don't know what that means to me ; it is death. I left Africa without a tear, my real life is here, and if I leave England, though I live for fifty years, still I am dead. The one fixed unchanging dream of all my life was to come ; to have to go back makes all life a blank, nothing left. I was right in *An African Farm ;* a striving and a striving and an ending in nothing. Oh, God if I had health would I care what happened or what came ? I know now that I shall never be well again.

To HAVELOCK ELLIS.   ST. LEONARDS, 19*th Nov.*

I cannot explain to you how I feel because I do not understand myself. Do you know that all my life since I came to England is a mystery to me ? In all my life before (except at rare times with regard to my love for Theo and Ettie) my keen analytical intellect stood by watching, and *knowing* what went on ; since I have been in England I have never thought of myself. I have only lived and felt. I think it has been because I *dared* not analyse.

To HAVELOCK ELLIS.   ST. LEONARDS, 20*th Nov.*

I quite forget the part about Aunt Margaret [in *Undine*]. I don't know what her relationship to Frank was. I know that Ettie was in my mind when I drew her and Ettie's love to Theo. Not the woman of talent, the eloquent lecturer, but my soft-hearted sister Ettie who used to stroke my hair. I had quite forgotten that there was such a character in the book. I've never looked at it, you know, since I wrote it. It's not finished either ; I left off in the middle of the last chapter and tore up the half I had written. I ought to have burnt it long ago, but the biographical element in it made me soft to it.

To HAVELOCK ELLIS.   2 1*st Nov.*

If I went to Africa, of course I should take a situation as teacher and go back to my old life.

I was very well in my chest the first five months I was in England. It was as soon as I went to Endell Street that my chest got bad.

To HAVELOCK ELLIS.   ST. LEONARDS, 2 1*st Nov.*

Isn't Taine's *English Literature* splendid? I have not yet found one word that does not appear to me true. It seems to me a work of genius as much as any novel or poem could be. His remarks on Dickens are simply the perfection of criticism.

I am not adding to my book. It grows smaller and smaller. I am sure that all I am doing is improvement. Condense, condense, condense! But it's the most mentally wearing work. To cut out these few parts has cost me more than to write the whole. I generally write things off best at first; the passionate parts and leading scenes I never need to touch; but the little bits between, where there is not such intense feeling to guide me, have to be thought over.

I do not remember *Undine* at all. I think that Frank was Undine's step-brother, so no relation to Aunt Margaret at all; perhaps I meant to make out that he was her nephew and that she couldn't marry him.

To HAVELOCK ELLIS.   ST. LEONARDS, 2 3*rd Nov.*

My chest gets steadily worse. . . . I have read Webster's plays. After Marlowe and Shakespeare they are the best I have read. What a gulf between them and those Queen Anne and Stuart fellows!

To HAVELOCK ELLIS.   ST. LEONARDS, 24*th Nov*

Shall never have rest or mental or physical health while I am dependent on any other human creature. It is death to all the manly side of our soul. Take all from perfect love, but from nothing else.

To HAVELOCK ELLIS.   ST. LEONARDS, 25*th Nov.*

I must feel very near to you because I think I wouldn't mind taking *anything* from you. I wouldn't mind taking anything from my Daddy [Fred], if he wasn't married. Please find out for me whether the *picture* of the horned beetle is in Darwin's *Descent of Man* or in *Variations of Plants,* etc. I make Rebekah say in [it is in the] *Descent of Man.*

To HAVELOCK ELLIS.   ST. LEONARDS, 26*th Nov.*

I am going to Hastings [from neighbouring St. Leonard's] for a week and if I don't get better there I will ask my brother for money and go to Switzerland or Italy. I thought I was going to die this morning, the suffocation was so bad, but of course it was only fancy.

To HAVELOCK ELLIS.   ST. LEONARDS, 30*th Nov.*

Oh, my darling, I am getting worse and worse. The thought of you is all that helps me in this agony of loneliness. Where shall I go? What shall I do? If I had only gone to Switzerland or Madeira when I left London. I was still strong then. . . . I wish there were paying Hospitals to which one could go, not private, public, so that there was no cheating. Such an agony comes over me to think of becoming a real invalid and having nowhere to go. If I could only have written my book first, so that I could have got a little money.

To HAVELOCK ELLIS.   ST. LEONARDS, 1*st Dec.*

I am going to try and get back to Edinburgh Hotel [St. Leonard's] if they will take me. . . . I feel very desolate. You are always in my thoughts and close in my heart, but somehow we seem sad in body as if we should never be able to be near each other to comfort and help. You must let me see everything you write, like I let you see *Undine* and all the stupid things I write. I wonder if I shall ever write again. Yes, I *will.*

To HAVELOCK ELLIS.   ST. LEONARDS, 2*nd Dec*

You know I am really dead.   I only seem to be alive
You have made me live a little.   I am so grateful to you
Our love has been such a pure beautiful thing.   I fee
it so now. . . .   Ach, one day I shall get well and we wil
work together in heart and be the strength of each other'
lives as we are now.

To HAVELOCK ELLIS.   ST. LEONARDS, 4*th Dec*

If I had money, I could always have someone I love
near me, and I could help other people who are lonely and
comfort them.   Harry, how can I write hardly in my
books when I know how all important love and sympathy
are.   Life seems determined to keep pressing that on me
till it spoils me as an artist.   My feeling is that there i
nothing in life but refraining from hurting others, and
comforting those that are sad.   What kind of feeling i
that for an artist to be narrowed down to ?

To HAVELOCK ELLIS.   ST. LEONARDS, 4*th Dec*

If possible I am going to look for rooms to-morrow
and I shall get so strong, like I was at Fitzroy St., and
shall do everything.   Don't be a bit troubled about me
I am taking quinine four times a day—your quinine. . .
I don't have breakfast.   I get up about half-past nine, a
the early morning is the time I can rest, I walk up and dow
my room and lie down and try to read till one, then I g
down to lunch with the terrible old women, it makes m
heart sorry to see them, poor sad bitter old souls. . . .
think I shall have to go to Montreux the week after next
My heart gets cold when I think of leaving England, lik
ice.   When I come back to England, with my book a
written, then you will come to Paris to meet me ?

To HAVELOCK ELLIS.   ST. LEONARDS, 5*th De*

I am feeling so much better this evening.   I've worke
a little.   I slept well last night, after about one o'clock
Till then I was in such agony thinking there was n
Hereafter, that there wasn't a time when you and I an

Louie and my brother and all of us will know and understand each other, that death will be the end of all this living. How easily one understands how men invented Heaven—

> Where the blighted life re-blooms,
> Where the broken heart the freshness
> Of its fragrant youth resumes.

. . . I am writing such a funny, that is to say, singular, scene. I don't know how it came into my head, where Veronica goes to look at a man's clothes. It is in the place of a whole condensed chapter.

To HAVELOCK ELLIS.   ST. LEONARDS, *7th Dec.*

Worked this evening. . . . Generally I feel as you feel. But when my body gets weak the old original nature comes up and my soul cries out and I don't want to die. I don't want anything I love to die, nothing must lose its *individuality*. It isn't only that I'm weak. I always get into this state when I live utterly alone in England.

To HAVELOCK ELLIS.   ST. LEONARDS, *9th Dec.*

I am working. But my story gets smaller and smaller and smaller. I can't help myself. I am driven on to make it smaller. The last part of the book doesn't need any condensing or much touching. It is good I know. The question is whether anybody ever gets through the first. It's that abominable Veronica and John Ferdinand gave me all this work. . . . As I was writing my brother came in. He only stayed about 20 minutes. He came to say that I must not let money stand in the way of my going to Montreux, if I thought that would do me good.

To HAVELOCK ELLIS.   ST. LEONARDS, *10th Dec.*

Yes, *Undine*, the last part, isn't bitter, because I wrote it *not* at Ratel Hoek, but at Ganna Hoek when I was so peaceful and hopeless and spiritual. It was the feeling I had in that year that I paint in Waldo when he goes to sit out in the sunshine, that placid calm, and I say that it is well to die because I knew that if one lived the eager,

striving, passionate heart would rise again. I may have
copied it at Ratel Hoek. I didn't write it there, but in
my little mud-floored room with the holes in the roof at
Ganna Hoek. I am afraid I am getting into that sweet
resigned unpassionate state again. . . . I am not doing
any French or reading at all. I have only a little strength
and I spend that on writing.

To HAVELOCK ELLIS.   ST. LEONARDS, 11*th Dec.*

I belong to you. Even if I were married our friendship
could not be broken or done away with, any more than my
feeling for Willy Bertram could pass away. Afar off, it
has been the only thing that was like my feeling to you. . . .
The wind is howling, oh, so wild and mad outside. It is
so hard to paint that bright African world with this dark
wild world about me.

To HAVELOCK ELLIS.   13*th Dec.*

I have just done a scene. My work takes so much out
of me, and it is so little in quantity when it is done. It is
like being continually in love.

To HAVELOCK ELLIS.   15*th Dec.*

My other self, the little word I write to you, and the
word you write to me every day, just makes life livable. . . .
Just now I do not exist ; my book exists ; that is all, as
far as my daily life goes : Bertie sitting there that hot day
in the bush, with John Ferdinand. That is why writing
makes me happy because then my own miserable little life
is not. . . .   Before, you were just nothing to me compared
to what you are now. I was trying to fall in love with you
at first that I might " forget." Now I know I cannot fall
in love. If I love now it must be the slow long growth of
years.

To HAVELOCK ELLIS.   16*th Dec.*

Yes, artistic work takes the life blood out of one. It
lives by just as much as you lose.

To HAVELOCK ELLIS. 17*th De*

I think it is my cold room here at the top of the house with nothing over it makes my chest so bad. I have never had a cough keep on week after week like this before. Oh, I want to be strong and vigorous. I don't mind any pain, any suffering, but not to be dragged down. . . . Fancy, I can't understand Balzac, even when I have the translation in my hand, and I can read *Manon Lescaut* almost without the dictionary.

To HAVELOCK ELLIS. ST. LEONARDS, 19*th Dec.*

I told Mrs. Walters you were perhaps going with me to Paris. She has been brooding over it ever since, I can see. If even she thinks so of it, what would other people think ? But they must be taught not to think.

I don't know that I think so very well of a Woman's paper. I object to anything that divides the two sexes. My main point is this : human development has now reached a point at which sexual difference has become a thing of altogether minor importance. We make too much of it ; we are men and women in the second place, human beings in the first.

To HAVELOCK ELLIS. ST. LEONARDS, 21*st Dec.*

Please tell me who F. W. H. Myers of Cambridge is ? I have got a letter from him about *S.A.F.* [*Story of an African Farm*] and he seems to fancy I must know who he is and have read his books. . . . I made up my mind three years ago never to let a man care for me whom another woman thought she had any claim to.

To HAVELOCK ELLIS. ST. LEONARDS, 23*rd Dec.*

I have not yet written anything to-day. Ah, here is my letter ! I am reading it, I have just read the first page. Oh, Harry, how sweet that you think of me *so much*. No, I wasn't unselfish then, but I was trying *hard* to be, now I don't try, it's becoming natural to me ; I mean directly my interest conflict[s] with anyone's, I *want* to give up mine, I don't care for it. Of course always,

ever since I could remember, if I loved a person really, like
I loved Theo and Ettie and Ellie, then I had *no* self, they
were everything, they were me, but I don't call *that* being
unselfish. What lay before me like an intellectual ideal
then has become part of me now. Not that I'm as unselfish as I want to be but somehow it's quite different. I
always thought: " I'm cold and selfish now, but one day that
great good man will love me, and I will be it all then."

To HAVELOCK ELLIS.   ST. LEONARDS, *Exmas morning*.

I like Roden Noel's poems. " Byron's Grave " and
" The Two Magdalenes " are as wholes the poems I like
best, but these lines in " Northern Spring " are to me
wonderful :—

> A bird hath a nest in a twilight of leaves,
> All woven of mosses and lichen and down ;
> An eye there is glistening, a bosom there heaves ;
> You may see there love's miracle when she hath flown—
> Four delicate ovals flecked faintly with wine—
> She is guarding the mystical marvel of life.

They seem to me to reach the high water of poetry. Perhaps
I feel so because I am so one with animals and animal life,
for I can't tell why the lines affect me as they do.

Ach ! I want to go back to the old life. I want to
go away from this life. But if I went back could I live
the old life ? To my little mother it seems that life
was so hard because I was half-starved and had to work
so hard. If anyone could know how beautiful it was !
And the six months at Eastbourne where I had every
comfort and luxury, were the bitterness of death to me,
because I was of no use to anyone.

To HAVELOCK ELLIS.

4, ROBERTSON TERRACE, ST. LEONARDS, 28*th Dec*.

My Harry, can you come on Monday ? I like Myers'
poems better and better the more I read them. Fancy, I
know some of them by heart from hearing my brother Will
saying them, without knowing there was such a man as
Myers ! His favourite was " Oh, somewhere, somewhere,

God unknown." . . . This cough tears me to pieces. . . .
Come for three days and bring your microscope. . . .
(*Later.*) I can't think, I can't work, what shall I do !
For eight days I've not written anything. I'm in a dream.
What is the matter with me ? . . . It is not good for a
human being to live absolutely alone as I live ; one is apt
to go mad. . . . (I wrote this the other day.) I have
just had a new wonderful idea for a wild story. Not at
all like my usual ones, but it will be splendid *when* I am
able to write it. The idea is the conscious transmigration
of a soul. A wild weird impossible thing, real of course—
the feeling. It flashed on me just now when I was reading
Maine's *Ancient Law.*

CHAPTER III

LETTERS WRITTEN IN 1885

To HAVELOCK ELLIS.　　　4, ROBERTSON TERRACE, 4th *Jan*.

I have read some of Myers' essays. He writes well and I like his mind, it is a fine broad mind, but he does not step out quite fearlessly after the truth, anywhere, anywhere. I like his essay on Victor Hugo. He and Swinburne are all sound and form, no truth and no thought. After Ibsen how small all writers and thinkers seem !

To HAVELOCK ELLIS.　　　4, ROBERTSON TERRACE, 5th *Jan*.

I dislike the article of Myers on Renan very much. His assertion that George Sand was a Christian is simple folly. . . . I'm getting more and more power to live out of myself in things that have no personal relation to me. My own life gets less and less. I love my work so. . . . You and I *do* take the long path together because we are going on the same road to the same end. Such a feeling of blank desolation, I mean spiritual desolation, came over me this afternoon, but you and I are together.

To HAVELOCK ELLIS.　　　4, ROBERTSON TERRACE, 6th *Jan*.

When I've had something to eat (I am faint now, lying on my back on the bed, with my feet up high and my paper against *Early Law and Custom*), I am going to sit down and try if I can dash off an article for the *Fortnightly* at one speed. If I can't I'll leave it alone and go on with my darling book. Why do I love it so ? . . . I can see the ships far over the sea. I feel so happy.

To HAVELOCK ELLIS.   4, ROBERTSON TERRACE, 9*th Jan.*

I have been in a dead dream all day. To-morrow I mean to work all day. Myers sent me both volumes of his essays. What you say of him is true. It is not truth but pleasant beauty he looks for.

To HAVELOCK ELLIS.   4, ROBERTSON TERRACE, 10*th Jan.*

Keep me close to you. I have of late such a *dead* feeling emotionally. I think it is the result of my physical illness. Do not you ? I have been in a nightmare all these months and it is not gone. Somehow my life is ebbing away from me. I don't fear death. What I fear is a long life of dying. To live month after month, and year after year, and watch yourself ebb and ebb. To be at your own funeral. It is because my heart is full of this bitterness, and I do not like to show it you, that you feel me far from you. Sometimes visions come to me of waking up and finding my old life again. Perhaps I shall. Oh, if it were just once again for a little time ! . . . I have taken no chloral to-day ; and have tried to write without leaving off since I got up. I have written a few lines. The pain in the left side is getting steadily worse. . . . The writing to you this evening rests me because I'm just telling you all the weak selfish feeling there is in my own heart about myself. I have been crying this afternoon and I cried much of last night.

To HAVELOCK ELLIS.   4, ROBERTSON TERRACE, 10*th Jan.*

Last night I couldn't lie and rest. In my half-asleep state I prayed and I cried. I wanted someone I didn't see to put its arms around me and comfort me and help me to bear. It's interesting as showing how in states of the greatest weakness our childish habits and thoughts come up as the higher nature sinks lower. It shows of how little worth those deathbed sayings are. I hope I shall die with my head clear. . . . Afterwards I got up and put a cold compress on my chest. The relief was immediate and immense. Do you know, long ago, when I broke that blood vessel it was the thing that saved me. I wore one [cold compress] for three months because as soon as I

took it off the expectoration and pain came back. Dr.
Fergus showed me how to make it. He was a young doctor,
something like you. . . . Send me Marcus Aurelius if
you have him.

To HAVELOCK ELLIS. 4, ROBERTSON TERRACE, 11*th Jan.*

Oh, Harry, I want to be good, I want to be good, not
good in the ordinary sense, good to my idea. Never mind
telling me if you think I'm ever wrong ; if you see the
faults in me you must blame me.

To HAVELOCK ELLIS. 4, ROBERTSON TERRACE, 12*th Jan.*

Yes, I used to have that feeling of a power bearing me
up, that would lead me. Now I have a kind of feeling
that it has done ; a blank wall now.

To HAVELOCK ELLIS. 4, ROBERTSON TERRACE, 17*th Jan.*

That nux vomica is good for me. I feel so strong in
the head to-day. I can remember everything ! My legs
are still the same, but it's only the " lymphatic system."
I was up much last night with asthma, but took chloral.

To HAVELOCK ELLIS. 4, ROBERTSON TERRACE, 19*th Jan.*

I remember when I walked up Regent Street with
S.A.F. [*Story of an African Farm*] in the rain, thinking
everyone could know that what was stuck under my cloak
was a rejected MS. Oh ! so heart-sick. . . . If without
trouble you can quote me Darwin's exact words from *Descent
of Man* with regard to the Boers having been at the Cape so
many years and not changed colour, I shall be glad. You have
the *Descent*, have you not ? It is in the middle of the volume.

To HAVELOCK ELLIS. 4, ROBERTSON TERRACE, 20*th Jan.*

Could you find out what the price of rooms in Gower
Street is ? . . . My legs are bad. Three cheers for Olive
Schreiner ; she's the best doctor going. Old Pennie says
it *is* the " lymphatic system " ! ! I look upon that as
a stroke of genius, for I didn't know what a " lymphatic
system " was ! . . . If I only add one line each day I
mean to go on, I shall go on.

To HAVELOCK ELLIS.   4, ROBERTSON TERRACE, 26*th Jan.*

My brother came to see me last night. He was so wonderfully *tender* to me. It seems like a dream. He talked so nicely of you. My other self, you are part of me. . . . Perhaps if I wait I shall have the power to work brought back to me, too. But, oh, Henry, it would be so beautiful just to lean my head back as I am sitting here and die. I am just satisfied now. . . . You know all I have suffered in my life has been my own fault nearly. If I had been wise and unselfish I wouldn't have suffered, but ——

To HAVELOCK ELLIS.   4, ROBERTSON TERRACE, 27*th Jan.*

The doctor has been and I put my rug round me and sat in the chair when he came and told him I was much better and that I thought he wouldn't need to come again. He says that if I go to Mont Dore I will get quite well. Do you know anything about the place? Please find out.

To HAVELOCK ELLIS.   4, ROBERTSON TERRACE, 28*th Jan.*

My chest is getting worse, but my head is wonderfully clearer. To-day I resolved I would get up, and I went in a bath-chair ; now my legs are bad. Oh, it isn't my chest, it isn't my legs, it's I myself, my life. Where shall I go, what shall I do? [Then twelve more pages, all in the same strain ; also asking if she should go to London for the day to consult a doctor.]

To HAVELOCK ELLIS.   4, ROBERTSON TERRACE, 29th *Jan.*

I can't tell why it is that when it begins to get dark in the evening till about 9 o'clock it is so terrible. After that, I get exhausted, but sometimes it goes on till ten or eleven. Oh, such hopelessness, such despair. If I had only a human being to speak to me ! . . . Oh, Harry, think, there are hundreds of human beings in London, and everywhere, lying alone with their physical suffering, and not anyone even to love them like I have.

To HAVELOCK ELLIS.   4, ROBERTSON TERRACE, 30th *Jan.*

Alfred St. Johnston is going to publish my life after I am dead. He wants his children to know about his dear friend, he says. A fine life it will be ! And besides, I'm not going to die yet, eh ? The funny thing is that he doesn't know about my being ill or anything. What puts it into his head that I should die ? And he's so earnest about it ! I won't give him any details. I don't want my life written by anyone. . . . I wouldn't like you to come and see me now, dear, for more than a few hours while I am so ill. It would only be wasting your time and love, my darling. [Alfred St. Johnston died long, long before her. So far as Ellis recalls she had seen him but little, though liking him. Johnston wrote one or two books about the Pacific, as his nephew also is doing now.]

To HAVELOCK ELLIS.   4, ROBERTSON TERRACE, 31*st Jan.*

Please look out for rooms for me for to-day week. My chest is getting much better, so if I can get strong I shall be all right. Please, if you can, get a bed with curtains. It makes such a difference in asthma. I don't know why. . . . Will that paper do to join the " New Life " ? [This paper cannot be found.] . . . I am dead ; I need rousing. Oh, to wake up and be my old self for only one day ! I am getting better, except my legs. But it's no use driving myself mad. I can't work when I can't . . . You are so good to me.

To HAVELOCK ELLIS.   4, ROBERTSON TERRACE. 1*st Feb.*

I am better. I am coming to London on Friday. It's glorious to be better. I could stand on my head.

To HAVELOCK ELLIS.   4, ROBERTSON TERRACE, 2*nd Feb.*

Is that George Sand ? It's funny that when I looked at it as I took it out of the envelope I thought : " That would be a nice mother to have ; but a wife or mistress ! " Woe to the thing that tries to chain that Lion ! It's wonderfully like my mother, more like her than any likeness. . . . I am better. Just think, I am sitting at the table and going to write ! If it's only six lines it will comfort me. . . . If you *could* get decent rooms in Bloomsbury I should be glad.

To HAVELOCK ELLIS.　　4, ROBERTSON TERRACE, 3*rd Feb.*

I'm as lively as a young cricket this morning. I'm 'oing to try and write. . . . No, I'm not more Greek than Christian, I'm both in equal parts. . . . I can read *Manon Lescaut* nicely. [She frequently refers in the letters of this 'eriod to reading French books. Ellis had urged her to his, and had at times read French books with her, to give 'er practice.]

To HAVELOCK ELLIS.　　4, ROBERTSON TERRACE, 5*th Feb.*

I am getting so much better that I really don't *need* o go to London. I wrote to-day a little. . . . Last night cried for hours, I don't know why. It was like a mad gony come on me.

To HAVELOCK ELLIS.　　19, CHARLOTTE ST., 10*th Feb.*

I am vaguely conscious that in moral questions I am still, as I have been for the last two years, passing through a crisis like that which followed the break up of my religious ideas. I am willing, perfectly willing, to follow what is right, as I then was to follow what was true. But I didn't quite know at first what was true, and I don't now see what is right. Some day I shall see clearer. But one cannot hasten sight ; it has to grow clear slowly. When one breaks away from all old moorings, and shapes a higher path of morality for oneself, and perhaps for others who shall follow one, it cannot be done without suffering (I am not explaining rightly what I mean, only I dimly see it, and know what I mean, though I can't express it.) I *do* desire as sincerely to do what is right as I used to desire to know what was true when I couldn't see truth anywhere. . . . What help and comfort you are to me I hardly think you realise.

To HAVELOCK ELLIS.　　HASTINGS, 23*rd Feb.*

I am always giving you trouble. Now you have to go running about my bag again ! I'm glad it's found. I thought I saw you carry it down. . . . I have worked twelve hours already to-day, and am going to work some more

before I go to bed. I feel so well in spite of a little col
have *enjoyed* my work so. Life would be too beautiful
one were always well. If I could keep on feeling like th
my book would be done in four weeks.

To HAVELOCK ELLIS.   HASTINGS, 24*th Fe*

After my fifteen hours work of course I lay awake a
night. Up early this morning and for a walk. Now goin
to have lunch, then to work again. I am trying to brea
myself into the habit of going to sleep before twelve an
waking very early. I wrote with such delight and enjoy
ment yesterday.

To HAVELOCK ELLIS.   HASTINGS, 25*th Fe*

I am *writing*, not walking and getting excited. Th
change my visit to London worked in me is wonderfu
My being so strong I have the feeling that always goes wit
that state.

To HAVELOCK ELLIS.   HASTINGS, 26*th Fe*

I have not read at all to-day, or thought about anything
but Bertie and Rebekah. I have such a nasty bit to revis
to-morrow. I don't think it's interesting because I didn
enjoy writing it. It's about two mean scandal-talkin
women, and I can't bear writing about mean people.
don't dislike writing about wicked ones, it doesn't pain m
if they're large. I have done with Rebekah's diary. I ge
on slowly though I work so much. You see I have t
copy the whole book as well as revise. . . . I don't seem t
have any self, I am all lost in my work. . . . I am goin
to do a little French before I go to bed.

To HAVELOCK ELLIS.   HASTINGS, 27*th Fe*

The part of my life that stands out almost more clearl
than anything else, like an imprinted picture, is one mornin
at [Crystal] Palace Road. It was the last awful Sunday
spent there. All night I thought I was going mad and la
on the floor and walked up and down ; at dawn, about hal
past four, I went to the chemist's just near the corner, i
that street that runs down at the bottom of Palace Road

stood there knocking for half an hour, but no one heard.
wanted bromide or something, to make me sleep. I can
e that scene just as it looked to me, printed like one of
Iogarth's pictures. While I stood there waiting a milkman
ame with his pails and he stopped at the house opposite,
nd a dirty, wicked-looking woman and a girl in curl papers
ame to the door and talked low talk with him and laughed
w laughs. The chemist came down at last in his night-
hirt and trousers and gave me the medicine. It had been
aining in the night and the street was damp, but it was a
ne morning.

'o HAVELOCK ELLIS.   HASTINGS, 28*th Feb*.

I sent the George Sand portrait to my brother without
aying anything. He says it's just like my Aunt Rolland
nd my brother Will. He doesn't mention it's being like
ny mother, but then he's never seen her since he was
bout twelve years old. . . . I have been working to-day.
3ut my mind is a little over-excited, and I am trying to keep
own feelings which bother me. I can't get on with those
wo scandal-talking women.

'o HAVELOCK ELLIS.   HASTINGS, 2*nd March*.

I have been looking at that life of Schopenhauer to-day.
f I had ever read him, or even knew before I came to Eng-
and that such a man existed, one would say I had copied
vhole ideas in the *African Farm* and *From Man to Man*
rom him. There is one passage of his on the search for
hilosophic truth that reads like a paraphrase of my allegory
n the *African Farm*. There's something so beautiful in
:oming on one's very own most inmost thoughts in another.
n one way it's one of the greatest pleasures one has. That
.ife [of Schopenhauer] by Miss Zimmern is very well
vritten. . . . The women's rights women are going mad,
t seems to me. The latest idea is to set up a women's par-
iament to legislate for women and children !

'o HAVELOCK ELLIS.   HASTINGS, 3*rd March*.

My Aunt Rolland is my mother's sister, married a
'rench missionary, and went out to the Cape. I am exactly

like her in face, except the nose. A painted portrait o
her, before she was married, has often been taken for m
She is the mother of Mrs. Orpen and Mrs. Hope. She
still alive, very old, over ninety I think, but still writes an
walks about like a young woman.

To HAVELOCK ELLIS.   HASTINGS, 4*th March*

I *am* going to finish off my scandal-talking wome
to-day. Somehow I can't bear them. I wish there wer
only noble people in the world, *intense* if wicked. Bu
there are so many of these others. . . . I am getting mor
and more to hate the world, dress, and material cares an
pleasures. I used to wish I could feel like this; now that
do I find it has its drawbacks ! I am entering Nirvan
when you are a little waking out of it.

To HAVELOCK ELLIS.   HASTINGS, 4*th March*

I've not worked yet to-day. Been doing all sorts o
little things. I am very well. I haven't *looked* so we
since I came to England. Lovely weather here.

To HAVELOCK ELLIS.   HASTINGS, 7*th March*

I had pretty bad asthma last night. . . . I'm glad I'r
a member of the New Life, but perhaps I shall never atten
any of the meetings. I doubt whether I shall come t
London again before I leave for Switzerland. . . . I wis
I had arranged to go to Brighton to-day. I feel so incline
to go somewhere. I have just finished a chapter. When
am in the middle of a chapter I don't care for going out, m
mind is dwelling on it so. I shall have to sit hard and fas
at my book if I am to have it ready by the time I leave.
feel that I must not expect much for it. It is too strong fo
that. If I only get enough to keep me independent fo
one year I shall be satisfied. The things I mean to writ
next are things that will pay better.

To HAVELOCK ELLIS.   HASTINGS, 9*th March*

I fight always so hard to keep all sad hopeless thought
from me, because they sap the strength I want for my work
. . . Don't let your heart get overweighted with the though

of all there is to do and the little time there is to do it in
us mine often gets. "*Without rest, without haste.*" I
keep saying that to myself.

To HAVELOCK ELLIS. HASTINGS, 10*th March.*

Miss Müller called to-day, but I didn't feel that I
wanted to see her. I sent down word to say I couldn't ;
to-morrow I go to her Woman's meeting, I think, but I'm
so afraid my brother'll come while I'm out. I have a
feeling that he's coming, You know I've only seen him
for a few hours in the last year and a half.

To HAVELOCK ELLIS. HASTINGS, 11*th March.*

I went to the Woman's meeting this afternoon. There
was only one really fine speech, and that was by a man.
It was a drawing-room meeting, there were only three men
there. He was a splendid fellow, a great advocate for
women's rights. He stood up at the end when asked to
second the resolution, and said it was because women were
such *cowards* that they didn't get what they wanted. " You
can't serve God and Mammon, or Mrs. Grundy, and yet
attain to what you wish." . . . I've just got your letter.
Isn't it funny, I felt ill just as you did last night, as if I
had fever, burning all over, and crying, but for three nights
I've seemed quite delirious. I feel to-day aching all over
but better than yesterday. . . . Perhaps I had better go over
to Eastbourne for a day and then I shall rest a little. I
can't bear it any more ; there just comes a time when
you can't.

To HAVELOCK ELLIS. HASTINGS, 12*th March.*

Miss Müller called to-day. We had a long and very
delightful talk. . . . No, I never feel " Without rest,
without haste." That's why I always have to keep saying
it to myself. . . . You never told me how glorious J. A.
Symonds' new sonnets are ; " Stella Maris "—isn't it fine ?

To HAVELOCK ELLIS. HASTINGS, 13*th March.*

I went to Pevensey in the afternoon. It was so beautiful. Here are three daisies I picked there. I sat in the fork

of a tree below the Castle. The rooks in the tall bar
branches of the trees were talking ; they seem to me t
be always *talking*, you can hear, it's conversation. An ol
church, too, a grave-yard, great flat marches, and the se
far off.

To HAVELOCK ELLIS.   HASTINGS, 14*th March*

Have been working to-day again. Going to Pevense
seems to have soothed me. . . . Read Montaigne's sig
nificant essay on repentance ; it is one of my favourites.

To HAVELOCK ELLIS.   HASTINGS, 16*th March*

I did such splendid work to-day. Isn't it wonderfu
what effect the trivial change has on me ? You know livin
here alone is something like solitary confinement in it
mental effect on me. It isn't length of time ; two day
do me perhaps more good than six.

To HAVELOCK ELLIS.   HASTINGS, 17*th March*

I send you a little present. It's some gorse I got thi
morning at the top of the hill at Ecclesbourne. It's th
walk Bertie went with the Jew servant. They went pas
there. Only it was misty, not beautiful and sunny lik
to-day.

To HAVELOCK ELLIS.   HASTINGS, 20*th March*

Can one talk of a " croning " laugh ? I say " Rebekal
laughed the small croning laugh she laughed only at Bertie.
I always use the word.

To HAVELOCK ELLIS.   HASTINGS, 21*st March*

All the last eight days I have a most terrible headach
that never leaves me. I feel so over-excited and full o
blood, like when I'm very miserable. But I'm not miserabl
at all now.

To HAVELOCK ELLIS.   HASTINGS, 22*nd March*

I have got up very early, have had an egg and some brea
and some squeezed lemon (my invariable breakfast) an

am going out to post this and for a walk. . . . Mrs. Walters is the one woman who sympathises with me in everything. . . .

To HAVELOCK ELLIS.   HASTINGS, 2 3rd *March.*

I begin to be afraid I shan't get much for this book. It will be so *very* small, one small volume after all this work. If people only know how easy it was to write three volumes, how difficult to write one ! . . . You know, darling, when I say I'm happy I don't think you understand. I think you think I mean something like what is ordinarily called happiness.   I don't think the feeling I call "happiness" has much likeness to that.   It means that *I am for a time in a condition to master my own feelings and keep them from rending me.*   I don't think you know what feeling is to me, how it can rend even my physical structure. When I was a little girl I came [out] of church one Sunday. I was sent out for something. When I got out it was all so wonderfully still on the Mission Station, no one was about in the mid-day, there was not a sound, and up in the sky there was *one* large white [cloud]. It was a thing I have never seen but that once. It was a large round mass of cloud, standing in the middle of the sky, and it [was] silvered over on the side facing the sun and dark on the underside and the top was all like turrets and castles. It was the most beautiful thing I had ever seen. I got more and more excited and quivering when I looked at it, it was so wonderful to me. I thought God had sent it just on purpose, when he knew that I should be coming out of church, that I might see it alone. I almost fell on the ground with feeling. I wouldn't be so foolish now ; but still I could pray like when I was a little child that I might not feel too much—— Just got your letter. Fancy, I didn't know till your letter came that to-morrow was my birthday ! I never shall be right about any date. . . . I feel a little bothered about this fullness of blood in the head, it's not headache, it's just as if my head and especially neck were full of blood. . . . I'll not be sad. Life is a battle to be fought, quietly, persistently, at every moment.

6

To HAVELOCK ELLIS.   HASTINGS, 24*th March.*

What a beautiful present ! . . . I have quite a grand
birthday. It is such a glorious day outside, only I feel sad
I want to cry. It isn't because it's my birthday. . . .
I must get to my writing and then I lose sight of my own
individuality.

To HAVELOCK ELLIS.   HASTINGS, 25*th March.*

I liked your letter this morning. I was miserable and
wanting to cry all day. I couldn't work. I held myself
in. If I once give way it may be weeks or months before
I pull together. . . . *The Story of My Heart* is *wretched.*
I shall take your Shelley to bed to-night.

To HAVELOCK ELLIS.   HASTINGS, 26*th March.*

I have been working pretty well to-day. My head is
troublesome, but only fullness of blood because I think
too much. (I should be all right if I could do my work in
the open air.) It is wonderful how strong and well my chest
is keeping. I am living at the same kind of high pressure
as that year at Dordrecht. I can *feel* myself growing intellectually. . . . You *perfectly* understand my old self, but
not in the same way my new self. It is this last four years
(on the 30th of this month) that makes the difference. I
don't understand myself now, and how should you ? In
years to come I will see what was the meaning of all this.

To HAVELOCK ELLIS.   HASTINGS, 29*th March.*

Only about 130 pages revised, and four or five hundred
more ! When will it be done ? Yet I can't quicken myself.
My mind must work at its own pace. . . . To-day I thought
of these things that always goad me up into life and work
again : my want to be independent, the thought that I may
die and leave my book unfinished. I shall perhaps send you
a couple of pages, revised and unrevised, and not tell you
which is which, and see which you like. Oh, I must work,
I must work. Death'll come and I've done nothing, and
I've so much I want to say and so much I want to paint.
You know my mind is beginning to feel a little like when
I wrote the *African Farm*, and at Ganna Hoek and Lelie

Kloof and Ratel Hoek. My work and my people seem more real to me than I myself. . . . This morning I looked at [George Sand's] *Elle et Lui*. How splendid it is in some parts ! That last little bit is like the grand parts of the Bible in style.

To HAVELOCK ELLIS. HASTINGS, 29*th March*.

Oh Havelock, when I have even £200 of my own, so that once again I can have that feeling of perfect freedom and independence ! If it were you or any other man it would be the same. I can't live on dependence. Ah, freedom, freedom, freedom, that is the first great want of humanity. That is why I sympathise so much more with the Herbert Spencer school than with the Socialists, so called. If I thought Socialism would bring the subjection of the individual to the whole I would fight to the death. But human nature will assert itself under Socialism as elsewhere. Better to die of cold or hunger or thirst than to be robbed of your freedom of action, of your feeling that you are an absolutely free and independent unit.

To HAVELOCK ELLIS. HASTINGS, 1*st April*.

If I was to be in love with anyone else and tell you about it would you be able to sympathise with me ? There is a young Jew singing in the next room, with such a beautiful full man's voice, and it seems to wake up in me all my old, old dreams of when I was about fourteen, I don't know why. I know it would never be possible for me to find that ideal love : but somehow, I can't say why, the longing wakes up in one again. My body even has the same feeling. Perhaps it's because his voice is just like my father's that it brings back the past. . . . I have been lying down all day, not able to work, but I have read [George Moore's] *The Mummer's Wife*. I like it very much, better than *Nana*, and I think it shows a great deal of genius, and I'm going to stick up for it.

To HAVELOCK ELLIS. HASTINGS, 2*nd April*.

I can't get out. I sprained my leg on that long walk. Roden Noel called yesterday, and to-day, too, but I've

not been able to see him. I like him very much, more than
Myers, he's more *real*. . . . I've never left off work since
I got up early this morning. If it were something new I
should get on quickly. I should like very much to sit
quietly by you and talk this evening. I have got a horrid
bit of my book to revise now ; then I have only one more
horrid bit ; all the rest is delightful to the end.

To HAVELOCK ELLIS.   HASTINGS, 3*rd April.*

I am going to work to-day. My mind is so full. I
ought to write much.

To HAVELOCK ELLIS.   HASTINGS, 4*th April.*

I am better. I am going nearly mad with my work.
I have written this half chapter out *nine* times. Now I'm
going back to the first, only I've torn it up.

To HAVELOCK ELLIS.   HASTINGS, 5*th April.*

My mind struck work to-day and I have been doing
needlework. . . . Roden Noel returns to London to-
morrow. He has given me a pressing invitation to come
and spend at least a day and night with them, and then I
shall be near you. I shall come up to town the 1st May
for good. Hastings is already getting too enervating for
me. . . . With regard to my scribbling, I have gone
back to the original thing. I think I get silly over my
work, I want more than I can have at last. I am getting so
disgusted with my work ; it seems I don't show people
at all what I mean. But I suppose the ideal perfection
is no more attainable in one's work than elsewhere. . . .
The only part of Hinton's teaching that is quite original
is his idea of polygamy as a remedy for prostitution (one-
sided polygamy) and this is just his false and weak point.
What Hinton did, the great good he did, was that by his
character and standing he got a hearing for ideas that many
other people might have preached in vain. As a man he
must have had genius, that wonderful personal power
which makes people listen and follow whether they will or
not. I think I should have liked Hinton very much if I
had known him.

To HAVELOCK ELLIS.   HASTINGS, 8*th April.*

I have just received this [from Eleanor Marx Aveling].
Please go and see them and tell me just how Aveling is.
If he gets dangerously ill I must go. If the Avelings are
very hard-up I must try to send them something, but I
am hard-up myself just now.

To HAVELOCK ELLIS.   HASTINGS, 9*th April.*

You know I think the brain works hard when one is
not conscious of its working. I told you this afternoon
I had not been working for some days. I'd sit at my table
but nothing would come, only a strange blank feeling in
my mind ; couldn't think, couldn't feel. Suddenly, this
evening, the feeling came to sit down and write. I have
been writing hour after hour, page after page. I could
write till to-morrow morning. I don't know where all the
ideas come from if they've not been forming slowly these
last few days while my mind has felt so blank. I have had
the same experience over and over again before. I work
very hard for some days, or think very intensely on some
subject day and night. Then suddenly my mind strikes
work. For a day or two days or three days I seem quite
passive. Then suddenly, as in a moment, it all bursts open
again, and I find all the thoughts that were half-formed
and in confusion when I left work, completed and ready.
I wonder whether other people have the same experience.

To HAVELOCK ELLIS.   HASTINGS, 10*th April.*

If you're a good boy when you come I've got a *lovely*
little story to tell you that came to me this morning when
I was in bed, quite a new one I never had before. It's about
a man and a little girl on a desert island. It's lovely.

To HAVELOCK ELLIS.   HASTINGS, 11*th April.*

I have been working all the morning, but now I must
give in and read French. . . . Long ago I used to think
that was quite a discovery of mine that there is as much
structure in prose as in verse. The difference is that in
verse (which is only a kind of style in which you set certain

To HAVELOCK ELLIS.   HASTINGS, 3*rd May*.

I have just discovered from Bagehot that what I am trying to do is to make my work classical ! That essay of his on the Classic and Gothic rather good, eh ? I am better.

To HAVELOCK ELLIS.   HASTINGS, 4*th May*.

I have been making observations now for many years and I have come to the conclusion that between the brain and the kidneys there is the most wonderful interaction. It seems ridiculous but when I work much and use my brain powerfully it *always* has an effect on my kidneys and causes a heavy sediment. And very intense feeling, connected with terrible over-excitement, has the same effect.

To HAVELOCK ELLIS.   HASTINGS, 5*th May*.

I think Eleanor [Marx Aveling] is coming to meet me at Charing Cross, but I have to hear from her again. Alfred St. Johnston has sent me flowers. . . . This morning it has been so beautiful on the sea, a bright wonderful light along the horizon, one of those beautiful scenes one never forgets. . . . I feel better to-night. I won't take any more bromide.

To HAVELOCK ELLIS.

30, DOWNSHIRE HILL, HAMPSTEAD, 30*th May*.

I am not able to come, my darling, but I want to see you. Can't you come Monday morning at 10 to National Gallery, and then we go to Grosvenor Gallery together if fine ? . . . Please think of some books for me to get. [This was a constant request.]

To HAVELOCK ELLIS.   HAMPSTEAD, 12*th May*.

Forty one was the number. I am going there to-morrow afternoon, if I can, to see Mrs. Hinton. I feel so well now I've been in the London air. I enjoyed to-day. I am going to try and work. . . . Philip [Marston, the blind poet] came this afternoon. He says he is going to invite some people to meet me, Theodore Watts, Swinburne,

Moore, etc   I will tell him to ask you if I go.   I don't like to go to any place without you now.   [This did not come off.]

To HAVELOCK ELLIS.   HAMPSTEAD, 13*th May.*

I have been searching all day for rooms near Manchester Square, etc., and found nothing.   I think it's no use.   You mustn't waste your precious time looking for rooms for me.   Let one of us at least be working. . . . I want to stay at home and see dear Mrs. Hinton to-morrow, and see D—— on Thursday, and go with you to the Academy, eh ?

To HAVELOCK ELLIS.   HAMPSTEAD, 16*th May.*

It was so sweet to get your letter.   I'm a poor miserable creature.   I feel really ill all over, and couldn't come to my boy. . . . I've got I don't know what the matter with me.   I can't read or walk, my head and all my body aches, like hay fever.   Perhaps I shall have to go back to St. Leonards.   I will meet you if I can at the National Gallery at 10. . . . You see I can't get better and work.   What is the matter with me ?   You know I am always feeling so ill now, even when I am what I call well, as if my constitution had no more strength. . . . Do not trouble about my monetary concerns.   When my book is out I am sure to have a couple of hundred pounds, and shall, if I live, have plenty of money one day. . . . If I don't turn up on Monday you must come to me.

To HAVELOCK ELLIS.

41, UPPER BAKER ST., LONDON, 17*th May.*

This afternoon Philip Marston and Rider Haggard called.   I had such a dreadful time.   In the middle of the visit my landlady burst open the door in a rage—I'll tell you all about it when we meet.   After they were gone the two women turned on me and stormed.   They asked me if I had so many men always coming after me.   Then they said they were much insulted that I hadn't asked them to come in and introduce them.   I began to cry. . . . I hope Roden Noel won't come.   They will think I have nothing loved another woman as a mistress before, and how she gets the other woman so beautifully to live with them. What Aldis says about monogamy being our present highest aim but something higher *coming after it*, is what I've so long felt but never seen expressed anywhere. No state will ever be final ; as soon as we have attained to it we shall cease to need it.

To HAVELOCK ELLIS.   UPPER BAKER ST., *9th July*.

Life would be so perfect, so beautiful, so divine, but I think I'm reaching a kind of Nirvana. I can't feel much personally, nor desire much for myself ; that is passing. *Self* seems to be dead in me. Other people want to kill self, but I want so to wake mine to life again, but it won't wake. You know I didn't kill myself two years ago, but I really died then. It's so funny, I can't make anyone understand, I don't think I could describe it in a book ; but I have died. It's strange Philip Marston feels this about me, without knowing. When I first knew you I kept thinking you would be able to bring my old *self* back to life again. . . . What you say about Hinton is true. His value, like the value of Emerson, is that of *stimulation*. He brings no new thought—when he does it is worthless—but he makes all thoughts live and throb, which is the work of true genius.

To HAVELOCK ELLIS.   UPPER BAKER ST., *20th July*.

Donkin says Gladstone likes the *African Farm* so much.

To HAVELOCK ELLIS.   UPPER BAKER ST., *23rd July*.

I don't know what is the matter with me that I long for quiet so, just for twenty-four hours without the sound of a cart or a wheel, just stillness in one's ears. When the carts have left off making a noise, when all is still to-night, I'll try to write to you. I can't write to anyone, not to my brother, not to Mamma, not a real letter to you.

To HAVELOCK ELLIS.   UPPER BAKER ST., *27th July*.

Maggie Harkness brought me yesterday Balzac's *Physiologie du Mariage*. It is very easy. I can understand it.

To HAVELOCK ELLIS.   UPPER BAKER ST., *2nd Aug.*

My asthma is still bad. I think it is the little close house.
I have been out on the hill and then I could breathe. The
place is very beautiful but I am afraid I shall not be able to
stay. I get plenty of good food—and can't eat it. I will
write a long letter when I wake up from my asthma.

To HAVELOCK ELLIS.   UPPER BAKER ST., *3rd Aug.*

I have been sitting out on the rocks alone till ten
o'clock. They are rough rocks that stick out into the sea.
I like to sit just perfectly still and think of nothing and
look at the water, black, dark water it is. . . . My asthma
makes me so stupid, but I'll soon be quite right when I find
other rooms. Please try to feel restful when you think of
me.

To HAVELOCK ELLIS.   UPPER BAKER ST., *4th Aug.*

Suffocated all night. Have been rushing all over the
place for rooms where I can breathe. Have found some.
Will spend the last farthing I have. Can't think of anything
but breathe.

16, PORTSEA PLACE, *4th Aug.* (*2nd letter*).

Havelock, all day to-day I looked for rooms till three
o'clock. Then I arranged to come here. All the afternoon I have been trying to get someone to bring my
luggage. Now it is late and dark and I haven't got it
yet. My face and eyes are so swollen I can't see anything.
I don't know where to go or what to do. Even here I cannot
breathe. It all looks so dark. I am lying on my back.

To HAVELOCK ELLIS.   PORTSEA PLACE, *5th Aug.*

I am writing to St. Leonards to see if I can go there if
I get worse. I feel very desolate.

5th Aug. (*2nd letter*).

I have been snuffing glycerine and can see a little better.
I have got out my papers and am trying to work. I see
nothing but sea ; it is very quiet. (*Later.*) Am not able

to work.   Have written to landlady at St. Leonards to hear
if she can take me.   (*Later.*)   Just got your letter.   The
rose leaves I like so much ;   they seem to comfort me
I'll never throw them away.

To HAVELOCK ELLIS.

16, PORTSEA PLACE, LONDON, 10*th Aug.*

My Havelock comrade, I am still so stupid and going
to bed.   (*Later.*)   I didn't go to bed then, I lay on the sofa
and read the *Pall Mall*.[1]   I feel so sad this evening somehow.

To HAVELOCK ELLIS.   16, PORTSEA PLACE, 11*th Aug.*

Have been lying down all day, but better ;   I am
going to sleep now, I am so sleepy always.   I wrote a
long letter to you in my head in the night ;   now I forget.
I try to comfort you what poor way I can.

To HAVELOCK ELLIS.   16, PORTSEA PLACE, 12*th Aug.*

Oh, how each of us has to live alone and bear our burden
alone. . . .   If I could work, if I were not quite so weak,
I should not feel plunged in this gulf of melancholy.

To HAVELOCK ELLIS.   16, PORTSEA PLACE, 14*th Aug.*

I was awake nearly all night with my cough and I
wondered if your tired heart was resting a little. . . . I
have got out my papers, but I can't work.

To HAVELOCK ELLIS.   16, PORTSEA PLACE, 16*th Aug.*

Have been so industrious writing since I got up early
this morning, without leaving off, except while I cut out
my dress.   Art thou working hard ?   I *must*, or I should
be very miserable.

To HAVELOCK ELLIS.   16, PORTSEA PLACE, 17*th Aug.*

Last night D—— came in.   He said a funny coincidence
had just happened.   He was leaving the Savile Club
and talking to a military doctor just come from Egypt.

---

[1] This was the time of the Criminal Law Amendment Act agitation and
outcry about the protection of girls.

D—— said he had to go (he was coming to me) and the minute after the man told him that last Sunday he was reading the most wonderful book he ever read, *An African Farm.* " Why," D—— said, " the writer of that book is the very person I am going to see." The man said he wanted to see me ; so D—— asked if he could fetch him, and they stayed talking till half-past eleven.

To HAVELOCK ELLIS.   16, PORTSEA PLACE, 18*th Aug.*

Sweet brother soul, don't feel far from me. I too am going now through a very dark and bitter moment of my life. Each one of us must go through his own alone, you yours, I mine. I have never before felt so tender to you. Any new thing that has come into my life cannot touch my feeling for you. It might touch other feelings, any feeling of passionate love I had ever had for anyone, but *not* my sympathy with your nature. I have been thinking just now with such longing of my little bedroom at Ganna Hoek with its hole in the roof and the stars shining through, and of your little hut in Australia where you too used to lie and look up at the stars through the roof. I have a strange feeling now that my life is coming near its end. Not at all because I am weak or ill, I feel very strong, but I seem to have nothing to strive for, all lust and desire of fame or even of love seem dying out in my heart. I love because I must, but I can also renounce.

To HAVELOCK ELLIS.
16 PORTSEA PLACE, 18*th Aug.* (2*nd letter*).

Oh, Henry, when passion enters into a relationship it does spoil the holy sweetness. But perhaps those people are right who say no such thing as friendship is possible between a man and a woman, only I can't bear to think so.

To HAVELOCK ELLIS.   16, PORTSEA PLACE, 19*th Aug.*

Yes, passion has its beautiful side, but it must be kept very much in the background, an underlying sweetness that one feels through other things. It seems to me that no one feels about these things just as I do.

To HAVELOCK ELLIS.   16, PORTSEA PLACE, 21*st Aug*.

I am writing hard. I am going to be strong, and not give way to any weakness.

To HAVELOCK ELLIS.   16, PORTSEA PLACE, 22*nd Aug*

Sweet comrade, you mustn't feel life blank like I do. . . . If you are made unhappy by the thought of my marrying, that needn't be, because I shall never marry anyone ; all such love is never for me.

To HAVELOCK ELLIS.   16, PORTSEA PLACE, 25*th Aug*.

I am going to bed. D—— came for a few minutes. He said a few words in his sweet respectful manner and borrowed Bebel's *Woman* and went. I am very tired. I wish I was away at St. Leonards or somewhere and could look at the sea. Oh, I only want to rest, to rest, to rest.

To HAVELOCK ELLIS.   16, PORTSEA PLACE, 2*nd Sept*

I am starting off to Ventnor on Friday, I don't know where I shall go, I shall only take my little black case, so I can wander anywhere. I can't sit still here. . . . The Doctor was pained with my note, didn't come to see me, only wrote a note.

To HAVELOCK ELLIS.   16, PORTSEA PLACE, 3*rd Sept*

I don't think I am going to the Isle of Wight. I can' afford it. I must stay quietly and work everything down I will try not to see anyone for the next week. In a hundred years we'll all be asleep quietly under the ground.

To HAVELOCK ELLIS.   16, PORTSEA PLACE, 5*th Sept*

Life will bloom over and over again for thee, sweet comrade. You mayn't think so, but your life isn't begun yet. My personal life ended a few years ago, and nothing matters very much now. . . . I went to the London Library this afternoon, and while I was there Huxley came in. He's a jolly old fellow with the bright eyes of genius and such a funny humorous nose. This afternoon, Sand with, the man D—— brought to see me, called and stayed

some time. I'm trying not to see anyone. If we have time
when you come we must go to Hampstead. I must be hard.
You don't mind ?

To HAVELOCK ELLIS.   16, PORTSEA PLACE, 11*th Sept.*

Sat up almost the whole of last night writing. So stupid
this morning.

                    11*th Sept.* (*2nd letter*).

Only fit to walk about outside and look at the street.
. . . I think I see the whole woman question in a way
I never did before, and more clearly than ever now. I
have not been wasting my time lately, though I seem to
have been.

To HAVELOCK ELLIS.   16, PORTSEA PLACE, 14*th Sept.*

Dr. Wilks and Mrs. Barnes [Sir Samuel Wilks and his
daughter] called this afternoon. Dr. Wilks and I had a
nice long talk about the expression of the mind through the
body. He is a fine man intellectually. They wanted me to
go there to-morrow evening, but I won't go out anywhere.
It will be right to go on the river to-morrow because the
fresh air will set me up.

To HAVELOCK ELLIS.   16, PORTSEA PLACE, 17*th Sept.*

Oh, my baby [as she styles Ellis] isn't coming, and I
put on my clean blue dress and did my hair. I got some
rumpsteak and I've just been out and got half a cold lovely
water melon. I thought I'd feed a hot baby with it, but
now he hasn't come. I shan't put on my clean blue dress
to-morrow, and I shan't do my hair ! Are you ill, "heart-
aar " ? [" aar "=vein].

To HAVELOCK ELLIS.   17*th Sept.* (*2nd letter*).

I have just got your card. Oh, my boy, you told me
yesterday you were all right, but I ought to have taken
more care of you. What is the matter with you, my sweet
other self ? You oughtn't to have told me you were all
right because I always believe you.

7

To HAVELOCK ELLIS.   17*th Sept.* (*3rd letter*)

I have not even tried to write or think to-day. Thi
morning I was expecting you, and this afternoon I fel
tired in heart and body. How is he [Ellis] this evening
. . . Do you know, Henry, that the real cause why I an
happier and stronger now lies in you. You satisfy tha
deepest yearning in my nature for sympathy so perfectly.

To HAVELOCK ELLIS.   16, PORTSEA PLACE, 18*th Sep.*

The thought suddenly came to me this evening tha
—— had come back. (You know he wasn't to come til
next week.) I knew it quite well. I put on my things an
went round to —— Street. The hall lamp was lighte
and there was a little light shining through the shutters o
the room. I came home, I was going to have my war
bath and was undressed when I heard a woman and chil
singing outside in the street. I went to the window t
give them some pennies, and when I looked out I saw hi
going away. My landlady said I was gone to bed. H
said he would come again to-morrow, and she mustn
tell me he had been. Do you like me to tell you all abou
myself? You must tell me if ever you don't.

To HAVELOCK ELLIS.   16, PORTSEA PLACE, 28*th Sep*

I have been reading *Diana of the Crossways* all da
Isn't it splendid ! I am going to write to poor old Meredit
they say he is so ill. My head is still so bad I don't kno
what to do. I wish I could come to-morrow, but if it's
cold I can't.

To HAVELOCK ELLIS.   16, PORTSEA PLACE, 29*th Se*

Yesterday D—— came ; he says I'm not to work f
a week. He took me to dinner at the P——'s. When
came back we had a talk. He talked so nicely of you.

To Mrs. J. H. PHILPOT.   16, PORTSEA PLACE, 4*th O*

I think *Diana of the Crossways* the most fascinating no
that has been published in England since *The Mill on*
Floss.

To Mrs. Cawood.   16, Portsea Place, *5th Oct.*

I've a great many friends who are very loving to me, but sometimes I feel very lonely. I want something really to belong to me ; there seems always one side of one's nature left empty when one lives alone like I do. I can't marry, you know, because I never can find anyone that suits me.

To Mrs. Cawood.   London, *5th Oct.*

Ach, I would like to see old Africa a bit, I would like to smell the mimosa trees. I often see the sun shining on that flat in Ganna Hoek. It never shines so here. It is only the people that make England so delightful ; our old Africa beats this old country through and through, but the people are so delightful that one forgives it. [She often made this remark to me in the first years of our acquaintance.]

To Havelock Ellis.   16, Portsea Place, *5th Oct.*

A splendid flash, a whole story, this morning, so lovely, about a rich grand prostitute. Oh, so splendid, you will like it so. I am going to sit down and begin at once. . . . I must work now for money. I shall have to beg my brother for a few pounds or work for it. It's so splendid to be quite without money and quite reckless. I feel like I used to.

To Havelock Ellis.   *5th Oct.* (*2nd letter*).

Miss Müller came and took me for a drive this afternoon ; we went to Wimbledon. It was such a help to me. I am so tired. I want to lose myself in my work. Don't wonder, please, if I don't write much, you are not far from me even when I don't write.

To Havelock Ellis.   16, Portsea Place, *6th Oct.*

I'm working at my dress to-night. I can't do stiff brain work. I have no control over my mind. I can only keep trying to distract it. . . . I am well physically.

To HAVELOCK ELLIS.   16, PORTSEA PLACE, 24*th* Oc.

It seems so nice to talk a little to you. I got bac
about 1 to-day. [She had been spending a few days wit.
Miss Carrie Haddon at Dover.] I wrote a letter to yo
at Dover and dropped it in the street. I really *love* Carrie
and her sister is just as nice. I would like to go to Dove
just to be near them. What beautiful unselfish lives
One feels the better for seeing them.

To HAVELOCK ELLIS.   16, PORTSEA PLACE, 26*th* Oc

Have just come back from Dr. Philpot's. Ray Lankeste
was there. He is the most *powerful* human being I eve
came into contact with ; he is like those winged beasts fro
Nineveh at the British Museum. What you feel is ju
immense force.

To HAVELOCK ELLIS.   16, PORTSEA PLACE, 27*th* Oc

I *don't* like Michael Field's [Miss Katharine Bradley's
letter, not at all. She's false and artificial. Clever, nothin
more, *very clever*. . . . Give my kind regards to Edwar
Carpenter when you write, and tell him I will be very gla
if he will come to see me when he comes to London, if h
has time. I am stupid, but I will, I will, I will try to wor
to-morrow. (*Later.*) Chest very bad. Couldn't see any
one this afternoon. Haggard, Marston, etc., came. Ju
had a letter from Arnold White who has come from the Cap
says he has read my book and wants to come and see m
[Arnold White was the representative later of the Sout
African Republic.]

To HAVELOCK ELLIS.   16, PORTSEA PLACE, 28*th* Oc

Chest bad but better. . . . I am going to write
that Arnold White ; it will be nice to see someone wh
comes from the Cape. . . . Why won't you let me s
Miss Haddon's letter ? I know she *will* look upon me
" one of *us*," just as the Christians do. It rather flatte
me to feel that however much I contradict people they w
persist in thinking I feel as they do !

To HAVELOCK ELLIS.   16, PORTSEA PLACE, 29th Oct.

My landlady has given me notice to leave at once
ecause I have so many men visitors. I am getting out of
ed to go and look for rooms.

To HAVELOCK ELLIS.   16, PORTSEA PLACE, 31st Oct.

Arnold White has been here. He's a tall, handsome
aan, rather stout, about forty. He is, I think, an aristo-
rat. He says Sir Charles Warren has read my book and
ked it so. He brought me heaps more flowers to-day.
Ie wants me to go to Greenwich or somewhere with him
or the day ! I've never had such a strange interview with
nyone in my life. He says my book is like the Bible to
im. You will laugh when I tell you all about it.

To HAVELOCK ELLIS.   16, PORTSEA PLACE, 3rd Nov.

I felt so sad last night, my comrade, I haven't felt that
ind of blank despairful feeling for almost a year. I feel
ie noise of the streets and to see those sad women, and I
lt as if you were so sad and far from me, and everything
d. I'm better now. . . . I read the whole of that novel
st night, fairly good, better, of course, than novels of the
nglish school, but it no more comes near Bret Harte !—
r even *Cape Cod Folks. That* was a work of genius. . . .
feel such horror of the people coming this afternoon.
long only for quiet. I wish for the next six months some-
ne would treat me like a baby and feed me and clothe me,
nd let me just lie and think.

To HAVELOCK ELLIS.   16, PORTSEA PLACE, 5th Nov.

Scribbling and thinking all day. How is it my mind
kes such a long time to satisfy before I feel that I have
ven got to the proximate truth about anything ? I shall
o to my grave still trying to make up my mind whether I
ave got to the bottom of the question.

To HAVELOCK ELLIS.   16, PORTSEA PLACE, 6th Nov.

I went to Mrs. Hinton's last night ; they were so nice.
ut if I am to work at all I must make a rule not to go about.

I think it's the streets that tire me *nervously* so awfully. I am
well and strong, very well muscularly. Miss Lord [the trans
lator of Ibsen] came yesterday afternoon and was very nice

To HAVELOCK ELLIS.   16, PORTSEA PLACE, 9*th Nov*

Harry, I feel tired and heartsore to-night. What i
there's nothing true, nothing real, in all the world ! Good
night.

To HAVELOCK ELLIS.   16, PORTSEA PLACE, 16*th Nov*

Never, except perhaps when I was at Dordrecht, has
my mind worked and expanded as it does now. Never have
I felt I was doing so much or had so much to do. It's jus
because of that that I feel no wish ever to think or talk o
myself, or to give way to aimless emotion of any kind. The
one thing that troubles is where I am to draw the line
between the duty I owe to all the many people whom I
feel I can help and influence (in what I at least think the
right direction), and my writing, which may influence people
at large. I often feel as if my real work lay with individuals
I sometimes am filled almost with terror at the sense of the
power I have over them, without wishing or trying to exer
it at all. I can easily understand the influence my books
might have ; but when people tell me, as Mrs. —— dic
the other day, that if she came near me her whole life would
be moulded and changed by mine, that already the world
didn't look the same to her, I feel a kind of wonder and
oppression. I can't bear the feeling sometimes. Even in
your case I can feel my individuality sometimes *oppressing*
you. You don't need me, I'm not good for you, I think
I don't know how it is, I've never analysed, I never analyse
nowadays. I just live on and act as my first impulse directs
Even to analyse and look at myself as much as this letter
requires is acutely painful to me. It's very funny why i
should be so. Perhaps some day I shall understand. Now
I just think and work on as I feel. I have grown in the
last six months ; I could do what I could not before. Per
haps I shall get back my old strength, with the added sym
pathy that these three terrible years of darkness and weak
ness gave me.

I have been working at my Man and Woman thing

with intense delight to-day. Even you don't understand the way I *love* to work, and this article will be all as real work as Waldo's death-scene. I am always satisfied if *I* see more, if *I* like my work.

It is strange, but sometimes, when I come near other minds, and we touch each other, I have the same sense of *joy* I have in my work. It is an end in itself.

It is late. I have been walking up and down in the dark and wet in Blandford Square alone. I'm beginning to like the fog. I've found out what a wonderful thing it is ; there's something so wild and uncanny in it.

Perhaps when my paper is done everyone will laugh at it. But it doesn't matter ; I know what I feel and I have the joy of writing. When I've done this paper and my book (I'm not going to hurry myself), then I'm going to live among these women [prostitutes] and know them. Good-night, my comrade, my sweet old helper, who is so dear to me and part of myself. . . . You *must* come to the *Ghosts* reading : Roden Noel is coming.

To HAVELOCK ELLIS.　　16, PORTSEA PLACE, 18*th Nov.*

I've been so troubled and despairing about the woman question. To-day I feel more hopeful and able to work again. Your hamstrings are cut when you lose your hope. You know it is possible that women are absolutely and altogether the inferiors of men. But still their suffering is real, and something must be done for it. When I look into my own heart, then I feel as strong and firm as a lion.

To HAVELOCK ELLIS.　　16, PORTSEA PLACE, 20*th Nov.*

Please, when you have time, put me down the names of six especially good books about syphilis. I have been work-ing all day, very happy. I have lit my lamp, and am going to make myself a little tea now. Oh, I will be so nice to everybody when my article and book are done ! Tell Louie [Ellis] I'll write her letters yards long then.

To HAVELOCK ELLIS.　　16, PORTSEA PLACE, 27*th Nov.*

I am just *sitting* down to my writing. I really am going to *sit* to-day. I'm all ideas, ideas for my book, ideas for my stories ; ideas for articles. I am very well.

To HAVELOCK ELLIS.   16, PORTSEA PLACE, *30th Nov.*

I'm so well, and that's the crown blessing, when I think of the agony in which I lay all this time last year. All that life at St. Leonards is such a nightmare to me.

To HAVELOCK ELLIS.   16, PORTSEA PLACE, *1st Dec.*

Shall I sign the Ruskin paper for you? It's just to say we feel real sympathy with him and think he's used his genius well and nobly, though we may not agree with everything he says.

To HAVELOCK ELLIS.   16, PORTSEA PLACE, *11th Dec.*

I feel so tired to-night. Have been crying. I thought I'd forgotten how to cry. Good-night, my comfort.

To HAVELOCK ELLIS.   16, PORTSEA PLACE, *18th Dec.*

I went to see an old woman in Bolsover St., she is a procuress I can see, and she has such a pretty girl with her whom I want to get away, and I'm just going to see the girl again. I love that girl.

To HAVELOCK ELLIS.

16, PORTSEA PLACE, *18th Dec.* (*2nd letter*).

My heart is getting worse and worse. I think it is the bad drainage. I am moving into another bedroom.

To Mrs. J. H. PHILPOT.   16, PORTSEA PLACE, *25th Dec.*

Life, from the time one enters it, seems to be a battle between the duty one owes to one's work of life, and the duty one owes to the fellowmen one loves and to one's own nature. If one was a little wiser, one would know how to combine all.

To HAVELOCK ELLIS.   16, PORTSEA PLACE, *26th Dec.*

My Havelock, a policeman wanted to take me to prison yesterday because I was walking with [a mutual friend] up the square at 12 o'clock. My God, my God, but I am mad! You will see my letter in the *Daily News*. Tell Louie [Ellis] I am too mad to write to her or anyone. Oh, Havelock, all those poor women! If you had seen the look of the wretch as he came up and said : " I don't want you, sir, I want *her* "!

To HAVELOCK ELLIS.   16, PORTSEA PLACE, 29*th Dec.*

The policeman has been to apologise to me, sent by [the mutual friend] but that makes no difference. I must write ; it is a matter of principle. . . . I am not going to see anyone who calls, I am not going to write to anyone, except, perhaps, a word to you when it rests me. A little more and I shall break down, for ever. Oh, for one month when I should not see a human face or hear a human voice. Carpenter is the only exception I would make if he called, but I don't think he will. What is his address ? Goodbye, my sweet, noble comrade. Write to me.

[PROBABLY 1885]

To MISS LOUIE ELLIS.

Thank you for your nice long letter. I've been dreaming about over my work all day but haven't done much that's visible. I somehow feel stupid. I got a nice letter from Roden Noel this morning, and I had written to him last night. He asks me if J. A. Symonds has written to me about *S.A.F.* [*The Story of an African Farm*]. I should like to know him (Symonds) because his tone of mind is so sympathetic to mine, and to Havelock's too I always think. I shall be quite sorry if you leave that old house because I can picture you all so nicely there. Yes, I wish you and I could be together for at least a week ; you don't get to know people really from just being with them a few minutes. I should go to have my likeness taken, but then I'd have to sew lace into the neck and sleeves of my dress. I feel so weak the last few days ; like Mrs. Dombey, " I can't make an effort," but I can sit and scribble and think well enough ! I'm very glad Havelock's going to have his taken but he'll put on his visitor face and then it won't be worth anything. He ought to be taken smiling, but then one never wishes to smile when one's undergoing that suffering. I'm going to go to Pevensey Castle next week one day to walk about in the ruins and wake up.

With my love,
OLIVE.

CHAPTER IV

LETTERS WRITTEN IN 1886 AND 1887

1886

To HAVELOCK ELLIS.   16, PORTSEA PLACE, *3rd Jan.*

[She had had a proposal of marriage from a mutual friend.] I can't marry, Henry, I can't, and some awful power seems drawing me on. I think I shall go mad. I couldn't. I *must* be free, you know, I must be *free*. I've been free all my life, Henry! Oh, they can't cut my wings!

To HAVELOCK ELLIS.   16, PORTSEA PLACE, *5th Jan.*

I think it is general nervous exhaustion. I can hardly bear to think even of any more strain. I must try and forget there are such things as moral questions. . . . I leave on the 14th for Shanklin, and if my asthma keeps away I shall remain for some months, probably till the hay-fever time. I shall let as few people as possible know I am there and write as little as possible to anyone. Before I go will you come and spend one long day with me? Or I will come to Redhill and stay with you. I am too broken down—not miserable only but worn out—to be able to write really a letter to anyone. . . . More and more I feel that marriage is not and cannot be a right thing for a nature like mine. If I am to live I must be free, and under existing circumstances I feel more and more that no kind of sex relationship can be good and pure but marriage. —— is so tender and sweet and reverent to me. My heart aches when I think I can never marry him. When I find a man as much stronger than I am as I am [stronger] than a child, then I will marry him, no one before. I do not mean physically strong, I mean mentally, morally, emotionally, practically. I do not think there is such a man.

90

To HAVELOCK ELLIS.   16, PORTSEA PLACE, 7*th Jan.*

Life is dark to both of us now. How strange these days will look to us in after years as we look back at them ! Yours always and unchangingly.

To HAVELOCK ELLIS.   16, PORTSEA PLACE, 8*th Jan.*

I went by myself to the Millais pictures this morning. I hate Millais more than ever—a cold worldly soul, without one touch of the true fire.

I am going this evening to the Metropole to dine with Dr. and Mrs. Chapman of the *Westminster.* . . . I don't think there is anything false in my heart to you or anyone, not even unreal. It is only that the feeling I have not for you or any man you all of you want. [She has not the feeling for him or for *any* man that all of them would like her to have.] Your little sister and comrade.

To HAVELOCK ELLIS.   16, PORTSEA PLACE, 12*th Jan.*

Just starting. All in a dream. Address Shanklin.

To HAVELOCK ELLIS.

ROYAL SPA HOTEL, SHANKLIN, 16*th Jan.*

Perhaps when I have been here a few weeks I shall begin to write letters again. You would love this place, it is so solitary, quieter than Derbyshire, much ; I am the only visitor in this huge hotel.

To HAVELOCK ELLIS.   SHANKLIN, 17*th Jan.*

You don't understand the horror I have of talking of myself and my own feelings, and you call that reserve. I talk much more of myself to you than to any other creature —more than I think of myself. . . . A long letter on woman question from Ray Lankester which I will send you. I am going to try and work out the whole woman question as far as possible here. It is so delightful to be alone. To feel there is no right and no wrong—no one to make miserable.

To HAVELOCK ELLIS.   SHANKLIN, 20*th Jan.*

I am changed, but it is not to you. An instinct, I think of self-preservation, is making me draw in, but not to you so much as to others. People with sympathetic natures like mine must shield themselves from their own sympathies or they must be cruelly crushed and life's work left undone. I don't know if you understand what I mean, yet you ought to, for in that silent passivity of yours you have always a shield up between you and the world. I have dropped my shield for the last four years, but I mean to take it up again. . . . If I marry now I will marry the man who needs me most. But I shall *not* marry.

To HAVELOCK ELLIS.   SHANKLIN, 23*rd Jan.*

I am much troubled about my head. I have a terrible feeling I shall never be able to work again, that those three years of agony have injured it—but I know it's fancy. Don't talk of it to me. I was made so happy by the note I got from you this morning. I wish so much you were here to walk on the sand with me.

To HAVELOCK ELLIS.   SHANKLIN, 31*st Jan.*

Yes, I have developed faster than ever in my life before, except that year at Dordrecht. Perhaps that is why I feel such horror at the thought of giving out. If only I could live quiet for two or three years, till I am thirty-three, and know I could have money to live on! One can't grow so much and keep on reproducing. Every day, every hour, I have new thoughts and combinations rushing in on me. I want to absorb, not to give out.

To HAVELOCK ELLIS.   SHANKLIN, 2*nd Feb.*

My Havelock, I send you Ray Lankester's letter to me [on the Woman Question] and mine to him. Will you do me a great favour? Read over mine carefully and see if it is mis-spelt. I have written it in such a dream that I am sure it is spelt backwards. I should have liked to copy it and keep both letters, they would be amusing in after years—but now I can't do anything. . . . I am not at all well.

To HAVELOCK ELLIS.   SHANKLIN, 4*th Feb.*

I can hardly walk, my legs are so bad.   I'm going to try Bournemouth.   I have such despairing letters from sweet old ——.   Oh, Havelock, why will not people understand I am not a marrying woman ? ...   I could work splendidly now, ill as I am, if I were not so troubled about others.

To HAVELOCK ELLIS.   SHANKLIN, 6*th Feb.*

Mrs. Hinton, without saying a word to me, wrote to —— that I was very ill, hadn't eaten anything since I came, looked like a ghost, etc.   He is coming to-day.   I am so miserable.   I don't want to see anyone.   I want to rest.   I really am not ill, only worn out.   It is so sweet of him to come.   Everyone is so sweet to me.

To HAVELOCK ELLIS.

5, SEAVIEW TERRACE, BOURNEMOUTH, 14*th Feb.*

Havelock, it was so strange when I got here last night, I had such a longing for you, almost like a child wanting its mother or a mother longing for her child.   I felt as if I *must* see you.   It's very funny.   I haven't longed to see anyone for months, not even my brother.   I have only longed to be alone.

To HAVELOCK ELLIS.   BOURNEMOUTH, 19*th Feb.*

I am very ill.   I shall have to go to London if I do not get better.   I am worse than I was at St. Leonards. Is there a place at Redhill where I could get a nice room or rooms cheap ?

To HAVELOCK ELLIS.   BOURNEMOUTH, 23*rd Feb.*

Much better, but doctor says I will have to keep quite still on my back for some time to come.   Am reading second volume of George Sand's letters.   So splendid. So different from George Eliot's.   If Cross had nothing better, then he ought to have kept still.   One has only one feeling in reading George Sand's letters.   *How great !* How much greater the wonderful woman than her work !

To HAVELOCK ELLIS.   BOURNEMOUTH, 24*th Feb.*

The doctor says that I must keep quite still. I feel so happy and quiet somehow, like I did when I was ill at St. Leonards. . . . I have been reading a little more of George Sand's letters, but one would like to see the letters they were in answer to. What a great strong impersonal soul it was !—a great, wise woman.

To HAVELOCK ELLIS.   BOURNEMOUTH, 27*th Feb.*

Your letter was so sweet this morning. If you go to Australia I'd like to go as far as the Cape with you. Only perhaps it wouldn't rest you then. I'm feeling *much* better ; better *mentally* than I have for months. It's the laying perfectly still.

To HAVELOCK ELLIS.   BOURNEMOUTH, 1*st March.*

Mrs. —— comes to see me every afternoon. She says it helps her so much. I feel so selfish because I would rather be alone because I am beginning to work now. But, you know, it isn't real selfishness because I do give my work to other people, and it may help more people than talking or writing to one. This question between the duty to the individual and the work is the agony of my life. Whichever side I decide for my conscience tortures me on the other. . . . I have been looking at *Towards Democracy* with such pleasure. I like that "Have faith." Please give my love to Edward Carpenter when you write, and tell him how I am liking him. I couldn't see him really in London, only the outward man, because I was crushed. I feel very happy and restful now. There is something so nice in knowing you must and may lie still on your back.

To HAVELOCK ELLIS.   BOURNEMOUTH, 8*th March.*

Sweet boy, I have had asthma. I am going to write a book *For Those in Physical Suffering.* You are to have it after I am dead and publish it without my name. You are to have *all* my papers when I die except any my brother wants. I am going to make a will ! I may live for thirty years, but I may also not.

To HAVELOCK ELLIS.   BOURNEMOUTH, 9*th March.*

My own, you must not expect me to write much.   For the first time, the last two days I feel the old passion upon me to work a glory and a delight.   It is because we have a little real sunshine.   My asthma is bad, I fight for breath, but it doesn't matter.

To HAVELOCK ELLIS.   BOURNEMOUTH, 10*th March.*

I never could ever have conceived of the problem till the last two years.   But now I feel that all the influence which I can have through my books is as nothing to the influence I can have personally.   Anything I can do in my books is only a little over-flood of that influence.   (But it lasts longer.)   It is because I love and enjoy that so much better that I chafe against individuals taking my love and thought.   And the two things are not to be combined. Exactly that life-blood which you give to your friends is what you in a lesser degree put into your books.   Take Mrs. ———.   The moment I am passive and sit still, as you do, she weeps and says that I am " far from her."   It is the same with ——— and everyone.   I sometimes feel as if I was bleeding to death.

To HAVELOCK ELLIS.   BOURNEMOUTH, 16*th March.*

My Havelock, I am as seedy as ever.   I am now in that state of mind in which one is quite resigned.

To Mrs. J. H. PHILPOT.   BOURNEMOUTH, *March.*

I had no idea *Romola* was so grand.   How George Eliot seems to live again in it, and one feels her grand old heart beating through it.

To Mrs. CAWOOD.   BOURNEMOUTH, 19*th March.*

Ach, dear friend, I do long so for a little Cape sunshine sometimes.   Everything else is delightful here, but we never see the sun.   Some day I shall come to have a look at him.   I have been staying at the Isle of Wight, but it was too damp there ; then I came here ; such a lovely place—but it's too damp, so now I'm going to try Harrow-on-the-Hill near London. . . .

There is a very interesting book you would much like to read, if you have not, *Variations of Plants and Animals*, by Darwin. There are many interesting experiments with grafting, breeding, etc. Do you subscribe to the Cradock Library? You can get it there. That dear little library! When I am rich I am going to send out £50 for it! It has given me more help and pleasure than anything else in my life almost. . . . I wish I could see some Boers and some Kaffirs. I think I should kiss them all.

To HAVELOCK ELLIS.   SOUTHBOURNE-ON-SEA, 22*nd March*.

I am so worn out I can't go on much longer. I must go and live at the Convent where I can have kindly human beings near me. You don't know what it is to have a mother like yours that looks after you. Give my love to her.

To HAVELOCK ELLIS.   SOUTHBOURNE-ON-SEA, 28*th March*.

The last chapter of *Undine*, I mean when she dies, is not so bad. Will you send it to ——. Please burn the first part of the book—no, I can't trust you to. I'll burn it myself. . . . I am very weak but my asthma is gone almost.

To HAVELOCK ELLIS.   SOUTHBOURNE-ON-SEA, 31*st March*.

I do not think it will be very nice at Kilburn. But I am getting resigned to knock about the world alone like this, being ill if it is " God's will," but I should like to do a *little* more writing work before I die.

To HAVELOCK ELLIS.   SOUTHBOURNE-ON-SEA, 1*st April*.

Sweet comrade, I walked on the beach this evening. I like walking against the wind. There were great white breakers and blue water, and one bright star. I took my Whitman with me though I didn't mean to read him. I have worked to-day so delightfully, am going to sit up and work more. I think it is the hope of getting away from landladies. I feel so grateful for being a little better. . . . Would you like to see the first half of my book when it is done or wait till it's finished? You are not to say *one word* about it to me if I show it you. I don't want to know what anyone says of it. Either now or ever.

To HAVELOCK ELLIS.　　SOUTHBOURNE-ON-SEA, 2*nd April.*

　Havelock, the only kind of woman being I don't like is landladies. That's why I'm going to the Nuns.

To HAVELOCK ELLIS.

THE CONVENT, KILBURN (ST. DOMINIC'S), 6*th April.*

　It is so nice and quiet here. You can't think what a feeling of being far from the world one has. What happy peaceful faces most of these women have got !

To HAVELOCK ELLIS.　　　　　　　KILBURN, 8*th April.*

　I see, before this book is done, I [shall] put it into the fire. The only thing that comforts me is that, one day just before I left, I sat with *The African Farm* by my stream at Lelie Kloof, at the place where I dug out my dicinodont, and such disgust came over me at the way I had expressed what was so clear to me, that I nearly threw it into the water and let it drown for ever. One day, if I live, I will do work that satisfies me, but all I have done I hate. It is *true*, but there is perfect beauty *and* truth.

To HAVELOCK ELLIS.　　　　　　　KILBURN, 10*th April.*

　I went to see Holman Hunt's Exhibition this afternoon. You *must* go to see it, my darling. It is splendid. Whether it was my mood or the work, I never have enjoyed pictures so much. You ought to go alone and be in a dreamy mood, and dream over them. The streets fill me with such agony and sorrow now, I can't bear it. Oh, when will the time come when we shall love each other and realise that humanity is one ! Remind me to tell you about a beautiful girl I saw ; but it's not only the prostitutes make me sad, it's everything. I am so glad to get back to my little white quiet bedroom, but want to help those women. . . . You say the MS. is splendid. Of course you would say so, whatever it was, to try and comfort me. You want so much to think so that you do think so.

To HAVELOCK ELLIS.　　　　　　　KILBURN, 12*th April.*

　I told you we were not to say anything about MS. What you say is quite true. I put that in the last day I

Southbourne. I was thinking of my sister Ettie knew it wasn't art and that I'd have to take it out. , I think, you don't see is that just at that point a ffer " *is* necessary—if you know what a " buffer " ; it's something that you put in to raise (or to lower) the *tone* to a certain level or to break a monotony of feeling. All through the book I have buffers that are only put in provisionally. I am taking out one because by raising the tone of the dialogue I can do without it. Sometimes a buffer comes in with grand effect (like the knocking scene in *Macbeth*). That buffer doesn't answer because it isn't related to the story, it's related to my sister Ettie.

To HAVELOCK ELLIS.　　　　KILBURN, 19*th April*.

I would like so much to have a child, but I couldn't *bear* to be married ; neither could I bear any relationship that was not absolutely open to all the world—so I could never have one.

To HAVELOCK ELLIS.　　　　KILBURN, 26*th April*.

I've not seen or spoken to anyone for eight days and I feel so hysterical that I'm going to Mrs. Hinton's this afternoon.

To HAVELOCK ELLIS.　　　　KILBURN, 28*th April*.

I'm going to stick up for Miss Haddon like old boots. Compared to those white-washed sepulchres, the Hintonians are simply saints.

To HAVELOCK ELLIS.　　　　KILBURN, 13*th May*.

Old Hartmann says all kinds of things I thought were such original ideas of mine ! . . . I had such a nice letter from —— this morning which I send. I won't see any-one any more for the next three months till my book's done.

To HAVELOCK ELLIS.　　　　KILBURN, 14*th May*.

On Saturday I leave for the Convent at Harrow. . . . I don't quite know what's the matter with me, I'm so much knocked down. Will my book ever, ever, ever, be done ? Every word of it is truth to me, and more and more so as the book goes on. It could not be otherwise. That is all that can be said of it. One thing I am glad of is that it becomes less and less what you call " art " as it goes on. My first crude conceptions are always what you call " art." As they become more and more *living* and real, they become what I call higher art but what you call no " art " at all. I quite understand what you mean, but I cannot think that your use of the word " art " in that sense is right, i.e. not misleading, and therefore *untrue*. If I understand what you mean, *Wilhelm Meister* is not art, one of Balzac's novels is. *Wilhelm Meister* is one of the most immortal deathless productions of the greatest of the world's artists, the result of twenty years' labour, worth any six of Balzac's novels, great and glorious as Balzac is. Yet if you were writing of it, you would, ridiculous as it would seem, be *obliged* to call it " not art." You seem to say " I will call ' art ' only that artistic creation in which I can clearly *see* the artist manufacturing the parts and piecing them together ; when I cannot see that, though the thing be organic, true, inevitable, like a work of God's, I will not call it art ; I must *see* the will shaping it (of course there always has been a will shaping it whether it is visible or not) or I will not call it art." This of course is not in justification of my method but touches what seems to me a weakness and shallowness in your mode of criticism. It *is* very valuable that the two kinds of art should be distinguished, but not that the one should be called art and the other not art. It would be better to call the one artificial and the other real art. But that wouldn't be just. I should rather call the one organic and the other inorganic.

To HAVELOCK ELLIS.
THE CONVENT, HARROW-ON-THE-HILL, 1*5th May.*

Got here an hour ago. Have a quiet dark room, and everything would be lovely but I have what I fear is hay asthma.

To HAVELOCK ELLIS.   THE CONVENT, HARROW, 16*th May.*

I'm not troubled about art. I'm trying to enlighten you ! . . . Oh, Harrow is so lovely. I think you'd like it. You must come and spend a whole day with me.

To HAVELOCK ELLIS.   THE CONVENT, HARROW, 20*th May*.

No, I deny that you can see how *Wilhelm Meister* was *made* ; you can see how it *grew*, not how it was *made*.   There is no *will*, no forethought, manifested in it.   It came like that, like a tree, not like a Greek temple.   You never know where you are going to turn next in *Wilhelm Meister*.   No more did Goethe—yet all was of necessity, nothing of chance.

To HAVELOCK ELLIS.   HARROW, 20*th May*.

I love Burns more and more.   I love that, "The Lark of Killyburn Braes."   The best line of Burns is in the 10th verse · "A reekit wee devil looks over the wa'."   No one on earth but Burns would have written that, coming just where it does.

[This, I think, as far as I know, is her one reference to Burns.   In later life she used to say she did not like Burns ; he was too coarse for one thing.   She thought "The Jolly Beggars" his best work.   She knew but little of his poems.   In "The Jolly Beggars" it was not the poetry that attracted her ; it was the delineation of character.]

To HAVELOCK ELLIS.   HARROW, 27*th May*.

I send you a bit of rough MS. as a specimen.   Is it good enough to send to Press in its present state ?   I mean as to legibility, spelling, words left out, etc. . . . You will think that long rigmarole on sex inartistic.   But it bears on the story ; it's all point—if only anyone will take the trouble to see the point.

To HAVELOCK ELLIS.   HARROW, 29*th May*.

Havelock, all day yesterday I was writing and thinking about the unity of the Universe and our love of truth arising from that conception.   I sat up till one writing.   I couldn't sleep when I went to bed.   For the first time for long, long, I thought of death, realised it, that wandering out of the soul alone ; that's what I always *feel* death will be, though I know it won't be.   I got that kind of suffocating

feeling I used to have at Ratel Hoek, as if I couldn't bear
to think of it, as if my physical heart was breaking. And
then, sudden, out in the garden in the dark, in a tree just
at my window, a nightingale began to sing, more beautifully than any sound I have ever heard. You can't think
what a strange effect it had on me, how wonderful. I'll
never forget it. In that utter still lonely night, when I
felt so, to hear it. . . . Thank you much for *Walden*.
I love it. . . . I haven't sent the MS., nor your books
yet, because I can't goad myself into walking through the
town to the post office. I can't bear to see people. I am
so happy alone. I feel just like I used to at Lelie Kloof

To HAVELOCK ELLIS.   HARROW, 31*st May*.

I've just come back from seeing Maggie Harkness.
Oh, the joy to get back here again ! I could have cried
for joy when I got out here at the station and walked up the
hill. I don't know how it is [that] I have been able to live
among the rush so long ; a little more and I should have
broken down for ever. Oh, this blessed, blessed solitude
and stillness. . . . If I had not my work I could be like
I was. What you and my brother and Mrs. Walters and
Mrs. Brown and —— and —— and my mother say :
" You are changed, you are changed," means simply that
I am not living in the world that surrounds me but in my
work. Sometimes I feel inclined to swear a big oath
and throw all my MSS. in the fire, and say : " Here I am,
I shall live as I have lived the last three years, never in my
work, never conscious of myself, but through and in the
people I love." My heart is sore, sorrowful about it.
And what, after all, is my work worth that I should sacrifice
everything to it, that I should torture myself like this ? I
won't say any more. Goodbye, my own darling, I wish
I were dead. But to-morrow I *will* forget all of you and
work. Oh, I am right in trying to get back into my old
state and work. Deep in my heart I feel that I am, but
doubts will come sometimes, and then I hate myself. I
wish you would come and see me here some afternoon.
You have been more help to me than you can ever know,
my Havelock.

To HAVELOCK ELLIS.   HARROW, 21*st June.*

I have had a fashionable prostitute here all day, such a sweet bright gentle woman. I think she loves me ; she says she is coming again.

To HAVELOCK ELLIS.   HARROW, 22*nd June.*

That prostitute is so darling. You would love her. Would you like to meet her ? She wants to read and be intellectual, it's quite pathetic.

To HAVELOCK ELLIS.   HARROW, 26*th June.*

I'm getting to love Landor so in your edition. I'm going to read all he's written. The more one reads the piece over and over the more one likes him. He's the genuine article.

To HAVELOCK ELLIS.   HARROW, 28*th June.*

This afternoon Dr. Donkin came. We went to the little inn and had tea in the garden. When we were sitting talking and laughing I suddenly felt that terrible illness just like death I used to have at the Cape. I really thought I was dying. I lay down on the ground, the cold perspiration pouring from me. All in a moment I got up quite well. *It was gone.* I feel particularly well now. It's always so just after.

To HAVELOCK ELLIS.   HARROW, 29*th June.*

I feel almost mad to-day, I've had such a succession of painful reproaching letters. I'm perfectly willing to allow I'm everything that's wicked and false and mean, but people who reproach you shouldn't end their letters by saying: " And when will your book be ready ? " I've been writing a long letter to Maggie [Harkness], but what's the use ? As soon as I've sent it someone else'll write just the same kind of letter to be answered.

To HAVELOCK ELLIS.   HARROW, 19*th July.*

I am working so hard. I've never worked like this since I came to England. I could write a whole book in a month like this. Isn't the weather splendid ? . . .

A beautiful letter from sweet noble old ——. You know I feel people love me more than I deserve, and it's sadder than being loved too little. I want to be able to love every human being back *more* than it loves me.

To EDWARD CARPENTER.   LONDON, 5*th Aug.*

I have been reading Whitman of late with much more enjoyment than ever before. I find he's not so good as you are when one is ill and wants help and strength ; one needs to be strong and in overpowering health *really* to enjoy him. I wonder whether you find it so.

To HAVELOCK ELLIS.   HARROW, 16*th Aug.*

"What did Goethe's *Faust* sell himself for?" What is the *one* thing which we, any of *us*, the peculiar children of this age, would be willing to sell ourselves for? . . . It is the glory of Goethe's *Faust* that it alone embodies the cry of its age, the cry which no other age has heard, yet which is the moving power in Whitman and in all the deepest inspiration of our age : " We will not only know all things, we will *be* all things."

To HAVELOCK ELLIS.   HARROW, 19*th Aug.*

Olive Schreiner can't write a sensational story, can't she ! I've written a devil of a fine sensational story. Whether when it's quite done I'll think so well of it remains to be seen. I want you to read it, and tell me which you think is best, it is *New Rush.*

To HAVELOCK ELLIS.   HARROW, 20*th Aug.*

My sensation story is lovely. " Olive Schreiner can't write a sensation story ! " Ach !

To HAVELOCK ELLIS.   HARROW, 27*th Aug.*

I've been a hateful girl this afternoon. I'm sure you're right. I shall see just as you do in a week or two's time. I'll go on with my work.

To HAVELOCK ELLIS.   HARROW, 29*th Aug.*

Mrs. [C. M.] Wilson came at 5. She is splendid. You ought to have a talk with her.

To HAVELOCK ELLIS.   HARROW, 1*st Sept.*

It's so hot and it's *horrid* to be so shabby.   The people in the streets laugh at me because I am so shabby, and I'm going to have a new hat one day and a dress and all ! . . . [At the British Museum.]   I have come here and find I'm too stupid to get the books I want.   I don't see how you are to find them.   I wish you were here. . . .   Do tell me if you know anything on the anthropoid apes I can get.

To HAVELOCK ELLIS.   HARROW, 1 3*th Sept.*

Podmore and Pearsall Smith were coming to-morrow. I've written to tell them they mustn't.   I can't see anyone. I'm going to try three months more, and then if I sink into the same state I was in last winter I'll kill myself.

To HAVELOCK ELLIS.   HARROW, 1 7*th Sept.*

My comforting boy, I have been sleeping all day.   I am only getting out of bed now at 4.   I *couldn't* wake up before.   All that is the matter with me is trying to do brain-work on insufficient food.   I'm going out to get a chop.

To HAVELOCK ELLIS.   HARROW, 2 2*nd Sept.*

Not able to go into town to-day [to " find cheap lodgings "].   It's just the old regular breakdown. Children ought to be brought up to understand that when they become helpless and a burden to others they ought to painlessly put an end to themselves ;   then no one would be pained.   My face is all drawn on a side this morning with neuralgia and I have asthma.   I don't think I'll ever finish even *Jan van der Linde's Wife*.   Tell me a little about yourself, please.

To HAVELOCK ELLIS.   HARROW, 2 4*th Sept.*

If I don't get better in London I must ask my brother for money and go out to the Cape.   I can't let *all* my life slip from me without work, and I have so much, so much to do.   [She went to London and was back at Blandford Square on the 4th Oct.]

To HAVELOCK ELLIS. BLANDFORD SQUARE, 12*th*

I have very nearly had brain fever. I am glad you
working hard. That is the one comfort we sensitive
people have. . . . Please tell me when next you are
coming to town, so that we may have a whole afternoon
to go to the Zoo. I have such a longing to go there
with you.

To HAVELOCK ELLIS. BLANDFORD SQUARE, 26*th Nov.*

I send you a rough draft of *Jan* [*Jan van der Linde's
Wife*]. Tell me (1) Whether you think printing it will
do my next book harm. (2) How *you* like it.
(3) Whether you think it interesting to the general reader.
(4) Don't make *any small* criticisms, it's not finished yet.
I have never written anything with more delight, but that
is just because it takes me out of this cursed London and
English life. (I don't mean really that it is cursed, but
it's so delightful to get back to my old life.) . . . I'm
not going to feel loving to anyone ; one feels so loving and
so loving, so loving that one can't do anything. Don't
you feel loving either. I try to do all I can to make you
not love me. I don't want anyone to love me ; it only
makes them miserable.

To HAVELOCK ELLIS. BLANDFORD SQUARE, 7*th Dec.*

I had called up both servants and told them if *you*
came you were to be shown straight up. I never dreamed
of my landlady's stopping you. Why didn't you tell
someone to come up and tell me you were here ? Do
always do that. I longed for you all day and listened
to every step in the street. I must have heard yours.
I've never had such *pain* in my chest before, though I've
been as bad in other ways. Do write to me, my friend.
My heart calleth to thee. . . . Oh, I feel so miserable
when I think of all the misery in the world. I will never
make a friend of a man again unless I love him better than
anyone else in the world. I haven't absolutely made up
my mind, but it seems to me that no woman should ever
allow a man even to kiss her hand unless she has absolutely
made up her mind, that, *as far as she can judge*, she will

never love any other man as well, does not love any man as well, and loves that man so well that she would willingly live with him all her life, bearing children for him. I would not base this on the idea of right and wrong but on the agony to both parties, to the one who gives pain and the one who is pained. It may be said : Oh, this is not sexual, it is an expression of friendship. But when the time comes it is found to be otherwise. Through what bitter agony we learn all life's lesson, and our dreams fall from us one by one. I am in a state of despair such as I have not known since I was a girl of fifteen. My ideal has been friendship between men and women as between men and men, but it *can't* be.

To HAVELOCK ELLIS.   BLANDFORD SQUARE, 10*th Dec.*

—— thinks *Jan* very bad, unworthy of me, not interesting, though it has power, he says. I think he's right. I'll not print it. I couldn't understand your thinking it good, but I think you see all I do as better than it is. I don't think anyone has ever, or ever will, feel to me as you have felt. It is given to a human being once in a life to be given such a tenderness as yours has been to me. I know that. . . . I am meditating to-day getting away from England next week as soon as I am better, without telling a soul except my brother where I am going. I feel in that old reckless devil state I felt in when I was fifteen and sixteen. . . . I'm still in bed. The doctor says I was almost dangerously bad on Monday.

To HAVELOCK ELLIS.   BLANDFORD SQUARE, 13*th Dec.*

I am getting on all right. I have a Hospital nurse. Give my love to Louie [Ellis] and tell her if she lived with me she would become a good nurse. . . . Come Wednesday if you can. I will be up then.

To HAVELOCK ELLIS.   VEVEY, SWITZERLAND, 21*st Dec.*

I was glad of your letter to-night. One's a bit more desolate than words can say here. Tell me all about yourself, it's about all of you I want to know.

To HAVELOCK ELLIS.   VEVEY, *22nd Dec.*

Mrs. [W. K.] Clifford called this morning, was very kind. I am going to try rooms near her at Clarens, the Hotel Roth, cheaper than this. I am to have a little room next the roof; it overlooks the lake. The next house is the one Byron lived in. . . . Harry, whenever my heart is sinking into agony and loneliness I think : Harry is thinking of me. I'm more tired than I ever was in my life before.

To HAVELOCK ELLIS.   CLARENS, *Christmas Day.*

This place is just like hell. Anything so hideous and so awful you cannot conceive ; you know the frozen sea in Dante's Hell. No, this sea isn't frozen, it's dirty and wet and the fog rises from it. I have seen no place in England so awful as this. The air is quite thick with water. I thought Geneva was the most awful place I had ever been in, but it's much better than this. . . . If I keep on getting worse I shall start for Davos or Mentone or God knows where on Tuesday morning. I ought to have gone to Italy at once ; it was insane of me to come here. There is no sun here ; sometimes through the fog an awful wan ray breaks on the water. . . . Your letter this morning was so precious, it made me able to get up. It seems to me as if it was many years ago since I left England, and I'd been in hell ever since. . . . No, I haven't kept a journal. If I can only keep sense and strength enough to pack my things, that's all I want. I have such a horror of getting quite helpless. But one can always kill oneself. Don't show this letter to my brother or ——. I don't tell them how I am.

To HAVELOCK ELLIS.   HOTEL ROTH, CLARENS, *28th Dec.*

I am quite settled here. Much better.

To HAVELOCK ELLIS.   CLARENS, *30th Dec.*

Anything to read would be welcome. I begin to feel I could read. Your letter was a great help. I'll send you a little allegory I wrote last month. Yes, solitude with

sunshine is heaven ; in the dark it is hell. You can form
no conception what the grey cold of these mountains and
this sea is. England has nothing like it.

1887

To HAVELOCK ELLIS.   CLARENS, 12*th Jan.*

I have never been so happy and restful. I am picking
up in physical strength. I am the devil in.[1] Never write
about me. . . . I long for solitude, absolute solitude,
where there shall be no living soul, scarcely an animal. . . .
Am thinking of having *From Man to Man* copied by typist
when I have money.

To HAVELOCK ELLIS.   CLARENS, 13*th Jan.*

You must save money so that you can come to Italy
with me in the autumn, to Florence and Rome. Also I
should enjoy the art ten times better if you were there. . . .
I'm going to try to work *to-morrow*. Day after day passes
and I do nothing. I am burdened with my work, which
grows and grows in my brain till the burden almost seems
greater than my strength can bear. . . . Don't think I'm
miserable. I'm as jolly as a brick-bat.

To HAVELOCK ELLIS.   CLARENS, 15*th Jan.*

Darling boy, tell me *all* about what you are doing,
please. I am not so well again. . . . You know I've
got a funny nature. I don't need other people should
love me if I love them. I love more impersonally than
anyone I know. I suppose it's because my imagination's
strong. I *become* that person.

To HAVELOCK ELLIS.   CLARENS, 21*st Jan.*

I am getting on. Going to work hard. . . . Leslie
Stephen came to-day. He's a tall thin ugly man, looks
nice though, of course not a touch of genius, which I think
Morley has.

[1] This is a literal rendering of the Afrikaans sentence, " Ek es die duivel in."

To HAVELOCK ELLIS. CLARENS, 1st *Feb*

I am very weak, feel as if all the bones taken out of my body. Your letters have been the one ray of external brightness that have come to me here.

To HAVELOCK ELLIS. CLARENS, 14th *Feb*.

I have just heard that my old friend Emil Holub, the African traveller, is killed [see pp. 133–4 of the *Life*]. . . . I am much better to-day ; all that is the matter with me is weakness. . . . Some day I will send you *I am an artist*. It wouldn't do to print. It's an artist lying by himself on the rocks here in the sun and just talking out his thoughts in the first person. How he loves a woman, first sexually, and how he's tempted to sacrifice his higher spiritual life for her, and how he breaks free from her love when she isn't true to him : and then after years he meets a woman whom he only calls " My little white face," who is almost dying of consumption, and how he loves her and worships her for her genius, wants nothing from her, not even a kiss, only feels that if she hadn't her mother he would take care of her. She wakes up all his old art power, all his higher life, all that seemed slipped from him forever. Then once he hears her talking, and she says to the person who is with her that he loves her, talks as though it were the common feeling that exists between men and women. Then she and the other person go away from the trees. He never wants to see her again. As he lies there in the sun he laughs to himself and plans his work, his great picture that has lain in his heart for years, and that only she has given him strength to finish. He laughs to himself. He has got all he wants of her. And then he plans how perhaps he will marry and have children. And he gets more drowsy lying there in the sun. And there's a description of Clarens mixed with it all. Can you see how it goes ? If only I was not physically so very, very weak.

To HAVELOCK ELLIS. 15th *Feb*.

I came here [Vevey] this morning in the boat from Clarens. It's more than an hour and the boat back hasn't come. I'm sitting in the sun by the lake on a bench. The sea (the lake is really a sea) is so beautiful, and dark blue. I feel so tired. I don't know why I'm so weak.

To HAVELOCK ELLIS.   CLARENS, 15*th Feb.*

I've been reading in the Baedeker's *Italy*, seeing where we'll go in the autumn. Harry, I'm so unwell, that's really why I'm so nasty. I have to save up my strength so. Do you know the feeling, sweet ? . . . I am writing rather a good paper on sex relationships. . . . Philip Marston is dead. I want to write a notice of him somewhere, and an Introduction to his stories, if there's nobody else.

To HAVELOCK ELLIS.   CLARENS, 24*th Feb.*

I'm writing such a lovely paper on sex experiment. I shall die easier after I've written it. But you know I won't like it when it's done, it's only when I'm writing it. There was an earthquake here this morning ; it was like being on a ship.

To HAVELOCK ELLIS.   CLARENS, 26*th Feb.*

Going to send for doctor to examine chest. Worst symptom is that I have become so angelical, sweet, and loving since I came here. Feel so happy too. If the doctor asks what's the matter I shall tell him that. Besides that, I expectorate much. But the first symptom is the worst. It's terrible to be so good. I love everybody. I forgive ———. I shall certainly go to Heaven if I die now.

To HAVELOCK ELLIS.   CLARENS, 27*th Feb.*

After saying I'm so angelically sweet I find I'm not. Devil in me this morning. . . . Ach, what does it matter ? Doctor says no disease in left lung but it has fallen in, and I breathe almost entirely with right.

To HAVELOCK ELLIS.   CLARENS, 3*rd March.*

Writing sex paper still. Getting to think it's worthless, but going to finish it. Don't *really* think so, but feel so.

'o HAVELOCK ELLIS.   CLARENS, 11th March.

I'm not miserable at all, but the *weight* of life seems
ist quietly crushing me to the earth sometimes.

'o HAVELOCK ELLIS.   CLARENS, 15th March.

My own boy, I am in a low fever, very nearly mad.
am starting off for Lucerne to-morrow.   Love me always.
Don't talk about me to —— or anyone ; they torture me.
'our little sister.

'o HAVELOCK ELLIS.   CLARENS, 16th March.

All my veins are on fire and I keep the people awake
y screaming all night.

'o HAVELOCK ELLIS.

HOF GERSAU, LAKE OF LUCERNE, 17th March.

I've been passing through about the stiffest time of
y life mentally and physically. . . .   My experiences
ith Mrs. —— were very terrible.   Some day I shall tell
ou. . . .   This is a little quiet place among the mountains,
tterly cold.   I like it, but have asthma.   To-morrow
go to Lugano, I think.   I hope I shall somewhere again
nd a resting place. . . .   I feel very tender and loving
· you.   I am now utterly alone in the world and I wish
so, because I only inflict suffering.   I want two or three
ears of *absolute* solitude to work in, and when I am a wise
d woman I shall return to the world.

'o HAVELOCK ELLIS.   MENDRISIO, 20th March.

I wish I could see you this evening.   I am reading
Iill's *Logic*.   It comforts me so.

o HAVELOCK ELLIS.   MENDRISIO, 22nd March.

Saturday or Sunday I don't know which.   My heart
irneth to thee.   Of course I'll never write to —— again.
wonder if my brain will ever be strong.   All these seven
ars the human beings have been pressing on it, and now
seems just to have given in.   It's so funny.   You know
can't bear any more.   Mentally I just lie helpless, and

To HAVELOCK ELLIS.   ALASSIO, 12*th April*.

You don't know *how* much you form part of my life, like the sun when he always shines here. One never talks of him. I'm sending you wild flowers I'm going out to pick, and a bit of olive tree with the flowers because they wouldn't look like Alassio without it. The wild flowers grow among them. You can go in anywhere and pick them. Nothing is walled off ; it's like the Cape. It's only in England people shut other people out.

To HAVELOCK ELLIS.   ALASSIO, 15*th April*.

I am working hard. Do you think " Towser the Dog " 1 good enough for Donkin's Hospital magazine. Don't go saying Yes, if you think it isn't. I think it's not. I'll send him a little allegory called " In a Far Star " if you think it's not. . . . You tell me so little about yourself, horrible old cat, and you aren't writing a big novel ! One day I shall get really well, and then, God, what a lot of work I'll do !

To HAVELOCK ELLIS.   ALASSIO, 16*th April*.

[Enclosing allegory " In a Far-off World."] 2 Excuse first draft. I made two new allegories last night after I was in bed. This I made about three o'clock. I've been for a walk to that lovely ruined church at Santa Croce, so lonely there. Now I've come back and just writing these out before I forget them. I love this one, I wouldn't change a word of it for the devil. You mustn't say it's not nice ! . . . I've got the climbing allegory right now. It's lovely, but I've not written it out.

To MISS LOUIE ELLIS.   ALASSIO, 19*th April*.

I am going to leave this on the seventh for Switzerland, because I'm afraid I'll die here and they'll bury me here and I don't like it. I'm going to be buried at Maderaner Thal. What is your grave going to be

---

1 In *Stories, Dreams, and Allegories*.   2 In *Dreams*.

like? This is a true and faithful picture of mine.

OLIVE SCHREINER,

CITIZEN OF THE
WORLD.

WHEN SHE

WAS A LITTLE GIRL

SHE LIVED AT

HEALD TOWN,

CAPE OF GOOD HOPE,

SOUTH AFRICA.

No I won't have a foot-stone. I'll send you lovely wild
flowers when I'm in Switzerland. I never go out here.
The little boys throw stones at me and I'm always writing
or trying to. There's a nice terrace one can walk up and
down all day long. Write and tell me what you think of
the boy [Havelock Ellis] when he comes back. Has he
developed much?

To HAVELOCK ELLIS.   ALASSIO, 2o*th April*.
        No, I have not finished my sex paper [see p. 354 of
the *Life*]. I was writing it for ———. I shall never send
him that or anything. In future years I may finish it.
Yes, work, work, work, if only one keeps one's reason, that
is all in life. Then one can help other women from
suffering as one has done oneself. Darling boy, I don't
mean to be selfish to you but I haven't power any more to
be otherwise than as I am.

To HAVELOCK ELLIS.   ALASSIO, 24*th April*.
        My old other-self, how are you? I wish so I knew.
I oughtn't to have written as I did, but I couldn't help it
at the time, sweet. Nothing in my life has been more holy
and sacred to me than your love. . . . I shall never feel
such sympathy on many sides of my nature with any

human being as with you. But now, my sweet, I am quite worn out and it will be many years before I have anything to give anyone. I have been bled to death. Darling, you know you have been such help to me, more help than anyone except —— has ever been, more help even than Willie Bertram. . . . It is all wrong this trying to shield others. We must be as willing to give pain as to bear it when truth requires it. Somehow all my life seems a mistake to me now, and no one else all through to blame but I. Perhaps some day, in the future, I shall see differently. . . . I've had a letter from Edward Carpenter. He's nearly the only human being I feel as if I would like to see.

To HAVELOCK ELLIS.   ALASSIO, 2*5th April*.

Harry, you *must* send me that letter of ——. I shall be absolutely mad in a few days. I have not slept or really seen anything since I got your letter saying you had written to —— after I had written begging you not to write about me. You will feel this one day. I am quite mad. I can't bear it. I am going out to walk on the hills now. Oh God! Oh God! Will you tell me what you wrote? Can you torture me like this? and leave me in this mad agony of suspense? Surely you will have sent it before. Oh, my brain, my brain, my brain.

To HAVELOCK ELLIS.   ALASSIO, 28*th April*.

I am just finishing my packing. All my heart turns with love to you all the time whatever I am doing. I try not to feel loving to you or to anyone, but I can't help it. It is a wild dark night, heavy clouds from the Riviera. I've been so untender to you, my darling, my true one, but you know I couldn't help—my head aches so, when anyone mentions——that I don't know what I'm doing. I love you so, my helper who has helped me so. I couldn't live without you. You could do much better without me. I am going to Genoa to-morrow. I am so glad to leave Alassio. I couldn't have stayed here even a day or two longer. . . . I don't know why the *Fortnightly* is so determined to have an allegory. When I get to Amster I'll be able to work and write a lovely one on " Woman " to send them. . . . Oh, sweet, my boy, my comfort. Your Olive. Never mind sending me the letter I asked for ; it doesn't matter ; it's all right. Your horrid, hateful Olive.

To HAVELOCK ELLIS.   HOTEL SMITH, GENOA, *2nd May.*

I left Alassio at 10 this morning ; got here an hour ago. This is a cheap little hotel kept by an Englishman, close to the docks in the noisy part of the town, but that doesn't matter for a little time. . . . I am going out now to see the place.

To HAVELOCK ELLIS.   BEELLINZONA, *4th May.*

On Swiss soil once more. I'm so glad. I slept last night at Arona. I meant to go on to-night only as far as Locarno on the Lake Maggiore. I started this morning in pouring rain and mist in the boat, and found when we had started that at this time of year the boat doesn't go to Locarno. . . . I am thinking of you all the time. Some-day, you and I and Louie will go to Italy together, and we'll be so happy and see the pictures. I never wish to see Italy alone again. In Switzerland one wants to be alone with the mountains but in Italy one feels so lonely. I'm so tired, I can't write any more. I haven't written to anyone but you.

To HAVELOCK ELLIS.   GERSAU, *11th May.*

I am going to work now. I have had terrible asthma all night ; even chloral didn't give me any ease ; and I'm afraid work I do in this state won't be good but I can but try.

Remember me to your dear mother, and how is my Louie ? Whenever,—in about a year's time perhaps !—whenever I've finished my book I'm going to hire two tiny little rooms in the East End in a quiet back street and furnish them myself. I shall never be able to live in England except for a month or two in the year, but I want to have a *home* somewhere, and you and Louie can always come and stay in them when you come into town. I've been so happy planning this when I was too ill to think of anything else, but the book isn't written yet, and I can't touch it except when I'm strong, and now I'm as weak as a baby with a could—*cloud* (I've been puzzling ever so long to find how that word was spelt wrong ; now, happy thought, I see where the "l" ought to come) over its brain. I hope the *Fortnightly* will like the allegory written in this state. Good-bye till this evening.

Evening. Asthma, and can't lie down. I never told you about that terrible Lady W—— who keeps writing and wants me to go to Bel Alp with her (I've never seen the woman !) and I've written the shortest letters I can to her, saying I *must* be left alone. I haven't got any work done to-day.

To HAVELOCK ELLIS.   GERSAU, 12*th May* (*Morning*).

Going away, getting worse and worse. Don't know where to go. Have written to Clarens.

To HAVELOCK ELLIS.   CLARENS, 16*th May*.

Tell me the address of a cheap respectable hotel in Paris. I am not better. I think I shall get well in Paris. Please be sure not to come and see me here. I want only to be left alone.

When I was getting out of the boat at Lucerne a man with such a sweet face, something like Carpenter, only handsome, who had been one of the passengers, came up to me, and said : "Fraülein, I am so sorry to see you so sorrowful," and then he said that brighter times must come, and something about his own life having been very dark and got bright again. And then he touched his hat very respectfully and said he hoped good would come to me and went away. Somehow it comforted me so.

To HAVELOCK ELLIS.

c/o Madame LAFARGUE, PARIS, 24*th May*.

Paris does my asthma good. But I feel very desolate here. Paris is a much worse place for a woman to be alone in than London. It must be glorious for a man. It is not so sad as London, but all my life is there. I sometimes think I am not going, but gone, mad. It's so God-forsaken everywhere. . . . Mrs. Lafargue [Eleanor Marx's sister] is like Eleanor, not half so nice, but very kind, she says Lafargue is a fine fellow.

To HAVELOCK ELLIS.   134, RUE D'ASSAS, 26*th May.*

Have got a little room here in a bad sort of house for ten francs a week, no cooking, spend most of my time in going out to get pennyworths of bread or milk ; no restaurants here, except filthy workmen's places. Paris suits my asthma, just as London does. But living is dearer, and not being able to speak one word of French makes living almost impossible. I like to think you were in Paris once and were happy here. It's so impossible to realise there is anything but agony in the world. When I see all the people in the streets it doesn't seem to me they are real. Everything seems to me just like a nightmare. . . .

To HAVELOCK ELLIS.   PARIS, 6*th June.*

I have been waiting many days to write to you till I felt my brain so cool that I could. I have now taken a dose of chloral, the first narcotic I have allowed myself to take for six weeks, and can write. I return to London on Tuesday or Wednesday. I feel as if seeing Carpenter would just save me. He has been suffering from great and terrible disappointment in human nature where he had trusted, but he is going back to the human he loves all right now. He has been great help and strength to me. I am writing to —— to ask him please not to come and see me if I come back to London. If he comes and heaps reproaches on me any more I shall leave London within twenty-four hours. Instead of going into the Convent I ought to have had the moral strength to refuse to see him any more. When you or Eleanor really see what my condition is I will not have to fear either of you ; you will leave me alone. I want to go to London because going to meetings and seeing strangers will be good for me, if I can only escape the people who think they have claims against me and torture me. They may have, I am quite willing to allow I am wrong and bad, but it won't help anyone that I should be sent *mad, mad, mad*.   One meeting with —— and his shrieking and throwing himself on the floor and it will all snap and go.   If I can't have peace in London I will go to the Cape.   I have written to Will.

To HAVELOCK ELLIS.   GORE ROAD, LONDON, 20*th June*.

Do you know, I'm going to finish my book.   I'm getting jolly hard, like I used to be at the Cape.   I can work now.   I don't want to see anyone this week ; so sorry Roden Noel is coming this afternoon. . . .   I went to the London Institution yesterday.   A clerk came up and said he believed I subscribed there before and that they regretted so much after I left that they hadn't known I was the author of *An African Farm*.   They wouldn't have destroyed any of my notes if they had.   He seemed speechless with emotion and I couldn't laugh.

To HAVELOCK ELLIS.   LONDON, 22*nd July*.

My eyes seem sometimes blinded by agony.   I don't know how I live.

To Mrs. J. H. PHILPOT.   LONDON, *Aug*.

I am reading Jowett's *Plato*.   God will have to give Jowett a front seat in the Kingdom of Heaven. . . .   I can't believe anything could be better.   I seem to have found a friend I've been seeking for all my life.

To Mrs. J. H. PHILPOT.

THE ROUGHS, YORKSHIRE, 18*th Aug*.

It's quite lovely here.   Solitary little house, miles and miles of barren moorland every way.   Not a soul to be seen.   I am sitting in the little stone-floored kitchen before a big fire.   It's damp and raining outside.   It's such a nice look as the grey mist steals over the moors.   I don't believe I shall go to the Cape.   I shall always come here. The old woman and her son are so nice, just like Boers. She and I and her son are going some Sunday in the old cart from here to Haworth, if it doesn't break down on the way.   That's the only dissipation I have in view.

To HAVELOCK ELLIS.   LONDON, 14*th Sept.*

I've come here [London Institution] to get books. Can't find anything I want, but this is such a delightful room to sit and read in or write letters. . . . I long so to hear good music. It would be so nice to go together. Somehow since I came back there has been such peace in my heart, as if I was dead. . . . I must go home and write to ——. You know we *must* love everyone in this world. It is only ignorance and darkness keeps us from it.

To HAVELOCK ELLIS.   ST. LEONARDS, 5*th Oct.*

Could you get me a room, if you are going up to town, in a cheap bed and breakfast place near the British Museum or Southampton Row? I can't ask —— or —— because I want to be quiet. My brain will go if I'm not. I'm going to try to get off to Italy by Thursday.

To HAVELOCK ELLIS.   ST. LEONARDS, 13*th Oct.*

My Havelock, I am thinking of you. You must write and tell me about yourself. Someday, when you are a broken down old man and I a young woman, I'll write much to you. You quite forget how much older I am than you.

To HAVELOCK ELLIS.   NEAR DOVER, 14*th Oct.*

Feel so glad to be off [to Italy]. Don't forget your old comrade quite.

To HAVELOCK ELLIS.

LUNGARNO ACCIAJOLI, FIRENZE, 18*th Oct.*

Florence isn't a bit like I thought. It's the coldest place in the whole world. The hills are covered with snow. It's something like Brighton but without the sea, big hotels and fashionable people. . . . My window looks down on the Arno.

To HAVELOCK ELLIS.   FLORENCE, 20*th Oct.*

I like Florence very much.

To HAVELOCK ELLIS.   FLORENCE, 29th Oct

Florence is beautiful beyond words. . . . The Pitti
Gallery is *lovely*.

To HAVELOCK ELLIS.

BOBOLI GARDENS, FLORENCE, 30th Oct

I am sitting here at the foot of a statue. It is as it
were the top of a hill, just outside Florence. The garden
is behind the Pitti Palace, such a garden ! Such a day !
As I look down below me is the Pitti and beyond Florence
and beyond the beautiful hills with an afternoon light
like the Cape on them. . . . I am leaving for Alassio on
Tuesday. I hope to work there, don't want anyone to
come and see me while I'm there, but in April or March I
want to go to Venice. I am working and so happy. But
to-day my landlady is in a rage with me because I spilt
the ink, so I am very sad. . . . Vernon Lee is a fine
woman. Nothing small or mean about her, but the devil
in if she likes. She's been kind to me.

To HAVELOCK ELLIS.   ALASSIO, 2nd Nov.

In my old quarters. Slept at Genoa last night.
Leaning Tower at Pisa splendid as seen from train. Seen
nothing in architecture I like so much as Westminster
Abbey or front of Notre Dame. It's the climate, the
streets, the people, the general effect that is so nice in
Italy.

I'm writing a long dream on Socialism, called " Dreams
of a City " [?" The Sunlight Lay Across My Bed "]. With
all these dreams coming I never get to any other work.
Can't help it—they *will* come.

To HAVELOCK ELLIS.   ALASSIO, 4th Nov.

I am so glad to be back in Alassio. Oh, I love this
place. " To-day there falls the dear surprise of peace."

To Mrs. J. H. PHILPOT.   ALASSIO, 4th Nov.

Have you read *Memoirs of Madame De Rémusat* ? It's
one of the most fascinating books ever written. It makes
me love Napoleon more than ever. If he had had a

*Lyndall thought him
the greatest man ever.*

nother like St. Augustine's, the world would have found its
oblest hero and saint in him.   It was only a case of bad
ducation. . . .

To Mrs. J. H. Philpot.   Alassio, 7th Nov.

I think I have passed through one of the happiest
imes of my whole life since I left England, especially
ince I came here.   I never since I left Africa seemed to
ome so near to nature.

To Mrs. J. H. Philpot.   Alassio, 13th Nov.

Yes, if one could live life over again with one's enlarged
ympathies, how different many things would be.   When
one looks back one understands the people one knew long
go so much better.   I always feel that about my parents
nd brothers and sisters.   One loves them more and more
s time passes.

To Havelock Ellis.   Alassio, 15th Nov.

Got nice letter from Canon MacColl.   Got nice letter
rom Gladstone's daughter [Mrs. Drew].

To Havelock Ellis.   Alassio, 21st Nov.

I have been sitting up to finish writing out a dream
I am sending to Canon MacColl and Mr. Gladstone's
laughter to look at.   I'll tell them to send it on to you,
f you care.   It has been dark and raining for many days
now, but I keep very well.   I think it has been very good
or you, my darling, that I have been quite removed from
you.   I see no one, live quite alone, except at meal times.
It is a comfort to have meals regularly, and to get plenty
of food.   I think that's why I'm so well.   I'm longing
or my darling sun to come out to-morrow.

To Havelock Ellis.   Alassio, 23rd Nov.

My Havelock, I don't know why my heart turns so to
you to-night.   I'm thinking of your old face and its
beautiful smile and your perfect truth and all they have
meant to me, all the help in my hour of need that you have
been to me, my sweet boy.

To HAVELOCK ELLIS.   ALASSIO, 24*th* No*v*

What work I do is splendid, but my heart is somewha
like stone. Perhaps it is when one is so altogether dea
that one's work lives. . . . Isn't it curious I have droppe
all my friends, I never write to anyone, never hear fror
anyone. It is as though God had suddenly struck me wit
paralysis ; and it is good. The great lesson I have had t
learn in the last three years is that one must be true t
oneself in the first place and think of your fellow me
second. I had to learn the opposite lesson in the fev
years before. Perhaps now I shall keep the balance
—at least as long as I don't see a human being. Yo*v*
have never needed the first lesson, nor certainly the second
I am working whenever I can. Can you send me a volum
of Heine's poems ? Living absolutely alone is the onl
life possible just now, but I'm glad of books.

To HAVELOCK ELLIS.   ALASSIO, 10*th* De*c*

I love my new book so, a hundred times better than
ever loved *An African Farm*. . . . I feel such horror o
England now, I never wish to see it again.

To HAVELOCK ELLIS.   ALASSIO, 13*th* De*c*

I wish you were here this evening and you and I woul
sit down on the floor before the olive wood fire and tal
till 12 o'clock. I want to talk with you to-night. . .
You know I feel I am so much in the right path to b
here. I am now on the path that I lost when I left th
Edinburgh Infirmary. I would like to get away fror
Alassio but I know I mustn't. Do you feel in the righ
path ? You are gaining what is very useful. Why don'
you put down shortly, in the way of a vivid diary, wha
you see among the factory workers [at Blackburn] ? I
years to come it will be valuable to know what their condi
tion was now. . . . Isn't it wonderful, I feel inclined t
write the first time for months ? Have seen wonderfu
beautiful things I never saw before. Such an odd kind o
peace and rest is with me ever since I made a scene to-da
in which Rebekah talks to her little son. What a grea
beautiful thing life is in spite of all its suffering ! It wi

take me about twelve months steady work to perfect what I see. You know I feel like I used at Lelie Kloof and Ratel Hoek. . . . I would like to talk to you, much more to hear you talk. You know when feelings of love come into my heart to you I restrain myself because nothing but sorrow comes from expressing love to anyone.

To HAVELOCK ELLIS. ALASSIO, 12*th Dec.*

I thought out that about Greece and Rome having fallen because of conditions of women by myself. What's the use of thinking ! Someone else will do it, the same thoughts come to all.

To HAVELOCK ELLIS. ALASSIO, 14*th Dec.*

I am working. But the last days I've got into the allegory state.

To HAVELOCK ELLIS. ALASSIO, 18*th Dec.*

Am working hard. Never come back to myself sometimes for a couple of days and that is the only way in which work can be done. *From Man to Man* will be quite different from any other book that ever was written, whether good or bad I can't say. I never *think*; the story leads me, not I it, and I guess it's more likely to make an end of me than I am ever to make an end of it !

To HAVELOCK ELLIS. ALASSIO, 22*nd Dec.*

I cannot tell you what this air and blue sea and sky are to me now I love them. I am working. I seem at last to have conquered, I think for ever. It may be not. . . . It is unlikely I shall get any publisher in England but Vizetelly to take this book. I am getting so hopeless on the question of earning money. The Devil comes to me sometimes for a moment and says : " Wouldn't it be better to sell your soul and work for money, and so be free and independent ? " I shall work night and day for a year or two years more, and then what shall I get for it ?

To Havelock Ellis.   Alassio, *Christmas Day*

I send my love to you. The sun is shining. I haven'
done any work, quite well, but can't pull together. Perhaps
by this time next year I shall pass whole hours withou
thinking of Mrs. ——. That would be heaven. . . .

CHAPTER V

LETTERS WRITTEN IN 1888

To HAVELOCK ELLIS. ALASSIO, *3rd Jan.*

Don't criticise my allegory, darling. It isn't written. It came like that. Do you think it good enough to print? Just say Yes or No. Good enough for *Fortnightly*? Please send it on to Eleanor Aveling. I want £5. I'm working most splendidly, but somehow I don't get any " forrader " ! "Work done most slowly Art most cherishes." Oh, does it? I think I'll die like old Paolo Uccelli : " *How beautiful is this perspective !* " And in the end nothing came of it ! Of course *I* have the satisfaction of seeing these wonderful works of art completed, but will anybody else? . . . I wouldn't like you always to have to work so hard as you have now, but I don't care for the next two years. I think it's good for you. My horror was that you would sink down into the mere literary man, like Leslie Stephen, or, worse still, something like Lang. It is the scientific side of your nature will save you. Are you learning to talk? I am getting silent as I used to be in the Cape. I mean I've a horror at the thought of having to write to anyone even, and I'm curled up. If you come to Venice you'll have to talk. . . . Try and get Karl Pearson's book, *The Ethic of Freethought*, as soon as you can. [She wrote a review of this book for the *Pall Mall Gazette*.]

To HAVELOCK ELLIS. ALASSIO, *24th Jan.*

On one side your nature is like ――'s, and unlike mine. When I want to go to Trafalgar Square and fight the enemies of Freedom of the hour wildly and get my head broken, *you* say I am a fool, and you are *right*. When I

The question is not : Is Pearson a genius ? Is he original
Can a flaw be found in his argument ? But is he givin
utterance as a social thinker and teacher to views we ca
sympathise with ? A reviewer is writing, not, as the essayi
and artist, for himself, but as a critic he stands between th
public and the thought and literature of the day, to guid
and lead them. To me the work of the reviewer is as sacre
and high as that of the poet and the thinker, or rather
is like that of the preacher. . . . I have been working i
great mental agony to-day. Sometimes I get almost pra
tically blind, I can't see before me when I am walking, an
then small external things crush me. I am writing abou
those two terrible women, Veronica and Mrs. Drummon
It is so terrible to have to realise them and grapple wit
them. I bear all kinds of wickedness, but not meanne
and smallness. I shall be so glad to get back to Bertie an
Rebekah, my beloveds. If they are ever so real to anyo
as to me, how real they will be ! . . . You know, if I ha
been married when I was twenty three, ten years ago, m
life would have been quite different and my strength muc
greater. This celibacy has not been good for me ; b
it would have been worse to marry any man I have ev
seen ; except *possibly* one. I mean that I am sure celiba
is not good for the brain of a continual [brain-worker
Schopenhauer, Goethe, Shakespeare, no really great stead
thinker has ever been celibate. You must marry some da

To Mrs. J. H. Philpot.   Alassio, *Ja*

Please post the enclosed letter. I hope it's not rud
but I get so many letters that one doesn't know how
reply to. This lady says that she sees there are man
things I am not able to grasp, but as I am young there
still hope ; and she writes me an allegory to convert m
She says her Heavenly Father gives her whatever she as
him for, and if I would ask him he would give me to
What funny people there are in the world. She ends h
letter by asking what colour my hair and eyes are. . .
There is an old clergyman's wife come here and two ol
maids. They made for my clothes the other day and sai
I was shabby, which is quite true ; so two days I've take

some bread and meat and an apple and gone up the mountain
to have my lunch by a ruined chapel. It's much nicer.

To HAVELOCK ELLIS.   ALASSIO, 1*st Feb.*

I don't need anything just now ; I've no time to make
the dress if I had the material. I'll get a lot of things when
you come out. . . . Italian is such a lovely language.
They say as people get older they get less able to take things
in. But I never in my life was able to take in so readily
and with so much pleasure as now. You know, I'm not
suited to living in a city. I must always live alone in the
country.

To HAVELOCK ELLIS.   ALASSIO, 7*th Feb.*

I have begun Italian. I shall get on very fast. Have
you Boccaccio's stories in Italian ? It would be a good
book. If not I will get it here. Going to send you picture
of my Ruined Chapel, my beloved Santa Croce.

To HAVELOCK ELLIS.   ALASSIO, 9*th Feb.*

I am all wild on the Mary Wollstonecraft Introduction.
Will you tell me more about the mill hands (women) in
the north ? I only go on my own slight experience. Do
you think I am too strong in saying that they are equal
(almost ?) to the men, that motherhood in them does *not*
prevent their working and being jolly, etc. ? I would like
something I could if necessary quote in a note. Don't
exaggerate, let it have the exact truth. This is so important in social questions when one can so easily put things
too strongly without being conscious of it. . . . I shall
do an immense deal of work and thinking and in the end
there will be three little pages. It's the exact truth that's
so damned difficult to get at.

To HAVELOCK ELLIS.   ALASSIO, 9*th Feb.*

You are quite wrong about my working a few hours
every day. The way in which *my* brain must work (at
imaginative work) is altogether or not at all. My great
mistake is that I read the things as soon as I have done

them and then burn them instead of not looking at them
again for a few months, when they would seem quite nice

To Mrs. J. H. PHILPOT.   ALASSIO, 18*th Feb*

I get to my work which is sometimes writing, more ofter
walking up and down my room and thinking things out
. . . I never see anything of them [the visitors at the Hotel]
After lunch I sometimes go out for a walk to my favourite
ruined chapel, Santa Croce, but lately I haven't been out
I read or write or walk up and down, " thinking out " al
the afternoon. At 6 we have dinner. Then I come up
to my room again, generally leaving before dinner is quite
done, and I walk out on the terrace a bit and then read or
write till bed-time. I do *exactly* the same every day. One
day is as all days. It's a very delightful life. I've never
been so happy since I left my dear old farm in Africa. . .
I'm writing an introduction to Mary Wollstonecraft's
Rights of Women ; it will hold the substance of all my
thoughts on the man and woman question.

To HAVELOCK ELLIS.   ALASSIO, 20*th Feb*

Working night and day at Introduction to Mary W[oll-
stonecraft] ; love it better than anything I've written for
a long time. But I want to publish it first in *Fortnightly*
Do you think the editor will let me. I'm putting the resul
of all my work on Woman Question into it. It will be a
disgrace to get only £10.

[I have the unrevised manuscript of this, which does no
seem to have been touched from the time she first wrote
it, nor worth publishing in its present form.]

To HAVELOCK ELLIS.   ALASSIO, 5*th March*

That old terrible agony is on me to-night that come
whenever I let myself go. It seems as if all slipped from m
at once, as if at other times I never knew how I was re
straining myself. . . . It's been hanging over me for days
I suppose I must be physically ill without knowing it.
feel quite well in body though. I have walked all the wa
from Albenga here to-day, over the mountains. I cam
by the Roman road. I wanted to make myself tired.

To HAVELOCK ELLIS.   ALASSIO, *6th March.*

. . . You will enjoy Italy. I leave this on the 1st of
May for Venice. To live so many months shut up alone
in one room is very bad for the brain. Then when we have
spent a week or ten days at Venice I want you and I to go to
Innsbruck and on to Switzerland. There you can go on to
England and I turn back to Tyrol or Switzerland. . . .
The people here said it was no use my going to Monte
Carlo because they don't let people into the gaming rooms
under 21 ! I feel as if I was 100. I couldn't believe they
were serious ! [She was thirty-three.]

To HAVELOCK ELLIS.   ALASSIO, *9th March.*

Don't mention to anyone Carpenter being here. I'm
always trying to keep people from coming, and if they
hear Carpenter or you have been they'll think they must
come too. I've been curled up for some days ; feel weak.
. . . Don't ask about Mary Wollstonecraft. You musn't
speak to a little hen when she's laying her egg, otherwise
she just pecks it open. I've been making nice plans of
travel for us. I enclose £1 more as you won't tell me
what I owe you. Please order me an *Eastern Alps* Baedeker.
I'm spending all my money on Baedekers, so that when
the time comes to start I shan't have any for travelling.
. . . Many thanks for the *Zoology.* Can you tell me of a
good book about mammalia, giving their habits and family
relations ? Always tell me if you come across any good
thing about the higher apes.

To Mrs. CAWOOD.   ALASSIO, *? March.*

I am getting on well ; another person in health while
I stop out of English cold. . . . Who lives at Lelie Kloof ?
I'm going to buy it when I've made my fortune and Willie
must come and look after it for me, and we be partners.
It's full of fossils. I should love to come and rest with
you for a week and tell stories to the children, the new little
ones, and look at your face.

To Mrs. CAWOOD.   ALASSIO, *16th March.*

Yes, I will leave you something, my little brown box
with all my relics in it, the last pipe my father smoked, and

bits of letters and paper-cuttings and hair, that won't mean anything to anyone else but have all at some time meant something to me.   There's a little bit of African earth which I took from my little sister Ellie's grave more than twenty years ago, when I was a child, and tied up in a silk rag. Wouldn't I make a good worshipper of saints !   I love everything old, though my intellect stretches out always joyfully to the future and everything new.   I never forget you, Erilda Cawood.   You have been of great value and help to me in my life, not by anything you've done for me, but in the only way people can help each other truly, by being what you are. . . .   If I come out to the Cape I will surely come to Ganna Hoek.   But I can't afford it yet.   It would be so nice to look at your face again. . . . I feel very old, sometimes quite a hundred and eight.   But it's comical how people take me to be younger and younger.

To HAVELOCK ELLIS.   ALASSIO, 1*st April.*

My own darling boy, I wonder if you like to get letters or if you are too ill to read them.   I want to know if you have the quiet restful mental feeling one sometimes has when one is ill.   Sometimes one is so agonised and worries about everything.   If Harry boy were here, he would like so much to sit out in the sun when he gets better. . . .   Isn't it funny that I felt that you were ill and were unhappy *before* your mother's letter came.   But perhaps the fact that you didn't write to tell me you'd got home made me fancy something. . . . I feel as if you *must* need me.

To HAVELOCK ELLIS.   ALASSIO, 10*th April.*

I'm so glad you are better.   I'm not nearly so affectionate to you as I was ! . . .   I've stuck fast in my work. I've been agonising over it but it won't come right.   I've been praying over it ; sometimes that helps.   When I stand up from my knees things come clear.   I pray a great deal over this work.   Unless the Lord should help me I'll never get it done.   And it'll be a damned poor little when it is done.   It's wonderful what makes one work, what impulse *drives* one on.   It's a sort of instinct, like what makes the birds make their nests.   I'm going to pray some

more by the sofa now. What else can I do when I don't
know what comes next ? It's all about sex in the human
race. . . . Can you meet me at Boulogne to go on to Venice,
say 5th of May ? Write and tell me all about yourself as
soon as you are better.

To HAVELOCK ELLIS. ALASSIO, 18*th April.*

I am so very anxious about you still. You thought
me foolish to be so foolish when I first heard you were ill,
but the terrible thing about fever is that it kills as if in
play. People are well, and in a moment gone. . . . I
can get the money and come at once if you need me. You
must come out to Italy when you are better.

To HAVELOCK ELLIS. RIVA, LAGO DI GARDA, 6*th May.*

Are you quite strong ? You mustn't come out till I've
finished my book. I don't mean to be interrupted, and
don't mean to stir from Riva till it's done.

To HAVELOCK ELLIS. RIVA, 13*th May.*

I'm worse ; going to try Paris. If I telegraph when
there, can you come for a day or so ? I hardly know what
I am doing, vomiting and agony in stomach. Are there
paying hospitals in Paris ?

To HAVELOCK ELLIS. MAIDENHEAD, 20*th May.*

I have made up my mind to go out to the Cape the week
after next, and not to return to England. It's best for my
work, for me, for everyone, for you. We must have one
long quiet day together before I go, and we must go to a
concert together. . . . Goodbye, my brother. You must
get stronger. You must have a beautiful strong life yet.
I haven't quite spoiled it, have I ?

To HAVELOCK ELLIS. MAIDENHEAD, 27*th May.*

Is it nice in Devonshire ? I am looking for a small
workman's cottage in Surrey. I want a high dry place on
chalk, with a heath and no woods. I'm going with Maggie
H. to-morrow, if well enough, to look near Woking. . . .
You know I love you, but one must check the expression
of one's emotions or die.

To HAVELOCK ELLIS.   MAIDENHEAD, 5*th June.*

Can you come on Friday ? I go to-morrow to Harpenden to look for rooms. . . . I ask only one thing, and care for only one thing at present, not a straw for love or anything of that kind. I care only that my loathing for humanity should not be increased, more especially for women.

To HAVELOCK ELLIS.   MAIDENHEAD, 6*th June.*

Please come on Friday. I do love you in a kind of way ; it would come out if you needed me. But I feel such shrinking from all human creatures. We none of us sympathise with each other, none of us understand each other, each one only himself. The lesson of the last five years has been to me that there is no such thing as friendship, just as the lesson of the two before was that there is no such thing as sex-love, only sex-selfishness. We are good and true and earnest at heart, meaning the best, we humans. But we can't understand each other, and understanding is friendship. . . . Can you go with me to Harpenden to look for rooms ? We'll spend all the day there on the common.

To HAVELOCK ELLIS.   MAIDENHEAD, 11*th June.*

Went to Harpenden, found cottage, rent £16 a year, going to move in next week.

To HAVELOCK ELLIS.   HARPENDEN, 18*th June.*

I've been trying to get my tiny house cleaned out to-day. I haven't got my furniture yet. . . . I want to get a big puppy dog that will bark. I don't think the little house is very safe. Anyone can get in at my door, and I'm quite beyond anyone's hearing. The house is so built you can get in anywhere. It's a dear little house.

To HAVELOCK ELLIS.   Harpenden, 28*th June.*

Mrs. Walters has been here. I've been pitching into her and her paper more even than into you. I must find the faults in the work of the people I love. You know it's my way of showing love. Good-bye.

To Mrs. J. H. PHILPOT.   HARPENDEN, *June*.

Did I ever tell you about the people I found in Germany when I went to the place where my father was born, and I found some money (only a little) that was left to us by an old uncle (the last of my father's family) 25 years ago? It was all like a story.

To HAVELOCK ELLIS.   HARPENDEN, 1*st July*.

Your *Ford* [Mermaid Series] first rate. I am quite satisfied! Isn't he delightful, too! I am always in touch with him at once.

To HAVELOCK ELLIS.   HARPENDEN, 2*nd July*.

Your genius lies in the direction of keen most subtle and understanding criticism. I believe you to be, in reality, the finest critic, that is the finest judge of a literary or artistic production. I would take your opinion of a work of mine before that of any other person. Therefore, I feel it so bitterly that you should depend in any way on the tinsel which men who have no keen *perception* and nothing to say to the world must depend on. You are always true, always right and valuable in your naked simple idea. Why hide it and dress it? Why not write as you write your letters?

To Mrs. J. H. PHILPOT.   HARPENDEN, 7*th July*.

I'll like best of all a *tiny* workman's cottage unfurnished. I dare say that wouldn't be easy to get, and I'll have to take rooms. I want to have some place of my own, without a landlady! That's the grand idea. I should like to settle down in it for three months till I'm ready to go to the Riviera or Africa. Sometimes you would spare me your baby for a whole day, eh?

To HAVELOCK ELLIS.   HARPENDEN, 13*th July*.

You know the great thing that divides us is that you have no need of me. I mean that your nature and development does not now require mine. I can only be bad for you and oppress your development. In the same way I

hould not long be good for Carpenter and many other of
my friends. I help them up to a certain point. I have been
of great mental assistance to you in certain ways, and you
have been so to me. It's not anything else that divides
us, though it may seem to be. What my mind needs
and what your mind needs is different. It's not a question
of affection, it's one of growth. I am ——'s life just now,
but if she develops, as I hope, she will not need me in two
years time. Love remains. I *need* you greatly in my life.
I've asked Carpenter not to come. I don't want anyone
just now who does not need me. I should like very much
to meet you at St. Pancras some day, if you wouldn't feel
it wasting time. It would give me courage to face London.
It would be good for me.

To Havelock Ellis.   Harpenden, 19*th July.*

I have been reading your Ibsen essay. It is nearly
quite perfect. It is the first thing of yours I have read so
absorbingly interesting I could not lay it down. You will
develop into the first biographer of the age yet ; you have
the insight and sympathy necessary, and the width. . . .
I want to go down to that most beautiful of wild places
one day this week or next—Woking—for the day, to look
for a cottage. Would you be able or care to meet me there,
and we might have a little picnic on the heather, as I and
Carpenter had. It is much the nicest part of England I've
seen.

To Havelock Ellis.   Harpenden, 22*nd July.*

Yes, I can write better now than ever. My imagination has never worked so easily, my reason has never been
so strong, nor my grasp anything like so wide. What I
have lost is *wish* to produce for others. I think I *ought* to
wish it, but I don't care. It is a terrible thing to have become
so indifferent. There is nothing worth caring for is my
instinctive feeling, though I never let it come up. I *do*
care to save other people from suffering. Therefore, only
those things which I can imagine will have that effect will
be written of all the hundreds I make. . . . Please send
back Prelude [of *From Man to Man*]. Some little bits are

not in yet, one where she apologises to the baby for not having any milk for it. Poor little thing ! I do love her so. . . . Perhaps I could care more about life, and work more, if I could have my food cooked for me and my clothes made, like a man, and if I could have two hundred a year. Edward Carpenter is going to help me find a little £6 a year cottage in Surrey ; we are going to Dorking. Isn't it good of him ? I want to come into town and go with you to the Zoo, please.

To HAVELOCK ELLIS.

CHERTSEY, NEAR WOKING STATION, *5th Aug*.

I'm going to try to want to work. It's so lovely to make stories and so hideous to write them. . . .

You ought not to have put that unkind sentence about Miss —— . You ought to change it if not too late. We mustn't hurt other people. Life is such awful agony.

To HAVELOCK ELLIS.   CHERTSEY, 19*th Aug*.

Last night I woke up crying, and it seemed to me something was the matter with you. I always wake up crying in the night, but generally I don't know what is the matter with me. Are you well, dear ? . . . You have suffered so much, my Havelock. Only I can't quite *understand* that anyone should ever have suffered about me. I can *understand* that people should respect and admire me, but not that they love me. But you did once, and we all must let love die. . . . I am longing very much to get out of England, but I have yet no money, and I don't quite know where to go. . . . I want to have you here for a whole day to myself before I go, and I want to cook you a *nice* dinner. You must once in your life eat a real dinner I've cooked !

To HAVELOCK ELLIS.   CHERTSEY, 21*st Aug*.

I am going out to Alassio the end of next month, I think. I see they've got a nice little earthquake there.

To HAVELOCK ELLIS.   CHERTSEY, 23*rd Aug*.

I send my love to you. Work hard, get on, be strong. When once we lose our strength there is nothing in life worth living for. All good be with you, darling. I don't write to you about myself, I should but write sadly. Your little sister.

To HAVELOCK ELLIS.   CHERTSEY, 26*th Aug*.

It comforts me so that you say you love me a little. My brain and my body are breaking down together, and I am so humbly grateful to anyone who saves me a little.

To Mrs. J. H. PHILPOT.   HARPENDEN, *Aug*.

A little allegory is coming out in next month's *Woman's World*. It's not a good one, yet I love it almost best of all. I think I showed it you once. I only publish it because a friend wished it. I make allegories every day almost, but I never want to publish them ; they seem to me things that are for one self, and one self only, like one's deepest personal feelings.

To Mrs. J. H. PHILPOT.
                LONDON INSTITUTION, FINSBURY CIRCUS, *Aug*.

It will be many years before either of my books are ready, I think. My big scientific book [? on Sex] will take me five or six years ; my work widens and widens out before me, and it isn't the getting done that's beautiful, it's the working and the learning more.

To HAVELOCK ELLIS.   LONDON, 2*nd Sept*.

I've come in to get books and see Dr. Wilks but he's out of town. . . . I've been reading *Madame Bovary* ; I detest it, beautifully as it is written.

To Mrs. J. H. PHILPOT.   HARPENDEN, 5*th Sept*.

How stupid people are that they can't understand that, just because one feels that that complete union of mind and body, one man to one woman, is the only ideally perfect thing, therefore one hates all that is false and like such union only in seeming.

To HAVELOCK ELLIS.   HARPENDEN, 9*th Sept.*

Will you please send one copy of *The Woman's World*, with my thing marked, to Stead at the *Pall Mall* office, writing on the outside " From Olive Schreiner " ?

To Mrs. J. H. PHILPOT.   HARPENDEN, 13*th Sept.*

Don't trouble about it at all, dear friend. I am perhaps morbidly sensitive about saying anything of anyone else. It is perhaps because I myself suffer so much ; I don't think others do suffer so, because their natures often allow them to justify themselves when mine does not.

To HAVELOCK ELLIS.   HARPENDEN, 13*th Sept.*

You can come and see me if ever you feel inclined. Tell me the day before, so that we can have a nice duck. . . . I am working hard. When I die you can have a post-mortem and open my brain, and then you'll see how I've suffered all these years.

To HAVELOCK ELLIS.   HARPENDEN, 14*th Sept.*

My sex book would do for your Science Series. It is a purely scientific collection of facts. But it can't be done for two years more, at least. I think it will be very good. . . . Will you send me all Heine's poems ? I will take care of them. I love them so. You must read Scherer's *History of German Literature*, most fascinating.

To HAVELOCK ELLIS.   HARPENDEN, 3*rd Oct.*

I have bronchitis. I am very ill. If I am not better to-morrow I must get someone from London to take care of me and help me pack. Would Louie or Laura [Ellis's sisters] care to come ? Wire reply, and I will wire whether I am better or not. You will promise me not to press it. I can get a nurse, and there is an old woman here will do all the real work, but I feel helpless. Wire to Symons I can't come to-morrow.

To Havelock Ellis.   Harpenden, *3rd Oct. (second letter).*

Oh, it is awful to be a woman. These women are killing me. Give my love to Louie, but I don't want to see her or any other woman. I want to live *alone, alone, alone.* I don't say the fault is not in myself, but they are doing it all the same. When I am in Italy I needn't open any letters they write me, eh? Old Chapman has offered me £100 for *African Farm* for two and a half years. I must take it to escape abroad. I wonder if I shall ever come back to England among these women again. One must die at last, eh Harry? Oh, please see that they bury me in a place where there are no women. I've not been a a woman really, though I've seemed like one.

To Havelock Ellis.   Harpenden, *5th Oct.*

Louie was, as she always is, so splendid, and I was so horrid. Come and see me early in the morning. I feel so loving to you, I wish you would all come and live in town.

To Havelock Ellis.   25, Montagu St., W.C., *7th Oct.*

You know I love you, but my power of expressing any feeling but pity is gone. There isn't one human being to whom I feel that tender outflowing of love I used to feel to all the world. If you can come on Wednesday afternoon we can have a nice cosy talk before the fire, and tea, and, *if you like*, I'll ask Alice Corthorn, and, *if you like*, Louie can come too, it would be nice to have a long talk together. It's just possible I may start Wednesday morning.

To Mrs. J. H. Philpot.   St. Albans, *Oct.*

My chest has been much worse this time in England than it ever was before. . . . I got an old woman at Harpenden to pack my things, but it ended in my giving them nearly all to her!

A friend [Louie Ellis] came and brought me here. I don't know what I should have done without her. It's terrible to think of all the people who must die in England this winter because they can't get away.

To HAVELOCK ELLIS.   ALASSIO, 16*th Oct.*

Now I've got here the Hotel man has raised his price
though he said he wouldn't, and I shall either have to go
or take a dirty little room. I'm in such a tired state I don't
know what to do. Please write to me sometimes. I can't
even see it is Alassio. I long so for some human being to
love me just a little. . . . You musnt't be lazy, my boy,
you must work hard. You've got a wonderful life before
you.

To HAVELOCK ELLIS.   ALASSIO, 18*th Oct.*

Dear Havelock boy, I am very loving to you. Please
write and tell me about work and books and so on, when you
have time, and the names of really good books when you
come across them. . . . I have been very ill since I left
London, but this evening the cough is better and the tiredness. You would like this hotel, it is uncivilised and wild.
. . . Harry, isn't it funny to grow old, and have all your
life passed, nothing in the future ?

To HAVELOCK ELLIS.   ALASSIO, 21*st Oct.*

I long so much for human love the last days, more than
ever in my life before, even when I was in Africa. I suppose
one never kills out one's personal instincts entirely till death
comes and sets one free. The terrible thing will be if death
comes, and instead of rest the struggle goes on on the other
side. But I don't think it. I couldn't explain to anyone
what beautiful things I think of death. He is always to
me a beautiful snow-white [? angel] with huge silver wings,
and he smiles down and folds you in them. I couldn't
write Lyndall's death like that now ; it would be something
so beautiful.

To HAVELOCK ELLIS.   ALASSIO, 22*nd Oct.*

Mrs. Bland (" E. Nesbit ") was so kind to me before
I left London. I don't think I should have got away
without her. She came the last morning to finish packing
my things and see me off. Do you know, she's one of the
noblest women ? I can't tell you about her life, because I

mustn't, but it's grand. The last night she lay by me on the bed and drew me very close to her and pressed her face against mine, and, do you know, I have felt it ever since. I am going to get better. . . . Canon MacColl has written to say Gladstone wants very much to know me.

To HAVELOCK ELLIS.   ALASSIO, 26*th Oct.*

I am working, so of course quite happy.

To HAVELOCK ELLIS.   ALASSIO, 28*th Oct.*

I am very happy and peaceful here. This relief from physical agony is so glorious. It's so funny to think you can, all of you, open your eyes wide in England and lie down at night just as I can here. Oh, I should like to show you Alassio. . . . I always knew you would be successful, and success is the one thing you needed. You *need* a great deal of it. It will help you, not hinder, as it does certain meaner natures.

To Mrs. J. H. PHILPOT.   ALASSIO, *Oct.*

All goes splendidly with me. I am working hard and very happy. *Nothing but work makes life beautiful.* I am staying at a cheap little out-of-the-way Italian hotel. No English here ! ! And the servants can't even talk French. There's a big neglected garden where I can walk about and write. It's much nicer than the other semi-civilised end of Alassio. We are quite wild here.

To HAVELOCK ELLIS.   ALASSIO, 2*nd Nov.*

I am well and working, don't sometimes remember for two days who I am. The being able to breathe makes all the difference. The Kaffir woman said God couldn't be good because he made women, but I say because he made asthma.

To HAVELOCK ELLIS.   ALASSIO, 2*nd Nov.* (*second letter*).

Please order for me a copy of your *Ibsen* and send it to my brother Fred in time to reach him on the morning of the 7th which is his birthday. If you have one of Zola's novels in French you might send it me. I read only to deaden myself and stop myself from thinking ; puzzling over a difficult French book could not do that. But I *must* learn more French because I am probably going to Paris next year ; so please send it. . . . My Mary Wollstonecraft is going on. It is all poetry from the first to the last, except a few sentences. There are six or seven allegories in it ; I've tried to keep them out, but I can't. I have come to the conclusion that only poetry is truth. That other forms are *parts* of truth, but as soon as a representation has all parts, then it is poetry. As soon as there is the form and the spirit, the passion and the thought, then there is poetry, or the *living* reality. I don't mean that I attain to true poetry —all I mean is that what makes a man strive after and seek to see the thing in that way is that it is the reality. It's the other that's fancy and fiction, and this that is real. It's so easy for a mind like mine to produce long logical arguments, or strings of assertions, but when I have done it I feel such a "valch" against it : that is only the material ; it has to be combined and made alive. I know I shall die a beggar in my old age. You will have to support me. I shall write slower and slower. . . . I am very happy, as happy quite as I used to be in Ganna Hoek . [The "Ganna" was begun with L, and she was evidently going to write "Lelie Kloof."]

To HAVELOCK ELLIS.   ALASSIO, *3rd Nov.*

I'm not like old Tolstoy ! Everything he teaches, according to the *Pall Mall*, is what I believe. His falseness lies in this : instead of saying simply : " I see these things as truth," he wants to force them into the world under the old name of Christ. If what Jesus saw was truth, and in as far as it was, everyone who pierces as deeply into the laws of human nature and life as he did will find [it] again. Neither Christ nor Tolstoy nor any one of us now living has yet seen and preached that doctrine of love and forgiveness as it will be preached in ages to come. . . . The strife and agony of these last years has not been to forgive, it has not been magnanimously to overlook : that is easy enough. It is to *love*. If there be one soul you cannot love, then you are lost. . . . Please buy and send me a Bible, as like my old one in size and print as you can. I am always quoting from the Bible, sometimes for the Devil's own purposes, and I find as the years pass that my memory sometimes wavers with regard to the exact wording of a passage.

To HAVELOCK ELLIS.   ALASSIO, 7*th Nov.*

How splendid your Ibsen Introduction is ! The only bad line is about Congreve, and I believe it gave you more satisfaction to write than all the rest. You simply *grunted* with satisfaction. . . . I feel so loving to everyone. I love Mrs. ——. I'm going to begin loving everyone again. That's the worst of me.

To HAVELOCK ELLIS.   ALASSIO, 9*th Nov.*

I don't think overmuch of your theories about genius though they are true so far as they go. Once God Almighty said : " I will produce a self-working automatic machine for enduring suffering, which shall be capable of the largest amount of suffering in a given space " ; and he made woman. But he wasn't satisfied that he [had] reached the highest point of perfection ; so he made a man of genius. He was [not] satisfied yet. So he combined the two—and made a woman of genius—and he was satisfied ! That's the real theory—but in the end he sold himself because the machine he'd constructed to endure suffering could enjoy bliss too. . . . I'm all right, but so very weak. I sometimes find I'm sitting on the floor crying, but I haven't any idea what it's about. I seem to be always crying inside.

To HAVELOCK ELLIS.   ALASSIO, 9*th Nov.*

My whole theory is *Crime is disease*, treat it as disease.

To HAVELOCK ELLIS.   ALASSIO, 11*th Nov.*

I've been working hard at my Mary Wollstonecraft all day. What troubles me is that I have too many ideas. You say, why do I spend so much time over it ? How can I do otherwise ? Whatever I write, it must be the best I can write, given that time and these circumstances. When I die the angel of death will find quite pure in me the power of thinking and of seeking that was born in me. I have not once defiled it. If I was writing for ten thousand pounds or for three and sixpence, my work would be just the same. Perhaps when it's done you'll wonder that it took so long and see nothing in it, but I see. I expect when it is done I'll throw it in the fire.

To Mrs J. H. PHILPOT.   ALASSIO, 1 5*th Nov.*

I wish I could be as well anywhere in England as I am anywhere out of it. I was quite well when I lived with my brother in his great warm comfortable house [Eastbourne], but when I live by myself I seem to break down. I can't make it out. . . . It's not raining to-day, and I'm going to rush about on the sand on the seashore a little. There are no respectable people here, it doesn't matter how one dresses ; it's delightful ! (My bill is only 35s. a week, *everything* included.)

To Mrs. J. H. PHILPOT.   ALASSIO (*about same time*).

When I've finished this book and the next, I'm going to sit on the seashore day after day and play with the sand and do nothing else.

To HAVELOCK ELLIS.   ALASSIO, 1 5*th Nov.*

Yes, I get plenty to eat, etc. Yet I stop weak. . . . You know either my Mary Wollstonecraft is very, very bad or very, very good. I don't know which. My story work I always know exactly the value of. You don't know what it is I am feeling after and will grasp at last. I'm going to think the matter out to myself and then turn it into allegories and stories. . . . I have had a crime story, two, in my mind for years. In one the woman—oh, there's the lunch bell, and I'm so hungry.

To HAVELOCK ELLIS.   ALASSIO, 1 7*th Nov.*

I made a little Dream to-day, which I've sent to Miss Müller for her paper. Shall send it you. I've got such a curious agony of loneliness on me this evening, though I'm writing, as if something terrible were hanging over me.

To HAVELOCK ELLIS. ALASSIO, 29*th Nov.*

This house is unhealthy, the doctor says. How splendid it would be to have Louie with me for a week, and you. I have been ten days lying here, without seeing a human creature whom one could speak to really, unable to work, without anything to read—*think, think, think.* Do, do, do send me something to read. If I could afford to go to one of the larger hotels I should soon be well. It was really the house and the good food that kept me well at Alassio before.

To HAVELOCK ELLIS. MENTONE, 5*th Dec.*

My Havelock, I long to see you. I think if I had stayed much longer at Alassio I should have died. I've been here only twenty-four hours, but am already much better. I am the only person in the hotel. I like Mentone, it's beautiful.

To HAVELOCK ELLIS. MENTONE, 8*th Dec.*

It's such a beautiful day here, quite perfect. I wish I could work. I ought to, but I have no nerve power. So stupid people always feel. We just sit and look in front of us and see nothing, and feel quite happy. . . . I went such a superb walk last night up among the olive trees beyond the house, and when you get to the top such a view, Monte Carlo and Monaco and the great still bay, I watched the sun set behind Monaco. Do you remember that poem you sent me? It just expresses what Mentone is : " To-day there falls the dear surprise of peace." Alassio is quiet but not peaceful. It's the perfect motionlessness of the sea here that gives this wonderful sense of calm. Goodbye, dear. Tell [Arthur] Symons I'm going to write him a long letter about his poems [*Days and Nights*], they are too good, that is the fault I have to find with them, too much thought, too little feeling, too perfect in form. They are wonderful for so young a man. He may be a great writer and a great man, but he will never be a great poet. You can tell him this, as I mayn't be able to write for some time.

To HAVELOCK ELLIS.   MENTONE, 10*th Dec.*

There's a Swede at this hotel who is in love with me. He puts little flowers by my plate every day. He's like one of Ibsen's characters. He is always talking of the " ideal marriage " and the " ideal wife." He has all but proposed to me, and so I am keeping out of his way. He has such a beautiful childlike nature. Even a German isn't like that.

To HAVELOCK ELLIS.   MENTONE, 14*th Dec.*

Havelock, don't you know of anything I could take to strengthen my nerves ? It's no good taking bromide ; it simply weakens one yet further. What is given for hysteria ? (Awful sensitiveness in lower part of body.) Isn't valerian a good thing ? . . . If I tell you something you are not to talk of it to anyone. I'm coming to the Endell Street Hospital in May for three months. I *must* get some hard work which will not allow of my thinking or feeling.

To HAVELOCK ELLIS.   MENTONE, 18*th Dec.*

I have quite made up my mind to go to the Cape next winter, but don't talk of it ; things are never done that are talked of. . . . I can understand everything people say in French now, even when they talk fast. Do you know any good natural history books and travels ? Those are the only two things I like.

To HAVELOCK ELLIS.   MENTONE, 22*nd Dec.*

Don't speak about those Dreams to me. I'm mad enough about it, as it is. I wrote the last down dash in a hurry one night, and told Miss Müller to send it back to me in proof to re-write. Instead of that she prints it just as it is—perfect nonsense—and old Stead takes it over ! She writes to say she couldn't wait for my proof. Ah, well, the will of the gods be done !

_To_ HAVELOCK ELLIS.   MENTONE, 23rd Dec.

The enclosed is from the Swede. I value the love of people who don't know who I am and love me just in an instinctive way because they can't help it. . . . You will see shortly in the _Pall Mall Gazette_ how _I_ do the " damned fine horse " ! But you are not to " let on " to anyone that it's me.

CHAPTER VI

LETTERS WRITTEN IN 1889

To Mrs. MARY KING ROBERTS.   MENTONE.

Our first duty is to develop ourselves. Then you are ready for any kind of work that comes. The woman who does this is doing more to do away with prostitution and the inequalities between man and woman, and to make possible a nobler race of human beings, than by all the talking and vituperation possible. It is not against man we have to fight but against *ourselves* within ourselves. We have to rise. . . . It seems to me you and Dr. Roberts have such an ideally beautiful life with one another ; there is so much you can give him, and so much he can give you. I think marriage is much the highest condition physically and mentally, though it is not attainable by many of us in the present condition of society. . . . To help any woman to be independent, that is the *real Secret of Freedom*. Please don't give up your longing to be materially independent because your husband is noble and generous ; you must be lovers and friends and companions right on to the end of your lives, and not sink into the sad old groove. It is this which matters, not whether one signs one's name in a register or not. . . . Please don't mind all I've said in this letter.

To Mrs. MARY KING ROBERTS.   MENTONE.

With regard to my view of the marriage question, it is very simple and just what it always has been since I was thirteen and began to form a view at all. The one and only ideal is the perfect mental and physical life-long union of one man with one woman. That is the only thing which for highly developed intellectual natures can consolidate marriage.

All short of this is more or less a failure, and no legal marriage can make a relationship other than impure in which there isn't this union. How we should arrange that this great pure form of marriage may be oftenest and most perfectly reached seems to me a great problem.

To Mrs. J. H. PHILPOT.   MENTONE, 4*th Jan.*

I've had such a happy day, working all the time. People think I have a sad, lonely life, but I believe I'm the happiest person in the world ; whether my work is artistic or scientific, I feel as if I were in Heaven when once I am absolutely in it. The terrible part is to think I will ever have to publish it.

To HAVELOCK ELLIS.   MENTONE, 7*th Jan.*

Is it you putting old Stead up to say I'm like Tolstoy ! It's an extraordinary thing when there's no man in Europe I hate so much.

To HAVELOCK ELLIS.   MENTONE, 8*th Jan.*

I made a great mistake in not seeing —— even in the distance before I left . . . . When my father died, for months I agonised, and when once I had saved up money and gone to that white grave stone at Balfour and looked at it I was *perfectly quiet.* I have never been otherwise when I think of him since. . . . I wish you would send me a prescription for opium pills, like those two you sent me at Alassio.

To HAVELOCK ELLIS.   MENTONE, 19*th Jan.*

My Havelock, I am writing to you from simple out-going of the heart this afternoon. It's a perfect day, the first like this we've had for a long time. I've not been working. I've had too much pain and headache, but I'm better this evening. . . . I think no one would ever understand what I have suffered from my periods the last two years and a half. The only time I have quite escaped the agony was when I took that opium pill you sent, but I suppose that was chance. You must study this matter of women's suffering some day. Something ought to be done for us. . . . Yes, it's best I go to the Cape, dear. Then after 5 or 6 years I may come back to Europe. . . . Harry, one does get to a kind of Heaven at last, a Heaven where one doesn't care.

To HAVELOCK ELLIS.   MENTONE, 1*st Feb.*

Havelock, I am so well and happy I can't understand it. It feels as if I don't mind anything ; not anything anyone could say or do. I suppose it's my work makes me so happy. You know there's one little line in my Prelude [First part of *From Man to Man*], not in what you saw, that I love so. When you read it you must guess which it is. If you don't find out I shan't ever love you because it is the most beautiful thing I ever saw. It surprised me so when I saw it. It's a tiny thing. . . . I wanted so much to get into the Endell Hospital, but they don't answer me.

To HAVELOCK ELLIS.   MENTONE, 2*nd Feb.*

Don't you pitch into me, Henry Havelock ! I'm just learning you to do the damned fine horse ! Wish you'd say the things a person wants to hear said about them, when *you* write, not all the things they don't ! . . . My Prelude is too lovely for any words. I had a lovely time this afternoon. I went on to the top of a hill near here and lay and slept half in a sweet dream kind of way with joy that my Prelude was done. I'm going on at my book [*From Man to Man*] and Mary Wollstonecraft [and] everything else can go to the D——. Tell Rhys so ! [The Mary W. was to appear in a series edited by Mr. Ernest Rhys.] The worst of this book of mine is that it's so womanly. I think it's the most womanly book that ever was written, and God knows that I've willed it otherwise ! . . . I'm singularly well and strong ; the dirty food here doesn't seem to do me any harm. . . . Goodbye, my old Harry Boy, the one person that ever quite truly loved me. I shall be glad when you marry, and yet, you know, something will be gone out of my life.

To Havelock Ellis.   Mentone, *5th Feb.*

Harry Boy, it's a lovely morning, I'm going to work, but am shuffling out of it for a few minutes by writing to you. I'm in a hurry for your *Criminal* book to be done. Yesterday I was reading in my [Nicholson's] *Zoology* (that fertile source of ideas) and looking at the diagram of the nervous system in vertebrates and invertebrates. Well—a new definition of genius, artistic genius at least. People of genius are those individuals in whom the sympathetic or instinctive nervous system is particularly well developed, or, rather, combined with that intellectual cerebro-spinal system peculiar to the higher vertebrate in a peculiar way. They are both highly developed and both strongly act on one another in case of artistic, and, I think, *all* genius. The man in whom the brain system alone is great and active is a man of talent, a thinker but not an artist. The man in whom the sensory automatic sympathetic system of abdominal nerves alone is highly developed and active is a fool. In the great artist his brain governs but his sympathetic system does the work, artistic work. This is why, after artistic or in any way creative work, your back gets tired, not your head—Don't you see, the sympathetic system has to pass through all the stages [in order] that your brain, which has the power of overlooking them, may become cognisant of them. The brain seizes and guides and chronicles the sympathetic system for its own purposes, as an artist. But it can't guide more than a very little way ; it mustn't interfere when the thing is working ; or it spoils all. What is called inspiration is somehow explainable in this direction. I haven't got the true theory, but I know I don't do any of my best work in my brain, by the process that is called thinking. It is as little thinking as your pinching my finger and my feeling it is thinking. I have millions of ideas always coming into my head that I would like to brood over and work out if life were longer.

To Havelock Ellis.   Mentone, *9th Feb.*

I've a little Dream about Poet and Thinker. It's good, at least true. . . . This house is full of prostitutes. No one talks anything but French at the table and the conversation is too awful for words. I profess not to understand, and I don't when people talk in such a way, but I can gather what it is. Something like in the worst of Zola's novels. The woman who sits next to me is a very pretty woman of thirty. I fancy I might get a little power over her at last ; at first she made fun of me and made all the men say rude things to me ; now, according to her orders, they all bow to me, and she's always trying to please me. I feel affectionate to her. She's just about the same kind as Nana, but I see what old Zola couldn't see, that she's yet a woman. This is a low hotel ; no respectable people come here, and no English. Don't say much about it in your letters because they might open them, and then come up and murder me. I'm at the very top of the house.

To HAVELOCK ELLIS. MENTONE, 10*th Feb*.

I am getting strong like I used to be at the Cape. I am somewhat curious to know if I could keep it up in England, or if the first twenty-four hours there will reduce me to my maudlin sympathetic condition. It's easy to be strong when there's no one you think it your duty to love.

To HAVELOCK ELLIS. MENTONE, 14*th Feb*.

I often—no, I don't often, but I did just now—wonder what all my work would be like when it is done. It's funny how one works on blindly in the dark, following an instinct, never knowing what one's work will be like. It's really not stranger than when bees make their nests ; it's exactly the same thing. . . . I am going to dedicate my sex growth book to you, I think. I'll never leave off loving you.

To HAVELOCK ELLIS. MENTONE, 17*th Feb*.

Terrible attack of asthma last night ; can't make out why. All right to-day ; working. . . . Harry, I *hate* being a celebrity. Why won't the people leave me alone ? I won't publish anything more. Some people like it, but I'm not suited for the rôle.

To HAVELOCK ELLIS.   MENTONE, 19*th Feb.*

I have just come up from dinner. I am sitting at my little table before the fire. The time of day I like best is just after dinner here. One feels a little tired and can't absorb oneself in one's work. If I thought smoking was good it would be a great comfort, but I can't get a good cigar here. . . . Harry, if I don't come back to England till August, and spend summer somewhere up the Rhine, won't you be able to come and see me? I couldn't bear to go to Africa and not see you again except for a few moments in London. I have so many things to talk about with you.

To HAVELOCK ELLIS.   MENTONE, 23*rd Feb.*

I send a little Dream. If you think it's good enough for *Fortnightly*, send it on at once to Harris. If you think it's not, send it to *To-Day.* It seems all right to me, but may not be.

To W. T. STEAD.   MENTONE (*evidently* 1889).

I believe in Marriage. The man who has a wife and children always to turn to must be stronger to fight the outer world. It is the perfect, the natural condition. But it is for those who are called. Some years ago I couldn't see a little tiny baby without an inclination to burst out hysterically crying, and to see a happy husband and wife with their children seemed to wake in me the same unaccountable feeling. Now I have entirely conquered it. I know my work and have accepted my little work in life ; and the real thing I am going to the Cape for is to see my brother's two small babies and play with them.

To HAVELOCK ELLIS.   MENTONE, 17*th March.*

Never since I first knew you has my heart turned to you so much as in the last two days, but it's not for a noble reason, it's because I'm in pain and I would like to lay my head against your knee. Something has happened that I can't write about, but that I will tell you of one day. It's nothing to do with my beautiful friend at —— or anyone you know. . . . I am, as soon as I've finished this, going to write out a Dream I made at the East End. I've tried to begin twice, but I've never been able to get the colour on to my pen. Yet this dream has lived with me for two years.

To Mrs. J. H. PHILPOT.   MENTONE, 17*th March.*

I wish I was large and strong and could put my arms round all the tired lonely women in the world and help them. The work of my life is to try and teach women to love one another. If we would leave off quarrelling with men and just love and hold each other's hands all would come right. Oh, I love the two women in my book so [Rebekah and Bertie in *From Man to Man*] I am getting to love women more and more. I love men too, so very much— only they don't *need* me.

To HAVELOCK ELLIS.   MENTONE, 18*th March.*

You remember that long ago I told you how, nearly twenty years ago, when I was at Dordrecht, I had such a horror of eating before people, I couldn't, and how I used to have to eat alone, and how it kept on, and I told you what unkind untrue things they said about it. Well, there came some people here ten days ago, from the Cape, I think, or they knew people there, and they have been talking to all the people at the hotel about it. They are low, rough people, you know the kind I mean, and they have heaps of money. They sit and jeer at me at the table. The man with one eye calls out across the table and asks if that young lady can tell what the word pickpocket means, and then everyone laughs. Even the servants won't say " good-day " to me any more. Only one prostitute, to whom I've been kind, speaks to me. Harry, you won't betray me. You won't talk about this to anyone. I'm hunted to death. If I stayed here a little time longer I must die. I am going to Florence. My cough is bad and I feel so weak that it has taken me all day to think clearly enough to write this. Harry, the world isn't fair, I haven't sinned so much more than other people to be hunted down so. If it goes on a little more I will kill myself. I wouldn't if I thought my ason would stay, but I know I can't bear much more. Oh, I've been so desolate all my life, Harry, I've never had a home, I've never had anyone to take care of me like other girls have. I was thrown out on the world when I was eleven, and even before that I hadn't a real home. Oh, you, who've never been turned out of a house, don't know what it is. Long ago I could bear, but now I can't any more. I know my reason will go. Oh, Harry, if you knew how helpless a woman [is]. I've borne now for four and thirty years alone. . . . Soon the bell will ring and I must go down to that room full of human creatures. I am many years older when I come out than when I come in. I dare not stay away. Twice I have. I must seem to feel nothing. I will go away to Florence next week if I can. I will try to finish my book and then I will kill myself. But,— oh, Harry, it seems as if my brain was going now. They surely wouldn't try to hunt a human creature down if they knew what it was. Harry, I've never willingly hurt a human being. . . . Oh, Harry, why didn't my mother put a garter round my neck the day I was born? I am a fine genius, a celebrity, and to-morrow all these people would tread me under their feet. I can't go back to Africa, they will torture me too much. I want to go somewhere where no one knows me. It's harder than if the things were true, it's so cruel. I never told you the cruel things Mrs ——— [a South African woman] said to me, when she came to see me in London last summer ; it was that broke me down so. . . . Read my Prelude and tell me what you think of it. Harry, if I could be alone I would finish my book, and then when it was done I could die. Harry, you mustn't talk about this to anyone. Everyone will say again I am wandering without a motive. I have never moved without a motive ; the hidden agony of my life no human being understands. Harry, you are young and fresh ; you will marry and find love ; you are not cut off from your fellows. Oh, this fame is so terrible, I shrink from it so. . . . I enclose a cheque for £20. Please cash it and send it out to me, £5 at a time for safety. Please send the first £5 at once. I can't leave till I get it. If people ask where I am, just say travelling in Italy. . . . P.S. I have opened my letter again ; the thought has just struck me to go to Paris instead of Florence. I can live very cheaply there, and you can come over and see me. What do you think ? If I wire the one word " Paris " you will know I have come and that I want the £5 sent to Oxford and Cambridge Hotel. Don't tell anyone where I am.

To HAVELOCK ELLIS. MENTONE, 19*th March.*

I am better this morning with the thought of coming to Paris. I get to Paris at 9.15 on Saturday in the morning. Can you meet me at the station where the Marseilles express arrives at that hour ? If so, telegraph, as soon as getting this the one word *Paris.* You can with full truth tell you are going for a holiday to Paris and to see about the possibilities of your living there. In fact for yourself alone it will be a good thing to come, but I am asking you selfishly. My brother Theo and sister Ettie and four of my nephews and nieces are coming to England the week after next, and if I am in Paris I am sure Theo will come over to see me. Please wire the minute you get this. I am going to tell everyone about my being in Paris, because I want nothing secret. But I don't want to tell heaps of people, and you needn't mention me unless anyone specially asks.

To Mrs. J. H. PHILPOT. PARIS, 26*th March.*

I am making dreams here at a great rate ; I always do in Paris. Only they are all about God, and my friends pitch into me when I make dreams about God. I can't help it, they come.

To Dr. KING ROBERTS. PARIS.

I went to Notre Dame to-day. Isn't it glorious ? It seems to me something I have been looking for and longing for all my life when I see that. I love it better than any building I have ever seen. . . . There's an idea built into Notre Dame in stone that we of this age and the ages coming will have to build up again into our social forms. It won't be stone next time. It will be men and women ! ! I go to it every day nearly when I'm in Paris, and it seems to me as if I'd seen it this afternoon for the

It's blank verse, only some words have to answer : *sitting*, *suddenly*, *starting*, and if I could put all *l* and say *starling* it would be more right.   It's very interesting because I'm so bitterly opposed to all versified forms and think my own prose so much higher ! and here I am drawn unconsciously into doing the very thing I hate.   " There's a deal o' human nature in Man."   What bothers me is that it isn't the right sort of thing, it bothers me a great deal.   I don't like that lilt, and if I try to get out of it I only get into something still worse.   Damned if I shan't write plain prose now, right on to the end, and get the thing done.   It's an awful temptation to go on with that sort of thing, because as long as you do there's such a delicious sensation going all through your body as if the whole of it was keeping time.

To HAVELOCK ELLIS.

25, MONTAGU ST., LONDON, 15*th April*.

I came on Saturday evening, late.   I like to think you are near.   I am very tired, but I want to write a word to you, I long to see you.   Come and see me when you come to town. . . . I'm afraid I shan't be able to work in London, my chest feels bad as soon as I get here.   I am going to try to work, and, if I can't, go to Germany.   It's the climate.   I don't mean to let people trouble me so much. . . . I like Plato.   I'm reading him.

To HAVELOCK ELLIS.   LONDON, 19*th April*.

Havelock, I think I felt nearer to you yesterday than ever in my life before.   I felt as if we understood one another. I shall look for you and [Arthur] Symons on Wednesday afternoon.   All good be with you, my boy friend.

To HAVELOCK ELLIS.   LONDON, 25*th April*.

[Arthur] Symons is a remarkable man.   One can hardly say what he will be.

To HAVELOCK ELLIS.   LONDON, 26*th April*

I am going down to Knaphill, near Woking, on Saturday.   Alice [Corthorn] will be there till Monday afternoon

Can you come on Monday morning and help me to decide about the house? . . . I am very glad Symons liked being here. I thought I was so tired he would be bored. I'm always tired now. Are you in love that you suddenly look so handsome? If you would rather come when I am alone, come on Tuesday and perhaps we can go to Hindhead for the day.

To W. T. STEAD.

25, MONTAGU STREET, RUSSELL SQUARE.
(*Date doubtless* 1889.)

If the woman a man loves were brave and faithful she would *for the sake of* her love for him not endure he should fail in openness and sincerity. I feel less and less able to call that relation love in which one draws the other from the higher for the sake of possessing them. You will understand what I mean when my book is published. I can't express myself satisfactorily didactically.

To HAVELOCK ELLIS.   EASTBOURNE, 9*th May*.

I'm in a daze. Can't write. Going back to my little cottage at Knaphill to-morrow. You must come and see me there as soon as you come back from Yorkshire. I'm lodging in a little workman's cottage. The Countess of Aberdeen and a lot of folk are going to come and see me, but I don't mind if I can keep out of London. Isn't it funny I can't feel any more.

To HAVELOCK ELLIS.   KNAPHILL, 15*th May*.

I don't know when anyone has seemed to be as vividly present to me as you were on Monday night. I kept starting up and hearing your voice and hearing you laugh. You and I will have some grand walks here.

To HAVELOCK ELLIS.   KNAPHILL, 17*th May*.

Have very bad hay fever, am going to Brighton to look for rooms, and, if Brighton does not do, look for rooms at Deal. I wish you were down here.

To HAVELOCK ELLIS.   KNAPHILL, 20*th May*.

Am leaving for Brighton on Thursday. But I doubt very much whether I *ever* shall be able to work my brain in England, it's not warm and clear enough. Do you remember those three clear hot days we had last summer? I never forget them.

To Mrs. J. H. PHILPOT.   KNAPHILL, 20*th May*.

When all my work is done I'll go into Society—in another world. You know I would like society if men would accept me as a man among men, but now I know they never will, and I'd rather just go on alone. . . .

To HAVELOCK ELLIS.
           MEDINA VILLAS, WEST BRIGHTON, 26*th May*.

I don't think genius is at all less common among women than men, rather more so. What they lack is the strong controlling *impersonal reason* behind the genius. Mrs. Browning had just as much of the genius element as Browning, rather more. She was all genius. But she lacks his powerful reason and his massive strength, which has nothing to do with genius, therefore she is as compared with Browning as valuable as a little finger compared to a whole body. How many women writers there are at the present day with a touch of genius but so pitifully *small*! The genius is all right in Ouida, Miss Mulock, etc., but the intellect is wanting.

To Mrs. J. H. PHILPOT.   BRIGHTON, 29*th May*.

Yes, I'm going to lunch with Gladstone and Bret Harte.

To HAVELOCK ELLIS.
           LADIES' CHAMBERS, CHENIES ST., LONDON, 10*th June*.

I can't work or think so I'm as well here as anywhere. I've done nothing all day but write letters and this evening went out for a walk in the dark up Gower Street, and Tottenham Court Road, and then went on a bus. It must be nice going about there in the north.

To HAVELOCK ELLIS.   LONDON, 23rd June.

Yes, I am better than I have ever been in England. I am wanting to see you. That Friday night when I went to see *Nora* [Ibsen's *Doll's House*] did me good.

To HAVELOCK ELLIS.   LONDON, 6th July.

I was very well and strong till —— and —— came ; I now feel like a little child hardly able to creep from one room to another. You can't understand that to feel any human creature hopelessly false is more terrible to me than all poverty, all loneliness, all death. The fact of such a nature as Edward Aveling's, for instance, is more terrible to me, does more to cripple my power of life and work, than all the close personal sorrows of my life. The thing which is great to me, and which alone touches me quite close, is anything bearing on my conception of human nature. It's not a theoretic thing with me, its my *passion*, just as other men's desire for love or ease or fame is, and as my hunger for knowledge pure and simple used to be. Personally, I care nothing for fame or success and still less for love, ——'s or anyone else. I want —— to be noble, and want myself to be so. That vision of the human soul which I have seen slowly growing before me for years and years, forming ever since I was a little child, *is* the work of art ! The perfect, the beautiful, which alone I desire. . . . You know I don't mean that I am beautiful. I only care for beauty and ugliness as part of the general. [She was beginning to write after " general " " beauty and ugliness," but struck it out.] It only *haunts* me, as an ideal, like beautiful arms and legs haunted Pheidias till he made them and *saw* them. But the beauty I seek is, I more and more realise, intellectual, and it can only be attained through the intellect. It is all-wise, all-knowing. Therefore the instinct which seeks knowledge *first* is quite right. After long years I shall understand fully what it is I am now doing and seeking, but now I can't explain to myself and still less to you, as little as when I was a little child I could have explained to anyone, or myself, why I had to pray and think all night. I know now. It's very easy to see. You are so beautiful to me, so much more noble and true and perfect than I, just as Ettie always was than me—and, yet, you can't understand. . . . It's so beautiful to think of you in Yorkshire. I'm going to have a splendid time, too, in the winter, get quite up to Nature somewhere.

To Havelock Ellis.   London, *5th Aug.*

Will you come to see me some time next week? Ettie leaves on Friday and after that I shall be free. We must make a plan to go out for a day into the country. . . . I am trying to get my allegories into order for a book. Please send me any you have, and bring *all* my MSS. that you have, please. It's too much to bring all at once. Bring it bit by bit. I shall want my desk too, some time.

To Mrs. J. H. Philpot.   London, 12*th Aug.*

Stead came to see me on Saturday. I attacked him so violently for what I considered all his shortcomings as Editor of the *P.M.G.*, that I thought he would never forgive me. So few people can understand that fault-finding is the truest sign of friendship, I'm glad he has [understood]. I think his nature is sincere and good in its lowest layer. . . . I have been reading Kant and Hegel. I wish I could feel that Hegel was genuine at the heart's core. He always seems to me a mind that seeks more to gain its point than to find the reality. I've also been reading a life of Kant by Stuckenberg, very well written. I get to love my books so I take two or three of them to bed with me every night; I like to feel them lying by me when I wake even when I don't read them. The other morning I got my breakfast ready very nicely and set it out on the kitchen table and then came up to my room and began to write ; after an hour or two I began to feel faint, and wondered what it was and when I went down I found I had cooked my breakfast and forgotten to eat it. One gets in such a funny dreamy state when one lives alone month after month, and you get at last to dread seeing people even if you love them. . . . This is the longest letter I've written to anyone in the last two years." [The extracts given are more than half of it.]

To HAVELOCK ELLIS. LONDON, 28*th Aug.*

This letter of Amy's [Amy Levy] may interest you.
. . . I am going to St. Leonard's with Amy Levy from
Saturday to Tuesday as my chest is getting worse.

To HAVELOCK ELLIS. LEAS HOTEL, FOLKESTONE, 31*st Aug.*

We had to come on here because Amy Levy didn't like
St. Leonards and besides rooms were very expensive. We
are going on this morning to St. Margaret's Bay. My idea
is to ask you to meet me at Canterbury but I can't say. I
don't like travelling with anyone else because it costs so
much more, but I'm able to breathe and lie down the whole
night.

To HAVELOCK ELLIS. LONDON, 3*rd Sept.*

I'm back. Fancy, when I think of leaving England
the thing I mind most leaving is you. Isn't human affection a funny thing ! Come and spend Friday with me, if
fine, and let us go up the river to Kew, eh ? and we can make
further plans.

To HAVELOCK ELLIS. LONDON, 7*th Sept.*

I hope you will come on Monday. I shan't be able to
go out for the day because it's Theo's and Katie's last day,
but I shall like to see you in the morning or afternoon.
The asthma kept me up all night, but I'm better now. . . .
Good-bye, it was very nice in the boat yesterday and the
rowing did me much good.

To HAVELOCK ELLIS.
EDINBURGH HOUSE, ST. LEONARDS, 17*th Sept.*

I am writing this at once because I want you to get it
before you start to-morrow. I hope it will be nice in Paris
and shall be glad when you come back. Explain to Symons
how disappointed I was that I was ill. I think I shall get
better here. Goodbye, dear old brother.

To HAVELOCK ELLIS.   LONDON, 25th Sept.

I am glad it was enjoyable in Paris. I am going up to
London to-morrow to pack, to get done by Friday. Then
I go down to Eastbourne. My brother has invited me to
stay there till I leave. I shall be very glad to go and rest
and be quite quiet at Eastbourne.

To HAVELOCK ELLIS.   EASTBOURNE, 1st Oct.

I got here all right. Old landlady stormed at me for
walking up and down. Am out looking for rooms. Only
saw Fred for one minute last night. Not seen any of them
this morning.

To HAVELOCK ELLIS.   EASTBOURNE, 3rd Oct.

Am all right to-day. Doctor injected morphia last
night. My brother and sister are so good to me, and I've
got a nurse, so there's no need to be anxious. Too stupid
to write more.

To HAVELOCK ELLIS.   EASTBOURNE, 6th Oct.

I shall sail on Wednesday. Coming up to London
by the early train. I have a nurse and a doctor, he injected
morphia again last night. They will not have my allegory
in the *Fortnightly*. I am very lonely here. I would like to
see you.

To HAVELOCK ELLIS.   LONDON, 7th Oct.

Am better this morning. Will write or telegraph soon
as I know hour of sailing.

(Same date.)

Will you try to meet me at London Bridge on Wednesday morning and go with me to the Docks? It's a hard
time here, Havelock, and seems to have killed out what
little power of feeling was left in me. You will not mind
if I don't seem to feel anything? I will be better when I
get to Africa. It is just possible when I get to the Docks
I shall pack my cabin there and then go on to join at

Dartmouth. I *will* if I have money enough. If you can go too, make arrangements accordingly. I want to see you.

To HAVELOCK ELLIS.   LONDON, 8*th Oct.*

Better meet me at the East India Dock Basin, on board the " Norham Castle." We might miss at London Bridge. Don't fail. I must see your face. My brother is coming up with me. . . . Harry, I'm so dead, dear.

To HAVELOCK ELLIS.   " NORHAM CASTLE," 9*th Oct.*

Thank you for coming. I will write long letters. You must get on with the *Criminal* book. I'm all right.

To HAVELOCK ELLIS.   LISBON, 12*th Oct.*

Got here an hour ago. Going on this afternoon. Better, only so weak. Write to me often. I have been all in a dream since I left England. Haven't thought or felt anything.

To HAVELOCK ELLIS.   CAPE TOWN, 6*th Nov.*

I feel very loving to you. Please write to me. It is so nice here. I am so numb and can't feel anything and can't think.

To HAVELOCK ELLIS.   CERES, 16*th Nov.*

This is a little up-country village among the mountains. I got very ill at my beloved Visch Hoek [Fish Hoek] and the doctor ordered me up here.   You ride half a day or eight hours by train from Cape Town and then get out at a little railway station in the middle of a wide plain with mountains all round, and then you hire a cape-cart (if there is one to be had at the little solitary inn) and, by one of the most beautiful passes in the country [Michels Pass], one comes up into the mountains, great wild rocky mountains covered with wild untouched bush and ferns and flowers. When you get to the top you break out suddenly into a little plain with mountains of every form and kind piled up all round its edge, and in the centre of it lies the tiny green village, if one can even call it a village. There is such a sense of surprise in finding human habitations here among these wild rocks that adds to its beauty. The air here is splendid, high, dry mountain air, and yet beautifully calm and sheltered from winds with the peaks of the mountains about it. I am telling you all this about it because I remember what you said about living at the top of a mountain, and if ever you come to Africa you must come here. When I look out through my open door as I write I see through the branches of the trees the glorious still high sky and bits of the bare stone mountain.

To HAVELOCK ELLIS.   CERES, 17*th Nov.*

I shall be so thankful when I can find a resting place to work in. Please send the £21 at once. I can't afford saddle. I need every farthing for living. It's *much* more expensive here than in England.

To HAVELOCK ELLIS.   CERES 18*th Nov.*

It is a beautifully hot day, such heat as is not known in England, hot and light. I shall be glad of the sex book [Geddes and Thomson, *The Evolution of Sex*] and any books. Please write *at once* to *Pall Mall* office and ask them to send my paper to Mount Vernon, Cape Town. I have not seen an English paper, nor heard anything of the world, since I left. People in this country are very much impressed by *An African Farm.* Even the man who keeps this little place has it on his table and gives me the best room in the house and strawberries on its account ! It is a bit sad to think it would have pleased the little solitary girl who lived in Africa long ago—and now what desires I have run in such far other directions ! I want one woman to be converted. Do you think she ever will ? It is the sky that is the glory of this country ; it is better than I had thought.

To HAVELOCK ELLIS.   CAPE TOWN, 23*rd Nov.*

Thank you for the book [Geddes and Thomson] ; it looks interesting, but, as far as I've glanced at it, mine would have been much more profound and original and

well composed and beautiful.   Mine is a work of art !—
but it'll never be finished now I'm so tired. . . . I would
like to talk with you, even about intellectual things.   I
have not talked about anything that was in any way impersonal since I left England.   The people in Africa are three
hundred years behind the times.   I have not seen one man
or woman (except Will of course) that was within a few
hundred miles of oneself, except an hotel keeper in Ceres.
I got very ill at Ceres and have come back here.   I have
been better since I came back to town.   My continual
illness is a little disheartening ; I have not drawn one easy
breath since I left.   My little sister-in-law [Mrs. W. P.
Schreiner] is very kind to me.

To Havelock Ellis.   Grahamstown, 27*th Nov.*

I heard my mother was dying ; the doctor telegraphed
for me ; I started on Friday evening at 7 o'clock from
Cape Town and we travelled without undressing or stopping
for an hour for three days and nights.   I got here at 5 in
the morning.   [The journey was by train.]   My brother-
in-law, Robert Hemming, came with me to take care of me.
We passed all through the Karroo and through Cradock
where I used to live ; it was splendid to see the old
sky and earth.   It's just like it was to me.   I was fighting
for breath all the way.   I am staying here with my cousin
Mrs. Orpen.   My mother is much better.   Mrs. Orpen
is very kind.   She sat up with me the whole of one night.
Robert Hemming sat up the next.   Everyone is so kind.
I am going down to see mother at the Convent this afternoon. . . . I rather fear that as long as I am in this country
I shall not find a place where I can lie down one night.   The
fight for breath is quite habitual now.   This is all the material
news about myself.   Mentally I have no news, having no
feelings or thoughts.   I go about as one in a dream ; seeing
all a hundred miles off.   I have only been touched or moved
once since I came to this country, and that was when I saw
in a colonial paper that John Burns was going to hold a
meeting of bakers in Hyde Park.   It is curious how life
repeats itself.   Just the old feeling of utter separation from
all the people about me, so good, so kind, so nice—and

Do you know it? It seems to me it will be so beautiful
to be quite old and have life with all its experiences lying
behind you, to look down on it all from the top of a mountain. . . . I am working and am so glad in my work. Every
time I look out at the sunshine the force comes running
into me.

CHAPTER VII

LETTERS WRITTEN FROM 1890 TO 1893

1890

To HAVELOCK ELLIS.

MOUNT VERNON, CAPE TOWN, *4th Jan.*

My Havelock, I am sending the MS. of the Allegories. Please take care of it as I haven't copies of some. Do you think " The Artist's Secret " worth putting in ? . . . No, I'm not short of money, as I haven't to pay rent. It's travelling that's so fearfully dear. But I like this country and I know it was right that I came. I don't like to think of you all in that dark damp foggy winter. . . . Can you send me a book you used to have giving all the different medicines and their uses and effects and antidotes [Farquharson's *Therapeutics*] ? I only care about scientific books now I am doing artistic work, and when I am doing scientific work I only care for poetry.

To HAVELOCK ELLIS.

CAPE TOWN, *7th Jan.*

You seem much depressed in your letters, Havelock. Perhaps it was only the weather. I have much to be thankful for in having the sunshine. I am very tired. I have been out all day. I went down to the market this morning, and this afternoon by train to Newlands to a strawberry garden. Newlands is the next station to Rondebosch where Rebekah lived. I always think when I go near Rondebosch I fancy I shall meet Rebekah coming down one of the avenues. Not Lyndall, not even Waldo, have been quite so absolutely real to me as she and Bertie. I cannot believe that they never lived. I *say* I believe it, but I don't. You see they have lived with me fifteen years.

To Havelock Ellis.   Cape Town, 11*th Jan.*

If you go to Paris, stop there, and, when I come back to Europe in a year or so, introduce me to all your French friends, and I'll come and live in Paris too. *I shall never live in London again.*

To Havelock Ellis.   Cape Town, 21*st Jan.*

There's a little verandah here before the drawing-room with a vine growing over it where I often go and I play Chopin on the piano a great deal. [She could not play, only strum simple tunes like a child]. . . . I am sending my Prelude to you by this post. Please give it to Eleanor Marx to typewrite, paying her the full rate.

To Havelock Ellis.   Cape Town, 30*th Jan.*

I am working delightfully. Yesterday I climbed to the top of Signal Hill. It was glorious lying there among the bushes, with the sun above and the blue Atlantic on one side and Table Mountain on the other. I am going to climb Table Mountain itself soon. Cape Town is the loveliest place on the whole earth. My heart is set on going up into the interior and I think I shall manage it some day, but it wants money.

To Havelock Ellis.   Cape Town, 6*th Feb.*

It will be lovely when you are in Paris. I shall *never* live in London again, but in Paris or Germany or Italy. . . . I had to-day a long letter from the German translator of *An African Farm.* She wants to call it *Leben und Lieben*, etc. It sounds sentimental to me. . . . I am perhaps going up to a desolate place called Matjesfontein in the Karroo. I will work better there. . . . I suppose love always makes people jealous. Women are divided into two parts with regard to me ; the women who worship me (quite falsely !) and the women who are jealous of me (quite falsely !). . . . I don't think nowadays. I note unconsciously everything, the lights on the mountains, the shapes of the trees, but I don't think. I have thought, thought, thought, night and day, for so many years, I

can rest a little now and *see* the external world again after
this nine years introspective trance of thought.

To HAVELOCK ELLIS.   CAPE TOWN, 1 3*th Feb*.

Everyone here is very kind to me.   Sometimes when
I go to pay a chemist he says he can't take anything from
the author of *The African Farm*.   It touches me so.   I
like people much more to like my work than me.   Sometimes when I lie awake in the night and feel lonely and
in pain, I think of all the people all over the world who
have loved my work and seem to feel them.   It's so
beautiful here, Harry.   I feel like I used to when I was
a little girl. . . .   Please remember that I'm going to
land at Lisbon when I come back, so if you meet me there
we can travel about a bit together in Spain.

To HAVELOCK ELLIS.   CAPE TOWN, 24*th Feb*.

Old Rumenyi, the great Hungarian violin player, is in
Africa.   I am seeing a great deal of him.   This afternoon
we went out for a drive together with a Mrs. S——.   I
would give anything if you could meet him in London or
Paris.   He is the perfect type of the child of genius—
fifty-five and a *little child*.   The people here hate him, as
stupidity always does ; they say he talks about Hell and
that he. looks like a young elephant walking on its hind
legs, and that he is greedy because he makes a rule of
eating only once in the day, at the middle of the day.   And
he says nothing unkind to anyone, goes on like a happy
child in a flower garden talking to itself—with his violin
and his curiosities and his abstract ideas.   It is so beautiful
and wonderful to meet such a person *here*.   His playing
is divine.   I use the word advisedly. . . .   How beautiful
genius is, Harry !   And it takes genius to understand
genius. . . .   That " Joy " allegory is the first I ever
wrote ; all except just the end was made years and years
ago, at Hertzog, walking about one spring morning when
all the fruit trees were in blossom.   I couldn't finish it
because I didn't quite see the end then.   I finished it in
the Isle of Wight when I first came to England.   I arrange
them according to the first part. . . .   I am working with

joy, but don't make much way because I'm trying to hold myself in—and get strong that I may do all the wonderful work I see before me.

To HAVELOCK ELLIS.
MOUNT VERNON, CAPE TOWN, *3rd March.*

Old Rumenyi used to know George Sand well.   He says I am so much like her in my ways that if I had ever seen her he would have thought I was mimicking her.

To HAVELOCK ELLIS.   CAPE TOWN, *7th March.*

I'm going to Matjesfontein on the 22nd of this month. . . . Isn't it funny ?   My whole emotional nature seems completely dead, and yet I am so happy.   The people torture sometimes, but I can always crush down the feeling, and be quite stiff like when I was in Africa long ago.

To HAVELOCK ELLIS.   CAPE TOWN, *16th March.*

Next week I hope to be at Matjesfontein and I shall have heard of your arrival in Paris.   If you like I will keep my journal on this paper and send it you now and then as MS., but you must save it as I may want to refer to it sometime. . . .   Dost thou know I have had some stiff things to go through since I came to Africa, but I have not said anything to you, because I feel like I used to long ago, that I can't talk of anything.   It is a great mistake to talk ; one is so strong to bear when one is perfectly quiet.   My brother Will is a grand old fellow, an ideal sort of character. I should like to paint him some day. . . .   I am very strong and well.   You have never seen me like this.   I have got the old hard muscle, and then one can bear anything.   You have none of you known what my physical agony has been through all these years.   I was very near to the end when I left England. . . .   Next year I am going up in the interior if I don't go to Europe, which is very doubtful.   I am slowly maturing my plans, getting letters of introduction to travellers, traders, and others who may help me on my line of march.   Money is all I need.

If my Dream book is a success at all I shall have enough. I am going to meet Cecil Rhodes, the only great man and man of genius South Africa possesses. If he backs me up at all I shall be able to carry out my plan. He likely will, as Will tells me he has been for years a great lover of the *African Farm*. I am reading nothing just now but African travels. . . . Please write to me often. In a way I am more solitary in this country than you can conceive, more lonely even than when I was a girl. I feel as if there were some ages stretching between me and these people. It's been a strange experience, how the same circumstances bring back the same conditions. I am perfectly silent ; seem almost to have lost the power of speech, except to Ettie. Ettie will soon be a free-thinker. She says now she has always believed all I say in *An African Farm* and her only regret is that she didn't stand by me in the old days ! So the world goes round. But I shall never be respectable, never rest, because, as the world comes on, one has had to go on too. I long for you sometimes. You are the only person in England I want to see, and a little Mrs. Wilson. I am going to have a cold bath now, and then I must sit and talk to the people a little, and then I will get away on to the dam wall. . . . Good-bye. Are you really in my dear old Paris ? Ach, I fear me I shall never see Europe again. I would like to see the pictures and all so, now my mind is quite blank like a little child's and I could take them all in.

To HAVELOCK ELLIS.   MATJESFONTEIN, 2 5*th March*.

I got here yesterday morning from Cape Town. It is early morning now. I have woken up just as I used to in the old days when I was in the Karroo and am sitting at the dressing-table before my little window to write. The sun is just rising ; the hill-tops are dull purple. Over the way at the railway station the coloured boys are at work already, digging the new foundations. I might be at Ratel Hoek as far as the sounds go. . . . Now I am going to put my hat on and go out for a walk over the Karroo. Such a sense of wild exhilaration and freedom comes to me when I walk over the Karroo. . . . I have now only a tiny bedroom in a little house built of iron, but in a few days I am to have three rooms in a brick cottage all to myself. I go over to the railway station to have my meals. This is a wide long plain with rocky mountains running down both sides. There are one or two little kopjes in it ; I am going to walk to one this morning. There are no farms or homesteads ; the only place is this. It consists of the railway station, Logan's house, and a row of out-buildings or cottages of which mine will be one. There is not a tree in the veld, nor a bush in the mountains as far as the eye can reach. The water is brought from a long way off in iron pipes. Even near the house there is not a tree or bush except a few little blue-gum saplings that Logan put in about four months ago ; they are nearly the only things that would grow here. The event of the day is when twice in the twenty-four hours the railway train sweeps by ; in the morning the Cape train on its way up to the Diamond Fields and Gold Fields stops about 9 o'clock and the people get out to have breakfast here, and they leave our mails ; again, about six in the evening, the train from the Diamond Fields passes and stops for half an hour. It is curious, and to me very attractive, this mixture of civilisation and the most wild untamed freedom ; the barren mountains and wild Karroo and the railway train. I know that at any time by leaping into it and travelling twenty-four hours without stopping I could cover the 500 miles between this and Cape Town. [The time is about 10 hours, the distance 195 miles.] If only my asthma keeps away, this is the ideal place I have so long been longing for.

To HAVELOCK ELLIS.   MATJESFONTEIN, 1*st April*.

Have had very bad asthma but am right again. Just moved into my new little rooms. Wild stretch of Karroo in front of my door, so glorious. . . . I like it so here, Havelock. I love the Karroo. I feel when I go out alone here on it that all the last ten years are a dream.

To HAVELOCK ELLIS.   MATJESFONTEIN, 5*th April*.

It is a wild windy night, a glorious full moon and big clouds, outside. It won't rain ; it's only the change from heat to cold. Our winter will soon be here. . . . I am sitting in my little bedroom. Such a nice new clean little room, but bare enough. Out of it opens a tiny square room with a little chair and two little tables, not even a carpet, which is my sitting room. Behind that is a room where I put my boxes and have my bath. So I have quite an establishment. I *think* I shall stay here till the end of August, unless I find I am getting on with my work slowly and steadily, but not brilliantly. I am so good ever since I came to this country, Henry ; I do nothing wrong. I am so patient, I don't hate anybody even when they talk against me, I bear everything, I restrain myself. But I don't feel " God " so near me as I did in England in all that agony and dark and conflict. Perhaps I am exhausted and cannot feel anything. I hope you will have written a nice letter for me to get to-morrow. You don't tell little Olive anything ; you don't love her ! Please write to me about Paris. Isn't it strange, I never feel any wish to live in London again, and such a longing after Paris and Italy and Germany. But England is dead for me. You know, you sometimes seem so near to me that I would not be surprised if you suddenly walked in. . . . I love the Karroo. The effect of this scenery is to make one so silent and strong and self-contained. And it is all so bare, the rocks and the bushes, each bush standing separate from the others, alone, by itself.

To Mrs. J. H. Philpot.   Matjesfontein, *5th April.*

I have never had such perfect health for ten years, never since I left the Karroo. [Description of Matjesfontein, etc., follows.] . . . I am every week more glad I came to this country. . . . Some English people who are here groan over it terribly, say " one can't live on sunshine and sky " and think it terribly lonesome. . . . Do you know I feel so happy since I came here like I used to when I was a little girl only more so. All my English life seems to me sometimes like a dream ; but sometimes a great wanting to see you all comes.

To HAVELOCK ELLIS.   MATJESFONTEIN, 6*th April.*

A bright cold morning.   I am working and feel bright and strong.   John Pursglove is coming this evening.   I went a long walk this morning away out into the Karroo and found some nice large [karree boom] trees in the dry river course.   I will make that my walking-up-and-down place.   I like very much being so free ; it is like having a house of your own without the trouble of taking care of it, and the roughness and bareness I like.   It seems as though something must happen soon—this being so well is too good to last !   But whatever happens it will be all right. . . .   I am a great smoker now.   You see I tell you all the things about myself and you tell me nothing.

To HAVELOCK ELLIS.   MATJESFONTEIN, 11*th April.*

It is late.   I am sitting up in my little room waiting for the mail-train from Cape Town to come past.   It will drop our post-bag at the station and perhaps there will be my English letters.   It is a sharp cold night, such a wonderful heaven of African stars outside.

To HAVELOCK ELLIS.   MATJESFONTEIN, 12*th April.*

It's funny that I write so little to you, and think so much of you !   If another woman were to ask my advice about spending her life so much alone as I have done I should say No.   You feel the knocks the world gives you too much, because there is nothing to stand between you and the world.   Close relations are like a casing of fat round you, you can feel the blows but they don't come straight on the bone.   I wonder how it goes with you in Paris.   I forget the number of the house where I stayed in the Rue d'Assas ; it was right at the very top where you could see the Gardens.   Oh, Havelock, I feel so alone in the world.   I'm sitting alone in my little room.   I'm so glad when I'm here, but I have to go and have my meals in the public room among the strangers.

To HAVELOCK ELLIS.   MATJESFONTEIN, 15*th April.*

I have finished a chapter this evening, so my mind feels nice and free.   Harry, you don't know what Philistines the

people in Africa are. The only two at all not Philistine
people I have seen are Sir Henry Loch, our Governor, and
a Mr. Fuller [later Sir Thomas Fuller]. I think [if] I
lived fifty years in Africa I should never make one friend.
There is one man I've heard of, Cecil Rhodes, the head of
the Chartered Company, whom I think I should like if I
could meet him ; he's very fond of *An African Farm*. I
can understand how bitter I used to feel against human
beings, and how I hated them, and felt myself utterly alone
among them, and only liked the Boers and Kaffirs. Fancy
a whole nation of *lower* middle-class Philistines, without an
aristocracy of blood or intellect or of muscular labourers
to save them ! In a few months I want to go up to the
centre of Africa. If I can't I guess I'll return to Europe
or go to America.

To Havelock Ellis.   Matjesfontein, 20*th April*.

    It is one of those glorious and beautiful days on which
simply to be alive is cause for " blessing and praising God."
It is perfect, so still, so still, the motionless Karroo with the
sunlight shimmering on it. The stainless blue, with just
one little cloud floating in it like a ship, one doesn't know
why. It is so strange to think that trees and grass are as
beautiful to you as this stern Nature is to me. I can't
describe to anyone the love I have to this African scenery ;
it is to all others as the face of the woman he loves best is
to a man as compared to all other faces. It is not like at
all—it is different. I am writing at my book, but I just
took it into my head to write a word to you. Now I'm
going on.

    Evening.—I have been sitting ever since this morning
with a poor woman who is dying of consumption. I have
just been making her some tapioca. I am afraid the end
is coming, and am expecting her daughter to come and
call me up to-night. The old, old mystery : What is it !
That old passionate questioning came back to me more
strongly to-night, as I sat by her and watched her gasp,
than ever since I was a child. Let us love each other ! In
the midst of life we are in death. I don't have to try not

to hate anyone any more. I couldn't hate if I wanted to.
But I can't love as I could either. I've no doubt I should
make a much better wife or friend now. But I don't think
I shall ever fasten myself on to any living thing again.

To HAVELOCK ELLIS.   MATJESFONTEIN, 2 5*th April.*
    I am well, very, and working. It is so strange after
these years of physical agony to be free again. But somehow, just now, I feel more fit for practical work, travelling,
climbing mountains, etc. I seem to drink in the external
world through every little pore. Never before, never when
I was a child, have I been able to live such an objective
life, a life in which I feel not the least *wish* to give out, to
express, seem conscious of nothing but an all-powerful
desire to drink in through my senses. I look and look at
the sky and the bushes and the men and the material
things as if I was just new-born, and was learning to know
them. I suppose it is after these long years buried in
abstract thought, in a way which even you have not understood, that I turn with such a keen kind of relish to the
external world. It's no use fighting against it whether
it be good and great or not. I must be as I am. Oh,
how my *eyes* love to look at the world and feed on it. I
have the same kind of feeling to objective things that a
person has to solid food who has been ill for months and
begins to eat again ; it is something quite different from
ordinary hunger. My nature craves it. I wish you were
here, too, to be so happy with me. I went out for a three
hours' ride yesterday on horseback ; that makes me so
strong. How much I should enjoy Paris and Italy
now ! . . .

To HAVELOCK ELLIS.   MATJESFONTEIN, 2 8*th April.*
    I am curiously alive and at work again. I am not
getting on very fast because it's so cold and I get blue and
stiff when I sit writing long, but I mustn't complain. I
have no fireplace. I am going to make myself a little
cocoa with my spirit lamp before I go to bed. I've no
clock or watch, so I don't know what time it is. . . .
They took an I.D.B. [Illicit Diamond Buyer] past this

morning in the train loaded with chains. It's terrible
to see a man with chains on. He was the real criminal
type, something like Aveling, but much lower. But it
isn't right to treat them like wild beasts ; Love is the only
thing that can save such men, when they are dead to everything else that can still give them a kind of humanity. I
would have liked to do something loving to him. He
reminds me also of that young man we saw in the
Morgue.

To HAVELOCK ELLIS. MATJESFONTEIN, 12*th May*.

I got your journal-letter and liked it. Isn't it curious
that I only wish to be with you in Paris ? I never feel
the least desire to see London again. Whether it will
wake up some day I don't know. . . . I have got quite
out of that objective happy state. I am working hard
and suffering greatly from depression. I am sure this
absolutely solitary life is good for no human being ; but
to take a change of a week, after every three or four weeks
of solitude, which would be good, is too expensive, especially
in this country. . . . The man to whom this place belongs,
Mr. Logan, is going to call the house I am in Schreiner
House, after me. I think that's the only news. I am
waiting now for the train to come that I may go and have
my dinner. . . . The *Spectator* says my *Dream* is quite
wonderfully written but shows not only a want of reverence,
but a lack of the power of feeling reverence. Please send
me reviews of it, if you see any, because I am so curious
to know whether ordinary folk will see what it's about at
all. John Pursglove thought it was about " drinking,"
and my mother says she doesn't know *what* it's about.
That's rather encouraging ! Except once when Will came
and put his head by me and spoke kindly to me, I've not
had anyone say anything gentle to me since I left England.
It seems to me I did not prize all the love that was given
me in England half enough, and I shall never go back
again. . . . The only French writers I know for whom
I feel sympathy are Renan and George Sand ; the others
I only admire, I don't like or enjoy. I *like* French people
best of all people ; I doubt whether I could ever get to

really love one ; they don't touch me, they are interesting
and nice. . . . I wonder whether the work I am doing
now is good ; there are times when I feel so indifferent.
You know I love my people and I should like others to
know and love them, but all—I don't know what to call
it, it's not ambition but it's the something that drives you
to express *to others*, seems dead. I don't *want* to tell
anyone, it's enough that I feel and know and have seen it.
Good-night. I've talked long enough. The wind is
blowing outside and it's very cold, and I'm getting faint
with waiting for my dinner. . . . This is a Karroo plant.
The plants here are so beautiful to me, and the red sand.
The plants seem to me like living things and I love them ;
I like to touch them. When I wake up in the night I
think I shall see them next day. They are the only things
I feel near to in Africa, and the sky and the stars and the
mountains. I like the ants too, and the little mierkats.
I could never love other nature in Europe as I love this.
The only thing I ever loved there was the Alps in winter
and the sea in the Riviera. I like to think you will see
Alassio one day and my ruined chapel. But it will be
quite a common place to you, like any other place, and to
me it is so wonderful. It seems so long ago since I was
in Italy. I have changed so. Good-night again. Your
little Olive.

To HAVELOCK ELLIS.   MATJESFONTEIN, 14*th May*.

Oh, Havelock, I have tried so to like the people here,
you don't know how terrible they are ! Fancy a whole
nation of *lower* middle-class people. I am sure they are
quite different in Australia. I am reading Dilke's *Greater
Britain*. It's very interesting comparing the Colonies.
There's a lot about Australia. Now you see how wicked
and uninteresting my journal is when I try to keep one !
Afterwards I'll go out on the veld and look at the Karroo
plants.

Evening.—I am sitting in my large new room. I went
out this afternoon and saw the little Karroo plants, and I
lay down on a big flat rock in the dry sluit [sloot] and looked

at the sky and the bushes, and when I was climbing about among the rocks I saw three Korans, big birds that make a loud noise. I am so depressed. I can't understand it. I'll tell you some day lots of little things that take too long to write.

To HAVELOCK ELLIS.   MATJESFONTEIN, 16*th May.*

My future movements are quite uncertain. I only see that for the present I must remain here and work. I wonder if my work is good and great or not. I do it in a kind of dream. I know it's all true that I write, but I think what I write seems to become less and less popular. Fewer people will understand it. Did I tell you that I'd at last discovered Wordsworth? I knew I should some day, and I have. No one understands your *New Spirit* here. They are simply horrified. As to my allegory, they are silent to my face, and behind my back say I am [?]. It is very curious, to be so absolutely isolated as one is in this country, but perhaps it is good. If you fall in love, will you write and tell me all about it? I've told you all about my life. I should like to get married now. It's very curious but I could now. It wouldn't impinge on my individuality too much. No one could reach me now. You know what I mean. I know I shan't marry, but now for the first time in my life I feel that I *could* marry. But I have also given up the thought of ever finding a human being I could so love and look up to that I could marry him. Now that I expect so little from any personal relation or from marriage, whether of mind or body, I could marry safely, there would be no disappointment. . . . I am getting so pretty again, you wouldn't know me! My complexion is beautiful, like it used to be when I was a young girl. All the people here think I am 20 till I tell them!

To HAVELOCK ELLIS.   MATJESFONTEIN, 23*rd May.*

Why don't I get on faster with my work? Why must I write everything with my blood? Other people don't. And I could write in water three novels a year! What is this terrible compulsion over me ?   There must be a God —or what is it ?   I am very lonely.   And I've nowhere to go if I leave Matjesfontein.   It snows and rains all the time.   We haven't seen the sun for two weeks.

To HAVELOCK ELLIS.   MATJESFONTEIN, 24*th May*.

Thank you for the journal.   It is so nice to hear of all you are doing and seeing.   I think I should work just as much in Paris as here.   I have always worked in Paris. It is London that kills my power of work.   There is a little sunlight upon the hills this morning.   I am so grateful for it. . . .   Of course you don't like tobacco, and I shouldn't think Symons would ;   it is carrying coals to Newcastle.   Louie would like it, and it would do her as much good as it would do you harm.   The effect of tobacco is like opium.   What you need is much more a glass of champagne than a pipe.   To me all stimulants are poison. "Calm me, my God, and keep me calm !"   I am being worn out by going too fast.   When I have smoked three cigarettes my nerves are not acting in the same slow fashion that many people's are without it.   I have given up smoking lately because I can't afford cigarettes [a few days later she incidentally mentions she is smoking cigarettes], but I have at once become more sleepless and high-tensioned. People are so irrational about these things.   Just because a stimulant raises my nervous irritability it will be poison to me though a medicine to you, when I am above the healthy normal average of nervous irritability and you are below it.   Of course there are sidelong effects of tobacco on digestion, etc., apart from its direct effect on the nervous system.   With me it increases appetite, not directly, of course, but indirectly by helping me to sleep.

To HAVELOCK ELLIS.   MATJESFONTEIN, 12*th June*.

Such a funny thing happened to me the other afternoon. I was very happy and well and went out to walk in the veld, taking Ruskin [whom she was reading just then] with me.   It was a glorious afternoon, everything was beautiful, the sun shining on the bushes.   Suddenly I found I was crying ; not quietly but in a wild convulsed agony, just as one cries if one has had some terrible and heart-breaking news.   And yet *I* wasn't crying.   I kept saying to myself ; "What is the matter ?   What am I crying about ?   *I* am quite happy."   It was as if some terrible things, quite beyond the range of my *conscious consciousness*, were affecting me.   It was the strangest mental condition I have ever experienced.   It was like the agony one starts up with sometimes in the night ; but I had not been to sleep and my whole mind was busily engaged with the book, and if I was conscious of anything else it was the beautiful peaceful sunset scene about me.   It is a new and strange evidence of that double consciousness which I am sure exists in the brain, at least in mine.   I am sure that these marvellous flashes, as when in *one instant* the whole of my Prelude flashed on me as I was sitting and writing things about Bushmen's heads, are not really a flash of revelation, but the result of absolutely unconscious cerebration that had been going on in my brain.   Tell me if, without your suggestion, anyone ever tells you of the same experience. I wish I could make you understand how wonderful the feeling was, to feel that conscious part of my brain which had been reading, looking on, perfectly calm and cool, at the other part which was in such agony.   All my English life is so clear to me now, all my faults, but I was nearer Heaven that time when you all turned from me four years ago than I ever was before or than I'll ever be again.   I shall live now, and work, but I shall always be much less, no one will ever misunderstand me now, because I am living like them, with the same aims, and no larger faith in humanity and my fellows than they have.   I have transferred all my dreams and hopes to the future, which is perhaps wiser.   It wouldn't hurt me so much if you were to try and murder me and —— published all my letters in *The Times* as those little tiny things did.   I can see now that my great sin was that I put, not one individual, but all my fellow-men, humanity, in the place of the Infinite. To set my fellow-men before deeper things, and doing right to humanity entirely before everything, that is wrong. One must hold the balance perfectly even between know-ledge and service of our fellows, never let it sink either

way, and never love human beings better but exactly as
well as inanimate nature.   We help them more so.

To Mrs. R. Cawood.   Matjesfontein, 16*th June.*

   You are very wicked not to like my allegories.   I only
wish I was half as good as they are ! ! !

To Havelock Ellis.   Matjesfontein, 18*th June.*

   I enclose letter to Blackwood.   Do the best you can
about the MS. [*Dreams*].   Take it to Unwin and
Macmillan.   I should prefer getting a royalty.   I don't
know how much is right.   You can arrange with Blackwood
or anyone else, as you think fit.   I can't manage it out
here.   *I hate business.*   If I have to make arrangements
for myself I shall never get anything.

To Havelock Ellis.   Matjesfontein, 22*nd June.*

   I am going to Cape Town on Tuesday.   I think I've
told you this about ten times.   It's the only bit of news
there is !   Mr. Seymour Fort [who was Secretary to the
Governor, Sir Henry Loch] is going to publish the second
half of his criticism on my allegory this week.   I am so
glad I have one friend in this country at last.   It makes
Cape Town seem different to me.   I think I shall meet
Cecil Rhodes too !   He's the man I saw on the steamer
the day Ettie sailed from England, and liked so.

To Havelock Ellis.   Cape Town, 25*th June.*

   If Blackwood doesn't want to have it, take the MS.
from him and do the best you can for me.   Unwin would
like to have it, but do as you think best. . . .   I go home
to my Matjesfontein in a few days.   I shall be so glad
to get back.   People stare at me here as if I was a live white
elephant, but with the exception of an old member of
Parliament called Fuller and a Mr. Seymour Fort just
from England, I have not seen one sympathetic human
being since I came.   It is so strange to feel yourself so
utterly cut off from all the inhabitants of a country in
which you live.   I think it's good to be among Philistines ;
they agonise you so that you fly to work.

To HAVELOCK ELLIS.   MATJESFONTEIN, 12*th July*.

I spent some days in Worcester with Ettie on my way up
and was very ill there.   But I got here early this morning
and am better.   You know I feel a little lonely sitting here
alone in my house after I've been among human beings.
I had a happy time in Cape Town ;   they were kind to
me. . . .   You know people do make fun of my not having
been able to eat with other people, and do perhaps tell
lies about me, but I don't think that anyone really can
believe it.   It seems such a ridiculously small thing to cast
such a shadow over a life as it has over mine.   It's so
bad to be ridiculous ;   however, it doesn't matter. . . .
I am well, but I'll never be quite strong unless I marry, and
I never will.

To W. T. STEAD.   MATJESFONTEIN, 12*th July*.

Thank you more than I can say for your sympathetic
feeling towards my allegory.   My stories I fancy a good
many people must like, but my allegories are so much a
part of myself that [it] is hard to publish them, and I
feel keenly any sympathy.

The only big man we have here is Rhodes and the only
big thing the Chartered Company.   I feel a curious and
almost painfully intense interest in the man and his career.
I am so afraid of his making a mistake, as he would do, as
I think, if he accepted the Prime Ministership of this
Colony.

To HAVELOCK ELLIS.   MATJESFONTEIN, 18*th July*.

I will come and stay with you and Louie, if you will
have me, and you are not married, when I come to London.
I shall be much happier than I used to be now.   I've given
up thinking that any of the ideals we have can be realised
here and now ;   and when once that happens everything
is right.   No man's heart was ever broken who hadn't
formed an ideal of something.   It is well to feel satisfied
with everything past, and everything to come !   I do.
I wish only I could feel a little ambition, a little anything
to make me wish that the world should read my ideas.

To HAVELOCK ELLIS.   MATJESFONTEIN.

I've been talking so much to you all this week that now I sit down to write I seem to have said it all. Please be sure Stead gets an *early* copy of *Dreams*. I am sending back the first pages of the book. I want the words added to the Preface and I've revised " In a Far-off World." . . . When I die I want them to have a post-mortem and open my chest. If I am anywhere near you, will you come ? In all my physical agony the thought sometimes comes to me, as the only consolation, that after my death some use might be made of my body, knowing what my disease had been. You will find it in my heart. That long asthma may have affected my lungs, and has now, but that isn't the root. It has always been a funny thing to me why opium and iron and prussic acid have been the only things that ever, though in quite different ways, really touched my diseases, and it was only last night, reading the book you sent, that I know why. They all three strengthen the heart's muscles. If I leave off taking iron for more than a week or two my asthma gets worse, and that terrible contraction and pain I get in my stomach, that I used to get when I had to eat before people, was really asthma.

To HAVELOCK ELLIS.   MATJESFONTEIN, 25*th July*.

I've just got your letter. Thank you, but it wasn't a sweet letter. But one's heart would break if one was always sweet. I am beginning to feel so sweet and to love everyone, just like I did long ago, and so soon my heart will break again. It's very foolish to love anything but Nature. . . . Please make any arrangements you think best [about *Dreams*]. I want this put as a dedication :—

TO

A small girl-child ; who may live
to grasp much, that for us is sight,
not touch.

O. S.

To W. T. STEAD.   MATJESFONTEIN (*no date*).

I've been living quietly alone for some months working. Soon I shall send home much work ; my five articles on South Africa [1] which will form a large book, and a thing dealing with the whole subject of sex,[2] as far as my ten years' work at that subject have yet brought me, and a large novel.[3] I've got a number of little stories too, but they will need revision. I am specially anxious to know what you will think of my sex work. I have thrown it into the form of a story ; a woman scientific in tendency and habits of thought but intensely emotional loves a brilliant politician ; she is going away where she will never see him again, she invites him to see her the last night, and they discuss love, the ideal of marriage, prostitution, and the evils of celibacy (which I think are very great, though at the present day for many of the best men and women inevitable), and the knotty question : " In how far have we the right to force the sexual ideal, right and proper for us in a higher state of evolution, on persons in a lower ? " More and more I see it is not by attacks on each other's weaknesses but by a drawing closer together, and a tender sympathy even with each other's vices, that we men and women will help and save each other, and solve our sex difficulties.

To W. T. STEAD.
    PINE GROVE, HOF STREET, CAPE TOWN (*no date*).

The Roman Catholic is the best and greatest dead form of Christianity. The only really living form is the Salvation Army.

If I fought on any side I would fight for Parnell, not because I have an intense shrinking from the man, but because I would feel it *just*. I would teach the higher sexual morality by educating people till the lower, brutal form of love were impossible to them. While most men

---

[1] *Stray Thoughts on South Africa*, published in book form since her death, together with subsequent matter by her, under the title *Thoughts on South Afri a.*

[2] " The Buddhist Priest's Wife," published since her death in *Stories, Dreams and Allegories.*

[3] *Saints and Sinners (From Man to Man)* not yet published.

and women of the world feel and act with regard to love as they do, I cannot feel it right to single out one from the throng and lay the sins of others upon him.

To Mrs. R. Cawood.   Matjesfontein, *Friday* (*? In* 1890).

I have very bad asthma here ; if it doesn't get better shall have to try Kimberley or Cradock.   I should be so sorry to come to you ill but a few days at Ganna Hoek might drive my enemy away.   If I can't come, do come here and see me.   How lovely it would be if you and I could go up to Kimberley together for a week or a fortnight ; then I would go back with you perhaps to Cradock ! Can't you come ?

To Mrs. R. Cawood.   Matjesfontein (*? In* 1890).

Does Mr. Cawood know Lelie Kloof, and if he does how much is it worth ?

To Havelock Ellis.   Matjesfontein, 30*th July*.

I am sending you old Chapman's letter to me.   His two years' right to *African Farm* ends at the end of this year.   This letter is all the hold I have of him in black and white.   Will you try to arrange with him for another two years ?   He gave me £100 for the last two.   Get this from him for the next, more if you can.   Ask him what he would care to give for my next novel.   Harry, it's so kind of you to help me so.

To Havelock Ellis.   Matjesfontein, 11*th Aug.*

Boy, you seem so far away from me, hundreds of miles. I am sitting here alone in my small room with the fire burning.   Outside there is snow all about the mountains and a fine sleet is falling.   I wish you could sit here with me. . . .   I wonder how it is no one takes my MS. [*Dreams*].   I have had many more letters from people about my allegories, and have gained much more reputation by them than by *An African Farm*, and I myself believe they have a deeper value. . . .   I don't like Moll's *Hypnotism* nor Mercier's *Sanity and Insanity* as well as the other books in your series. One has the sense of something rotten and unsound in the first ; and, in the latter, instead of giving an interesting collection of other people's views, he tries to give his own, which are worthless. Decidedly the two best so far have been *The Evolution of Sex* and *The Criminal*. . . .   Boy, did I pain you when I criticised you like that ?   I don't know why I feel so loving to you to-night.   I so seldom feel tender in the way that leads to words to any human being now. —— loves me very much, but now I keep all men who love me at a great distance.   And yet it would not have been well always to do so.   One learnt so much. . . .   It will be a great blow to me to hear you are engaged, as I shall do some day, but for your sake I shall be glad.   If I go up into the interior, when I have finished my book, would you care to come with me ?   It would not be wasted time. That is the only thing I look forward to in my life now, that journey to the interior.   Life is so very dear to me. I am quite happy, it's all right, you know—but so dead.

To Havelock Ellis.   Matjesfontein, 13*th Aug.*

I've been writing and am now going to bed (10 o'clock). I am in all things able to work as I used to at Ganna Hoek, but I get so terribly tired soon.   I can't keep on at a stretch for ten and twelve hours, in fact not more than half an hour, without feeling fagged.   It is colder here than I ever knew it in England.   A healthy dry cold though very painful.   My nervous system is so strong again, and so of course my head.   I feel now I could bear a great sorrow without dying. . . .   Do you know I have that old intense love of life, the animal love that I used to have, and that so completely died in my ten years' agony in England.   I am so glad when I wake in the morning, and I wish I could live for ever and ever in this beautiful world. You know I can breathe. . . .   Harry, will you forgive all the unkind things I said and did to you ?   You know, dear, I'd borne just as much as I could.   Do you quite forgive me ?   If you marry, will you call one of your little girls Olive Schreiner after me ?   If your wife will ? Good-night.

To HAVELOCK ELLIS.   MATJESFONTEIN, 26*th Aug.*

About Unwin's letter I'm sure you'll do much better than I should have done and shan't trouble my head about it.   It's all in your hands if I get anything or nothing. " A man's life consisteth not," etc. . . .   My friend —— is perhaps going to England on Wednesday.   Please try to like him.   He's very like you.

To HAVELOCK ELLIS.   MATJESFONTEIN, 30*th Aug.*

I'm glad you are having such a good time down at that place in Cornwall.   I hope you are a great deal of mental and moral comfort to those folks whom you attend, for it's sore little good you'll do their bodies !   I'm so well now. I never want a doctor, even I breathe perfectly, and my flesh is quite hard and springy, as it used to be when I was a child. . . .   No, I haven't any more allegories to give. All the others are too personal.   I believe the book will be a success.   You don't know how many more letters I've got about my allegories than about *The African Farm* even, if that is any sign of the way things are read. . . .   Goodnight.   I've just had a smoke and I'm going to bed.   You will be a successful man with children and everything ; I shall die a solitary wanderer.   Isn't it funny that since I've come back to Africa the old passionate love of life has come back to me.   Oh, life is so beautiful !   In all those ten years I was in England, Death seemed to me nothing but the beautiful great white angel coming to set me free. I am not afraid of death.   I could never be that, I can never cease to be part of this infinite life.   But this blue sky is so beautiful, I want nothing more.   I am satisfied. Even a childless solitary old woman living alone here, I feel it as such a beautiful thing to live.   Good-night again, Harry, how faithful you are.   I believe no one has ever loved another human being as truly as you love me.

To HAVELOCK ELLIS.   MATJESFONTEIN, 4*th Sept.*

I do not ever think I have misunderstood people, but I feel small things done in the dark against me, as much as some people would a plan to murder them.   When the people at that hotel in Italy sat laughing at me and calling me a thief (you remember that man who knew old ——) I was nearly driven mad with a sense of injustice and wrong in the world.   I suppose few people have suffered as much in the course of their whole life as I did in those two days, and thousands of human beings go through life without ever dreaming the possibility of such joy as I feel when I go out in the morning here.

To HAVELOCK ELLIS.   MATJESFONTEIN, 10*th Sept.*

You have been so strangely near me the last few days ; it's strange that never in my life before have I had the same drawing towards you. . . .   I have got your letter to-day, Havelock boy.   I am so very glad you are having such a happy life.   Your life will grow happier and happier as you go on. . . .   It's so wicked of me to want you to love me at all when I give you nothing worth the affection you have given me.   Everything Alice [Corthorn] has told me of Edith Lees [whom Ellis married later] makes me feel she must be exceptionally fine and noble, singularly sincere and straightforward.   I read a very nice article of hers somewhere some time ago.

To HAVELOCK ELLIS.   MATJESFONTEIN, 1*st Oct.*

Please correct all proofs finally for me and return to Unwin.   We can't wait for them to come out here.   Please make the best arrangements you can for me about Chapman. You are so good to me. . . .

To HAVELOCK ELLIS.   MATJESFONTEIN, 13*th Oct.*

I love Dürer best of all painters in the world.   Oh, I wish you could see his pictures at Munich !   So I would paint if I were a painter.   It is not any one picture I love especially, it's all his pictures, the spirit in them, whatever they are about.   He and Watts, but I love him more than Watts.   You know, when I say I love those gates at Florence [of the Baptistry], and Michael Angelo's four figures [in the Medici Chapel] and Notre Dame [of Paris] best of all works of art in the world, I mean that *I* feel one

with them.   It's such a curious feeling, that they are part
of your own soul, of your own individuality, that secret self
that you know, standing out there before you, and you feel,
the first time you see them, as if you were finding something
that you used to know, very well, long ago, and that you were
quite rejoiced to see again.   I felt like that to Notre Dame,
the first night in the gathering dark, when I walked up to
its front.   It seemed that I knew it when I was a little girl
and lived at Witteberg.   I feel like that to Dürer's pictures.
Oh, the wind is howling so.   I wish I could see you, my
brother, my dear true one, who has loved me more truly
and faithfully than anyone.

To HAVELOCK ELLIS.   MATJESFONTEIN, *4th Nov.*

I have the most extreme humbleness with regard to my
business faculties.   I could command a fleet, govern an
army, lead a nation, write an epic, sooner than make a bargain
about seven-and-sixpence.   You see, I want to be so just !
I shall never be able to act upon the difference in honour
which prevails in a drawing-room or a dinner-table or a
country-house.   You don't try to push a man off the most
comfortable seat, you don't try to eat all the ices and give
none to anyone else ! . . . Good-bye.   You have my
corrections of the " Ruined Chapel " and " The Sunlight."
The first copy of " Ruined Chapel " I sent I did in great
haste.   It's agony to me to think it was ever read by anyone so.   If you have received the corrections of these two,
then bring the book out.   The others are all pretty right.
Please revise carefully for me " The Sunlight Lay."   What
utter nonsense it was before, the second Heaven, the noblest
of all, clean left out.

To HAVELOCK ELLIS.   MATJESFONTEIN, *6th Nov.*

The pain in my stomach that I used to get when I had
to eat before people was really asthma in the stomach,
caused by the terrible excitement of my heart from nervous-
ness and misery.   I have an interesting letter from that
Miss A. P. ——   I told you of who suffered even more
than I did.   She has described *all* I suffered.   A——,
you know, also suffered in the same way, and Eleanor

Marx, I know, did. I am writing to ask her about it ;
I think she will speak frankly of it. But now here comes
an interesting fact. A——— P———'s sister is the most
terrible sufferer from asthma that I ever saw in Europe,
and Eleanor's sister, Jenny, suffered from her earliest
childhood till the day of her death from asthma. I think
I have often told you of the curious relation I found between
that convulsive feeling in the stomach and the asthma.
I will send you all the letters I get from women about it.
I will write to Eleanor and if she takes it in the same spirit
as the others she will give you her experience. Then you
might use all our experiences to write a valuable article in
some medical journal. . . . I do not say opium [really
morphia] *absolutely* cures, but for the first two months
I was in this country I was very bad, though the weather
was perfect. I then had the doctor who injected $\frac{1}{4}$ grain,
and *for eight months I never had an attack*. For the last
month I have been bad. Three days after the last injection
I climbed Signal Hill. Of course doctors often tried
morphia, at least twice before I came to England, but it
caused terrible vomiting, the $\frac{1}{2}$ gr. makes me vomit for
twenty-four hours after it is injected but not nearly so
much. Will you try it if you have any asthma cases like
mine ? It doesn't make me sleep. I lie awake for hours
after it, and then fall into a light natural doze. You must
remember that when I lived in Africa before I went to
England I had more attacks of asthma, pure and simple,
than I ever had in England, though I was stronger
generally. . . . I'm doing such beautiful work. This
life is so peaceful. I'm happy, like when I was living on
those farms, writing *An African Farm*. *I feel just the
same*. Life is so precious to me. You know I think in
this book I *will* say what I want to say. I mean I've
sometimes felt as if I couldn't make this book say everything I want to say as *An African Farm* said what I wanted
to say then. But it will ! All that is in that " Sunlight
Lay " is in it, only simply in an objective form—the first,
second, and third heaven. I send you an African rose.
Dear Harry, I'm loving you so. I'm always keeping my
eyes open and hoping I will see some good chance that
will bring you here. I would like to show you Africa,

my Africa. It's not a bit like Australia, so wonderful with its mixture of races and peoples, and its marvellous diversity of natural scenery. I'm glad I wasn't born in any other land on earth.

To HAVELOCK ELLIS.   MATJESFONTEIN, 22*nd Nov.*

I am very well and happy here in my solitude, but sometimes my heart goes out very much to you. I wish you could be here with me, dear, dear one. It would be so beautiful. Thank you for not laughing at me about what I told you. You know a person can't help these strange attractions. Those feelings *never* mislead one. The person may not be great or beautiful or good, but they are native to *you.* It's so wonderful how one's first impressions *always* come true. . . . I am so happy, dear, since I came here, never troubled about anything. I am getting on with my work well but slowly. You know, I wish I could be married to everyone, I love everyone. Do you know what I mean ? I shall always have to stay single, because marriage would tie down my sympathies, unless it was a very great personality I was tied to. . . . I saw Edith Lees once a long way off and liked her very much, felt she was true. Dear, if I could be jealous of *anyone* it would be of you. You seem so much mine—how could you love anyone else ? And yet I want you to marry. No one would be so glad as I, dear, if anything beautiful came to you.

1891

To HAVELOCK ELLIS.   MATJESFONTEIN, 13*th Jan.*

My Havelock, please do something for me. Write to the *Nineteenth Century,* the *Fortnightly,* the *Contemporary Reviews,* and ask whether the editors of either would care to see an article by me called *Stray Thoughts on South Africa,* by a South African. The article is not to be signed by my name, and its authorship kept strictly secret. . . . I will send it without fail next week. The article is most sympathetic, pitching into no one, or of course I should sign my name. It is my very best work, in a way as good as anything I ever did. Don't mention it to *anyone*. I want it to be a surprise to them all. The bird's-eye view of South Africa, its scenery, its peoples, its problems is, I think, good. Do this for me, dear. It will serve me greatly. . . . Buy me a copy of Hazell's *Annual*. Perhaps it would be better simply to write to Meredith about the lie in the *Annual*, but take no notice of it unless it is ever repeated. I felt it so much at first. I have killed out the pain now.

To HAVELOCK ELLIS.   MATJESFONTEIN, 17*th Jan.*

I am nearly broken down with trying to get my article done this week. I can't get through the revising. Will you try, even if I send it next week, to get it into a March Review ? Do try ! I'll be so grateful. I've a special reason for wanting it. . . . Such a funny thing happens to me every night. I find myself sitting up in bed in heartbroken agony, but I never know what it's about ; and I always have a pain under my left shoulder as if I were dying. I hope I won't have it again to-night ; I am going to bed now. . . . Get a copy of the book [*Dreams*] from Unwin and send it to Mrs. ——. Write the letters A.O.E.C. above the Dedication. I want her to know it's to her little girl but I don't want to write to her. . . . My dear boy, good-night. There are so many things I want to tell you. You know it will be a great blow to me ever to hear you are going to be married because that will end our fellowship ; but I would be so glad for you and would love the woman so much if she would let me.

To HAVELOCK ELLIS.   MATJESFONTEIN, 26*th Jan.*

I cannot send the article this week. I must revise it first. It is much longer than I had thought, a short book, but really the best thing I ever did, I think. For three weeks I have been in a dream living with it and nothing else, and loving it, which seems strange about such an article, but it is such a relief to me to write it. I will post it here on the 4th of February ; it ought to get to you on the 22nd. If you took it to the publishers at once in a cab

it would not be too late for March. If the *Nineteenth*
won't have it, try *New Review* and then *Fortnightly*. I
would give £50 to have it in the March number.

To HAVELOCK ELLIS.   MATJESFONTEIN, 2*nd Feb.*

I enclose names of places to be put at end of
allegories. . . . I am working still at the South African
article. It is almost a book. I am trying to bring it down
to the limit of an article. It's a fine article and will be of
intense interest, describing our problems and leading men,
Rhodes, etc. It's not the deepest, it's not the most intense,
but it's the most all-round and strong thing I have ever
written, and though it seems strange that on such a subject
one could give yourself away entirely, nothing I have done
has so absorbed me, soul, spirit, and body. For three
weeks I have thought of absolutely nothing else by day or
by night. . . . Dear one, I think I shall come to England,
for a few days in July. Don't tell anyone because I want
only to see you, Alice, Louie and Mrs. Wilson. Then I
shall go to Paris, correct proofs of book [? *From Man to
Man*] there, then go on to Italy or South United States,
and then return here in the spring to go up into the interior.
If I remain in such perfect health as I have now, it will all
be easy. You didn't send the morphia, but I've no sign
of asthma now. If I can only get through the winter
without ! I'd be so near to you, dear, now I am well.

[NOTE.—Up to this point not many of the letters Ellis
received from her had been destroyed ; but, from this
point, only a few exist—for the following twenty years
scarcely twenty letters in all. There was no break in
the actual correspondence. It proceeded regularly and
harmoniously, notwithstanding his marriage in Dec. 1891
and hers two years later, Feb. 1894. In 1917, however,
she began to become insistent that he should return or
destroy her letters (though he represented to her that it was
quite easy to adopt precautions to prevent the unauthorised
use of the letters), and at last became so urgent, even with
tears, that he agreed to burn her later letters, as to which,
though quite without reason, she was specially anxious

He spent some days in the painful task of destroying several
hundreds of the letters, and felt it so acutely that for many
months he neither saw her nor wrote to her. The experience
was the more trying as he was then in a state of mental and
physical depression after the long illness and death of his
wife.   His feeling in the matter appears to have been not
merely personal but also impersonal, for, since she had
spent so many years in writing and publishing almost
nothing, it seemed to him peculiarly sad that the flashes of
imagination and insight and criticism and reflection casually
thrown out in these private letters should be lost.]

To W. T. STEAD.   MATJESFONTEIN (? 1891).

    I am very grateful to anyone who wants to see me;
but I came out to Africa entirely that I might be alone,
and [have] gone through the bitter agony of parting with the
human beings I love best in the world in England, that I
might come to Africa for several years to work. Many
of my friends offered to come with me and more than I can
count have written to say they would come, but I have
begged them all not.   I have given up ten years of my
life utterly to people, and now I want two for work, then
I shall come back to work among people and give up my
time to them.   Even my beloved favourite brother and
sister have never been to see me here at Matjesfontein.
At intervals of four months I go for one week to see them
and their little ones and that is the only chance I have
allowed myself since I came, except once when I went to
Bloemfontein.   [To the Railway opening].

To Mrs. R. CAWOOD.   MATJESFONTEIN, 1891.

    [One of the Cawood daughters had died, the first of the
twelve children to go.]   My darling friend, it is very sad
to think I shall never see Elsie.   I am so glad she came to
Bloemfontein [Dec. 1890] and that I asked her to take off
her hat that I might look well at her.   She was so graceful
and sweet to me. . . .   To me death is such a beautiful
thing, I fear it neither for myself nor for others ; it is the
thought of any physical suffering or mental they have gone
through that hurts me.

To W. T. Stead.　　　　　Matjesfontein, 13*th March*.

Personally I believe Rhodes has the strongest antipathy to myself. His friends have told me so. But it does not in the slightest affect my sympathy with him in his work. . . . I am able to sympathise with and love many people who will never be able to sympathise with or love me. . . . All that I need to make my cup of happiness full is the Karroo and work.

To W. T. Stead.　　　　　Matjesfontein, 31*st March*.

How is it that great wide heart of yours cannot be a little more merciful to Dilke and Parnell? [1] . . . I believe you to be the most loyal friend I know. I would that thou wert also the most magnanimous enemy.

To Mrs. John Brown.
　　Schoonder St., Gardens, Cape Town, 17*th May*.
My dear Friend,

It seems so long since I wrote you. I've been bad with asthma for nearly a month and have taken this tiny cottage for a month to try the Cape Town air. . . . It is a pouring wet night, you know how it *can* rain here at this time of the year and it has rained since last Friday. My black girl has gone home and I am alone shut in for the night. It's a funny quiet little place quite on the top of the Gardens, no bushes behind me, only the mountain. [Table Mountain.] I have been very quiet since I came up here, but last week I spent with Mrs. Sauer at Kenilworth. On Monday Sir Sydney Shippard took us all, Mr. and Mrs. Sauer, Mr. Rhodes, Dr. Jameson, Miss Shippard and myself to Hout Bay for a drive. I think it's since you went that they made that wonderful beautiful road round to Hout Bay. We went by Sea Point and came back past Constantia. It was one of those days of perfect beauty and happiness that live long in one's memory and compensate for many shadows.

I can't give you any news about Cape Town people, because I know so few. Mrs. Sauer, Mrs. Innes (the

[1] Dilke 1886, Parnell 1890.

Attorney-General's wife) and Lady Loch are all the real friends I have, but they are splendid. Next week I am going to spend at Mrs. Innes's, and we are going to wander about my beloved pine woods at Rondebosch. But I like much better to be in the Karroo at Matjesfontein than here. Haven't I told you a lot about myself? My brother has a little baby called Oliver after me. His children are a great joy to me.

To W. T. STEAD.   (*No date or place.   ? Cape Town.*)

I am sending you a picture of Sir George Grey's statue. Of the three large English-speaking men who have during the last fifty years appeared on the South African stage—William Porter, Saul Solomon and Sir George Grey—I think the last was the greatest and the most unique—a "God's Englishman," if you like it. It is the thought that there have been such Englishmen that takes away one's despair of England's future. I have walked about the Cape Parliament, which stands just over the way from the statue, when debates were going on, in which the most talented and wealthy Englishmen in the world were voting for Strop Bills [for flogging Native Servants, which if passed would have made their condition not much better than that of slaves], and in which personal ambition and the greed for wealth and power showed at every turn, and I felt a curious consolation in coming across that statue.

To W. T. STEAD.   (*No date, no place.   ? Cape Town.*)

I shall never forget the stand you made for women eight years ago when my heart first went out to you. It is a debt that I, to whom all broken or oppressed things, be they prostitutes or South African natives, are dear as though they had sprung from my body, can never forget.

To Miss LOUIE ELLIS.   MATJESFONTEIN, 22*nd Sept.*

Thank you for your beautiful letter. Dear, I looked quite beautiful in my dress. [Louie Ellis made it for her.] I wore it once before I left town. I put a white flounce at the bottom. A friend of mine told me that after

I went out of the dinner-room her husband told her all the men were talking about how nice I looked and what beautiful arms I had ! ! ! ! So I must have looked all right. I've looped the sleeves up to the shoulder like baby sleeves and *I love the dress*.   Darling it doesn't matter about the brown dress.   I know it's not of man but a " judgment of God " on me for wanting a dress.   It's *all* so *perfect* in *make* and *taste*, what is wrong is that I'm such a curious little person I *can't* wear everything.   No one in the world *could* make a dress for me without seeing it on.   Don't you know some people look equally well or ill in anything ; I've long ago forgotten all about clothes.   I go about here in my dear old green dressing-gown or a funny old cloth dress I made myself.   Mr. MacNeill says I look a fright in it.   I don't care.   I'm reading Aristotle.   Dear do give a little treat to the girls with the money that's over, and tell me about it.   It would pay the fare and the boat, and they could bring their own food.   Yes, I'm coming to stay with you when I come.   At times I feel lonely here, mentally lonely ; not a soul in all this great country that shares a thought or feeling with me.   But I'm very happy, nature is so much to me, more even than when I was a little child.   It is the only thing I am ever meant to possess really and it's so beautiful to me to have that. . . .   Dear, I know how tired you must be of working sometimes, and what a great weight rests on you.   I wish you could come and see our African skies a little.

To W. T. STEAD.   MATJESFONTEIN, 24*th Sept*.

The only thing I didn't like was your putting me on a par with Rhodes.   He's much greater than I. . . .   He is now in Mashonaland.   One naturally feels anxious about him.   Any accident to him would, I believe, mean the putting back of our South African development for fifty years. . . .   I do not wonder at all at Rhodes' opinion of women.   If you knew Cape women you would not.

To W. T. STEAD.   MATJESFONTEIN, 23*rd Nov*.

You will be glad to hear that Rhodes has returned safely from Mashonaland.   Perhaps in no country has so

Matjesfontein
april 23/92

A funny idea has struck me about the enclosed cutting, that perhaps I am meant!!! So many lies have been told about me already that now I wonder at nothing, & I think feel pained at nothing, not even at being told that I am a Roman Catholic. What makes it like of that I am meant is that it is exactly the opposite of the truth, that I was always trying to cheer up any ... at ... for her, & ... that I found life so delightful & worth living

FACSIMILE OF OLIVE SCHREINER'S "SMALL, UPRIGHT" HANDWRITING, 23RD APRIL, 1892.

(See p. 146 of "The Life of Olive Schreiner," footnote.)

To face p. 206.

much ever hung on the life of one man. It is a bond of sympathy between us that you share my view of his genius.

1892

To HAVELOCK ELLIS.   MATJESFONTEIN, 23rd *April.*

[She encloses a cutting from the *Pall Mall Gazette* of 1st April : " Not many years ago two literary ladies—one of whom is widely famous—were spending a holiday at the seaside together, and both were indulging in very gloomy views of life. After discussing the question they both agreed to commit suicide and the younger hurried home and but too effectively carried out her purpose. The other happily thought better of the matter, and refused to fulfil her terms of the contract. The only pity is that she did not let the other party to the agreement know in time."]

A funny idea has struck me about the enclosed cutting, that perhaps *I* am meant ! So many lies have been told about me already that now I wonder at nothing, and I think feel pained at nothing, not even at being told that I am a Roman Catholic. What makes it likely that I am meant is that it is exactly the *opposite* of the truth ; I was always trying to cheer up Amy Levy (if it be intended for her) and professing that *I* found life so delightful and worth living. I've often felt since that, if I'd been more sympathetic to her melancholy mood, I might have done more for her. In her last note to me she said, " You care for science and art and helping your fellow-men, therefore life is worth living to you ; to me it is worth nothing," and the last thing I sent her was Edward Carpenter's " Do not hurry, have faith," which she sent back to me the night before her death with the words, " It might have helped me once ; it is too late now ; philosophy cannot help me." It's very funny how exactly the opposite of the truth are the stories in papers, a sort of inversion ! I should have minded once, but I think I'm getting hardened now.

To W. T. STEAD.   MATJESFONTEIN, 19th *June.*

I hate letter writing more and more ; it becomes almost a mental and physical impossibility to me. I saw Mr.

Rhodes once when I was in town at a dinner party at
Sir Henry Loch's. He came up and began to laugh at
me about some dream I had. I didn't speak to him or ask
him what he meant, but I guessed you'd been telling him
my dream all upside-down. [The dream of Rhodes being
injured, perhaps fatally, was told in a previous letter to
Stead, as evidence that Stead was wrong about the pre-
monitory nature of dreams.]

To T. Fisher Unwin.   Matjesfontein, 25*th Sept.*

Thank you for *Byzantium*. I couldn't write the book
you mention, it's not the kind of work I can do, and I
shouldn't like anything I wrote ever to come out in a series
in which anyone else had written, except an author whom
I particularly loved and admired.

I have too a large book of my own on South Africa
in quite another style to bring out.

I think the whole series of *Stories of the Nations* most
useful. But the flower of the series, as far as I have seen
it, is *Chaldea*, by Z. A. Ragozin. Is the writer a man or a
woman? It is a real "book," not only a compilation;
there is individuality and life in it; I've read it twice, and
have felt much interested in the writer. Two very able
judges whom I know have also been much struck with it.
I should be glad to think it was the work of a woman.

About the African Book. Why do you not write to
Mr. Theal, the great authority on South African History?
If he would do the work, it would be admirably done.
His *History of the Boers* is good, but his little book, *Cape
Commanders*, is high, first-class work; a book worth reading
again and again. Would you like me to send him the
letter you sent me, or would you like to write again to
him yourself? Cape Town, South Africa, will find him.
Everybody knows him. A most interesting volume for
your series would be one on the Native Races of South
Africa. Mr. Theal *might* be willing to write that also.
He is *without doubt* the ablest and best authority on South
African matters. If he can't, the Hon. A. Wilmot, M.L.C.,
might be willing to write either. His address will be
Grahamstown, South Africa. He has already written one
most admirable little book on the Cape and has a finished

literary style. If you can't get either of these two, should advise Mr. John Noble of Cape Town. His litt. *History of South Africa* is most reliable and valuable, but he has not the literary brilliancy of the other two. I should be glad if I could be of any service to you in the matter. I'm sorry I can't undertake it myself.

To T. FISHER UNWIN. MATJESFONTEIN, 26*th Sept.*

I insisted on *An African Farm* being published at 1/- because the book was published by me for working men. I wanted to feel sure boys like Waldo could buy a copy, and feel they were not alone. I have again, last year, at the request of my publisher, allowed it to be printed at 3/6 as I felt sure most poor lads would have it within reach. . . . *Dreams* is not published by me with the special intention of reaching the poor. I would prefer the rich to have it. If I dedicated it to the public, I should dedicate it " To all Capitalists, Millionaires and Middlemen in England and America and all high and mighty persons." It is a book which will always have its own public of cultured persons who will have it at any price. It will probably be a far more valuable property in 15 or 20 years than it is at present, as the younger generation grows up and the older dies out. I feel this with regard to all my books ; therefore except for a very large sum, I will never sell the copyright, nor any right except that of printing them during my pleasure.

To W. T. STEAD. MATJESFONTEIN, 12*th Oct.*

I am very happy in my work, but I wish the Gods would give me three hundred years to live in instead of a few score, that I might do some of the things I want to. Forgive Dilke ! It is like a blot upon your soul.

1893

To Miss ADELA VILLIERS (*later* Mrs. FRANCIS SMITH).
GRAHAMSTOWN, SOUTH AFRICA, 15*th Jan.*

. . . I'm having a very splendid time of rest and joy, travelling about. I am always so happy and so well when

I travel, and I think never in my life have I been so followed by love and kindness from my fellows as during the last two months. I have had a splendid time staying at different farms. Now I am in Grahamstown, seeing my little mother. I wish I could have shown her to you. She's one of the most wonderful little women in the world, such a brilliant intellect, *all* intellect in fact ; it's from my German father we all get our strong emotions.

. . . I sometimes think I must be going to die, everyone is so kind to me and everything is so happy ! But I think life does get happier as one gets older.

To W. T. Stead.   Matjesfontein, 19*th Feb.*

I shall be home by the second week in May. There was a woman I was afraid I should talk against to you if I saw you. I can't bear to talk against anyone ; yet, if other people talk of them, the thing I know or the opinion I have sometimes bursts out ; so I find it better not to see people who talk of them. Don't discuss other women with me *ever*, except in their political or public capacities, and don't expect me to know all your women friends, because some women are such an *anguish* to me they almost break my heart. Do you want for your paper a *first-rate* correspondent in South Africa ? A man with a keen condensed picturesque style of painting things ; a fearless outspoken thinker on political questions ? Don't forget to answer this. My friendship for him began by my being struck by the stand he took on certain political questions and by his artistic literary style. [This reference is to myself.]

To Havelock Ellis.   Matjesfontein, 18*th April.*

I'm so anxious to know how Edith is. It's so terrible when people we love are ill ; I know how you will have felt. One can stand anything better than that almost ; at least I can. I've no news of myself. You know I've overweighted myself with the number of stories and books I have written. [? want to write.] I don't see how I shall ever clear them off. If I could have a peaceful quiet home and could work out the rest of my life revising I might manage them. . . .   It's not my great great grandmother that is *supposed* to have been a Jewess (it's only a supposition, no one knows, and the whole thing may have risen from our Jewish eyes !), but my grandfather's great grandmother, which is my three times great.   We know that her grandmother was not a Jewess, but the idea is that her mother was.   [The legend has reference to the maternal grandfather of Olive's grandfather.   See p. 6 of the *Life*.] . . . I'm so tired, Harry, aren't you sometimes ?   It's different from the sort of *passionate* tiredness one gets when one's young.   One knows now it will never be different, and one is so tired, dear. . . .   I shall arrive in London about the 21st.

To Miss Louie Ellis.
New College, Eastbourne, 25*th May*.
I shall be back to-morrow.   You don't know how sweet and good they are to me here, but I shall come back to-morrow.   Thanks my darling for all your goodness to me.   You are all too good to me, dear Edith and all of you.

To W. T. Stead.   (*Undated.*)
To me you will always be a personality of the most absorbing interest, never to be forgotten, never to be lost in the mass of my fellows.

To Mrs. J. H. Philpot.
Millthorpe (Sheffield), 11*th Sept.*
The face [S. C. C. S.] has a very sweet almost child-like smile ;   in life its real charm lies in the mixture of intense strength, almost hardness, and intense gentleness and sweetness.   My only fear is that I am not sweet enough or large enough to deserve his love.

To Mrs. John Brown.   Sheffield, 15*th Sept.*
I am leaving for London on Monday to go to Eastbourne where I remain till I sail on the 6th October. . . . Cron has a wonderful, quite magnetic, influence on young men, and in some marvellous way seems to draw out what

best in them, so he might be of help to the Boy out
ere. [Mrs. Brown's son, Willie, who was studying
medicine and who, Olive suggested, should come out to
South Africa when he had passed his examinations.] There
are quite half a dozen young men I know who say they owe
all their intellectual life and strength to him, and he keeps
them straight, wakes up a kind of spiritual enthusiasm in
them. All his greatest qualities, come out in contact
with younger men.

To Mrs. J. H. Philpot.

ENGLAND (? MILLTHORPE), *? Sept.*

I send you two of my friend's photos [S. C. C. S.].
Please let me trust that you and Dr. Philpot will say nothing
about him to anyone. The photos do not do him justice.
There is a fire, a kind of light, like that of genius in his
eyes, which the photos don't give. He is really much too
noble and great for me ; but I will not absolutely resolve
to marry until I get back. . . . Whether I marry or not
I am going to buy a little farm high up in the Karroo as
soon as I get out. . . .

To Mrs. J. H. Philpot.   MIDDELBURG (CAPE), *8th Nov.*

I wish you could meet my friend [S. C. C. S.]. His
tenderness and goodness to me are something that surprises
me. I was so afraid that [if] I was very much loved and
very happy, I should forget to love other people. But it
seems to me I love all my friends and all the world better
than I ever did before.

CHAPTER III

LETTERS WRITTEN FROM 1894 TO 1903

1894

To W. T. STEAD.   MIDDELBURG (CAPE), *Feb.*

Neither on the subject of Christianity nor of sex have I gone from the standpoint of *An African Farm*, as people will understand if ever I publish one of my larger books.

To HAVELOCK ELLIS.   MIDDELBURG, 16*th Feb.*

My old Havelock, I'm going to be married on Saturday morning, the 24th. Cron and I will slip down alone to the Magistrate's Office and sign our names. You would love Cron. He's so manly, and withal with something so childlike in him. Sometimes it almost seems like genius. We are both so busy getting our little house right. Your little Olive.

To HAVELOCK ELLIS.   MIDDELBURG, 18*th Feb.*

My Havelock and Edith, I am to be married on Saturday morning. I will write you next week. Your Olive.

To HAVELOCK ELLIS.   MIDDELBURG, 19*th Feb.*

My Havelock, I am to be married on Saturday morning. This is Monday afternoon. Old Theo is kindly coming up all the thousand [the distance is about 603 miles] miles from Cape Town to be with me. We shall just walk into the Magistrate's Office and sign our names. I shall just wear my old grey dress that I wear every day. I am better, much better, in health. Some day you and Edith must come out and see us. I send you a likeness Cron took here of me in the veld among the bushes the other day. He sticks to it, it's the best that ever was taken. Havelock, dear, I love you so. Give my love to your little wife. My doctor says there's no reason I shouldn't have a child now. Your little Olive. Send back the photo or keep it safe as I didn't ask Cron if I could have it, and he *may* want it. Address—Olive Schreiner. If you ever write to Cron address—Cronwright Schreiner, Esq. [*Note by Ellis :* There was another long and beautiful letter of about same date not preserved, see p. 202.]

To Mrs. J. H. Philpot.   Krantz Plaats, 7*th Mar.*

I am very well, and peacefully very happy. My dear husband is so tender and thoughtful and good towards me. The 12 days I have passed here seem the most restful of my life. It is beautiful to see how all his servants look up to him and love him.

To Miss Louie Ellis.

Krantz Plaats, P.O. Halesowen, South Africa, 7*th Mar.*

I wonder how the world goes with you. I was married 13 days ago. We came straight to our farm the same day. I was married in the old blue black serge I wear every day. The terrible part was sitting down at the table to sign my name.

My husband and I are like two " chums." We feel like children when we are together somehow. I hope I shall have a little baby, Louie, but if I don't I shall be satisfied too. I was so glad when I heard perhaps you were going with Havelock to Italy ; but again he says he is going alone. Louie it's a wicked thing for human beings to live in great cities. One may be as poor as possible (we are poor) and be quite happy out in the open " veld " like this. You would like my husband ; he's a real *man.*

To Mrs. J. H. Philpot.

Beach Hotel, East London, 13*th Mar.*
[*Attending a Farmers' Congress with me.*]

There is a certain likeness in our tastes and habits, except that I smoke and he doesn't. . . . I think it's so sweet of my husband to take my name, don't you ?

To Miss ADELA VILLIERS (*later* Mrs. FRANCIS SMITH).

KRANTZ PLAATZ, CRADOCK, 21*st April*.

. . . You wouldn't know me again, I am so strong and well now. I spend much of my spare time in the saddle or bathing in the river before the house, and it's so beautiful to get out of the ice cold water and sun oneself on the hot rocks for half an hour after the bath before one dresses. My dear husband grows closer and dearer to me daily. I am much, much more happy than I had hoped to be.

I wish you *could* have this beautiful African sunshine dear. I have had asthma and was quite weak when I first came and now I am so strong. Life is so infinitely beautiful when one is well.

To Mrs. JOHN BROWN.   KRANTZ PLAATS, 31*st May*.

I know Cron would love you both. It is so beautiful to me the way in which he seems to open his heart to everyone who has loved me and whom I have loved. . . . Cron sends his love to you both. It is such a beautiful thing to me that every week we live together he seems to grow gentler and tenderer not only to me but to every living thing. His mother was here last week, and says he looks like he did ten years ago when he was a beautiful boy. It was very sweet to have her here for a couple of days.

To Mrs. J. H. PHILPOT.   KRANTZ PLAATS, 10*th July*.

There's a great fuss among the servants to-night. Kroon, the Hottentot herd (who figures in the group with the ostriches), has had his white cat killed by two of the little Kaffir boys, and Cron will have to act to-morrow as " Magistrate " to decide the rights and wrongs.

To Mrs. J. H. PHILPOT.

THE HOMESTEAD, NEAR KIMBERLEY, 8*th Aug*.

My husband says he's going to stay in the room all the while and never leave me [i.e., while the child was being born] ; I say the doctor and nurse will turn him out ; but he only looks as much as to say let them try. [I *did* stay in the room.]

To S. C. C. S.   KIMBERLEY, 2*nd Oct.*

Think out your speech for the Cradock dinner. I want it to be so good. . . . It's wonderful how few marriages are happy. I wonder why we are so precious to one another.

To S. C. C. S.   KIMBERLEY, 3*rd Oct.*

It's strange to think you'll be at the old place [Krantz Plaats], more instinct with intense emotion for me than any place on earth.

[A friend of Rhodes' called, a relative of hers by marriage.] I explained to him how strong my personal admiration for Rhodes' genius was and how strong my detestation of his methods, but mainly for the men who sucked the dust from his feet. . . .

I wish I could live always to be your little wife ; it's very nice.

Your tiny baby [it was not born till the end of April 1895] and I send our love to the Baas [Afrikaans : " The Master "]. It's getting quite a companion to me. . . . I'm very well.

To S. C. C. S.   KIMBERLEY, 7*th Oct.*

It's strange how the slightest uncertainty distresses and unnerves me ; I never knew any one quite the same in this matter.

To Mrs. J. H. PHILPOT.   KIMBERLEY, 3*rd Nov.*

I am writing the baby a little book ; every day I write a little to it ; so that, in case I should die, it will still have that, and I am writing it out a list of all the books I want it to read. I don't think I shall die, you know, but it satisfies me to think it will have that. . . . If my child is a girl I shall bring her up from the time she is quite tiny always to look forward to some definite work in life—though I should, of course leave the choice of a profession quite open to her. Cron is terribly anxious to have a little daughter but I should love a little son just as well. . . . I am reading all Walter Bagehot's books over again.

1895

To W. T. STEAD.   MIDDELBURG (CAPE), 10*th Jan.*

I am writing in haste. . . . I don't see how the relations of married life can be well and nobly, in any way ideally, arranged when there is not perfect and profound union of aims ; and when that is not, in the case of intellectual and mentally active people, I should say the marriage was a failure. When there is such complete unity there never arises the least difficulty with regard to friendships with third persons of opposite sex. In my own case marriage has not touched one of my friendships, and there is something almost comical in the idea that it might. When man and woman marry without this as the ground-work of their union, in many cases the sooner they part from each other for ever the better. Marriage, perfect marriage of mind and body, is such a lovely and holy thing, that rather than an imperfect travesty of it, I should say none was better. To me it appears that in highly developed and intellectual people, the mental and spiritual union is more important, more truly the *marriage*, than the physical. I should feel it (and I think any person who has reached a certain stage of growth) a much more right and important reason for terminating a union, that the person to whom I was united had a fuller, deeper and more useful mental union with another than that there should be a physical relation. Just the mental union, " for the begetting of great works " to me constitutes marriage. Of course there are millions, even in the most civilised communities, for whom physical attraction, affection and fidelity must constitute marriage. But for natures more highly developed I believe such a union to be wrong. Continuance of the physical relation when the higher mental relation is not possible, and when the affection is given elsewhere, seems to me a more terrible because a more permanent prostitution than that of the streets.

To S. C. C. S.   ? KIMBERLEY, 28*th Feb.*

While you are at Rondebosch go for a walk in my dear wood and see that old Summer House. That part is the scene where *From Man to Man* is laid.   Rebekah lives there when she is married and always walks in those woods.

To S. C. C. S.   KIMBERLEY, *6th Mar.*

Dear love, it is terrible to love anything so much as I love you.

To Mrs. JOHN BROWN.   KIMBERLEY, *7th Mar.*

Cron is away at Cape Town attending the Congress. . . . I and my funny little help are here alone.   She is a great character, a little off-coloured girl of about 17, who has no idea of cooking, but who is very fond of me and I of her. The other day she stood giggling and looking at me.   I asked her what was the matter and why she was laughing. She said, " Oh, because you're so funny.   You are just like a child, not like a missis."

To Mrs. JOHN BROWN.   (? *Date.*)

You know that in the depths of my heart I have such a yearning pity for you. . . . The infinite powers that shape human life may know that he is not more responsible for being as he is than if he had some physical disease.   I believe many men and women are born with many beautiful and emotional qualities, but without the will power to govern their action ; and men who would pity them if they had a drooping eyelid or a lame leg, hate them—but it is not right.

To S. C. C. S.   KIMBERLEY, 1*0th Mar.*

I am sure *no* child can ever realise what the feeling of a true " motherhearted " mother is for her child—not if it loves her ever so much.   A child believes a certain person is its mother because it is told so ; but the mother knows through every fibre of her body that the child is hers.

It's funny when you are away from me now, the picture that comes into my mind whenever I think of you, is you with that curious gentle little smile your face wears sometimes now.   Oh, my sweet one, it is very nice to be with you.

To W. T. STEAD.   THE HOMESTEAD, KIMBERLEY, 2 *5th Mar.*

My married life satisfies even the high ideal of what marriage might be which has haunted me ever since I was a little child.

You refer to that woman as the man's " mistress." But there is nothing to imply that the man supported her, and no woman can rightly be called a mistress and still less a prostitute, unless she sells her body in return for gain. To me the purity of a sex relation between a man and a woman lies finally in the fact that it is not a matter of material considerations. That is nearly the only point in the woman question on which you never seem to see clearly.

To W. T. STEAD.   THE HOMESTEAD, KIMBERLEY, *Oct.*

You talk of hymns, but who is to draw the line between hymns and poems ? Browning's " Grammarian's Funeral " has been more of a hymn to me than all the hundred hymns I learnt as a child.

1896

To S. C. C. S.   KRANTZ PLAATS, 1 *5th Feb.*

I must go to Mrs. Cawood's this afternoon because I fancy my being here gives old John [Pursglove] trouble though he doesn't say so. I'll like to stay at Ganna Hoek till you come, my sweet, if I can, I want to climb the mountain with you. . . . You are now in the cool part on the Stormberg : I'm so glad it will be cool for you. It seems as if one side of my body was pulled away when you are gone.

To J. T. LLOYD.   KIMBERLEY [*apparently early in* 1896].

Yes, I believe Rhodes has fallen for ever. My feelings are a strange mixture of intense personal sympathy with Rhodes in his downfall, and an almost awful sense of relief that the terrible power which was threatening to crush all South Africa is broken. I think we feel on a small scale as Europe must have felt after the battle of Waterloo. Yes,

it is an old, old plan, in Rhodes' mind, at least three or fou
years old. It is too terrible to think of what the results woul
have been if Jameson had *not* been defeated.

To J. T. LLOYD.   KIMBERLEY, 2*nd Mar*

What is the feeling at Johannesburg, that Rhodes wil
regain his power and carry out his Transvaal schemes o
not ? Answer this if you are able. At first I felt his plan
were at an end, but now I have a kind of feeling that he ha
bought a certain backing in England. Tell me what yo
know on this question.

To W. T. STEAD.   THE HOMESTEAD, KIMBERLEY, 16*th Mar*

I've never been so comfortably off and satisfied in my
life, and if I had more money I shouldn't feel it right to
spend it on myself, so *I* wouldn't be the richer for it.
would never, if I could possibly help it, allow a novel o
mine to appear in a magazine because it must then appear
in broken parts—like looking at a statue, a foot one week
a finger the next.

To T. FISHER UNWIN.
                   THE HOMESTEAD, KIMBERLEY, 13*th April*

Please remember me kindly to your wife [daughter of
Richard Cobden]. I have been reading for the first time
Justin McCarthy's *History of our Own Times.* I had no
idea before how beautiful and rare a character her father
was till I read this book. I had thought of him merely as
a successful politician—which is not much !

To W T. STEAD.
                 GRAVE STREET, CAPE TOWN. (*No date.* ? 1896.)

Each man's and woman's sex relations seem to me
something holy, sacred and personal to themselves and the
person with whom they enter on them. The pure and
beautiful ideal seems to me absolute love and friendship of
one man and one woman, the two blending into one. All

departure from it is to me evil, whether in marriage or not. But I do not feel called upon to crush those who depart from the ideal. Rather, I thank God when I see in them other great and beautiful qualities, and I say, let us make the most of these good things in our brother, and be thankful that none of our common human flesh is wholly removed from the beautiful. I think Dilke can be of great use to the world as a politician (but I don't know him personally, I have never seen him) and therefore I dare pass no judgment on his personal relations, which are entirely his own affair and those of the men and women concerned. When the Dilke case occurred some people cut me because I said I would still regard Mrs. Crawford as a woman if on meeting her we had tastes in common, not because I think it right to deceive one's husband, but because we are here in the world to love and help each other under all circumstances. I know you are angry with me. Be it so ! Years ago, when you were in trouble, I parted for ever from the human being I loved best in the world because he said the condition of our continued friendship was that I should not sign the memorial in your favour ; I have only seen him once since ; if I was willing to part with him then, I would also be willing to part with anyone now. You don't know how I value your friendship. But I could also give it up. I do not justify Dilke, I have nothing to do with his relations. I have only to do with his public political relations. I would all men were ideal. I would I myself were. *I never met one who was.* If we could have great all-loving, all-tender, all-true, all-wise men for our politicians and writers and editors, then the heaven of which we dream and for which we labour would be *here* already. Meanwhile we must prize any humanity or goodness or intellect in our fellows, and seek to develop it. If you are not too angry with me write a little word and say that if you think me wrong you can still forgive me.

To S. C. C. S.   THE HOMESTEAD, KIMBERLEY, *6th July*.

I love you, my dear one. When I think of you my heart runs all out in little ripples of love to you. . . . you've become so much a part of my life it seems funny to be without you. I'm always looking for something and it's my baas I'm looking for . . . Tell mother and B. about your throwing the water in that man's face at the Kowie, and of all your naughtiness generally.

To S. C. C. S.   KIMBERLEY, 11*th July*.

Did I tell you the day or so after you went I went to see Mrs. Solly [in Kimberley]. There were some lovely likenesses of a baby, one just like our baby would have been if she had lived, with big dark eyes. It was so like our baby. When Mrs. Solly came into the room I introduced myself, and said a few words and said what a pretty baby it was in the likeness, and then I burst out crying and had to go away. She must think I am quite mad. I will never pay a call again in Kimberley. You know that's the reason I don't want to go to England, I don't want to leave our baby's body. You don't know what that little brown heap is to me. . . . [The baby was then buried in our garden.]

To J. T. LLOYD.   KIMBERLEY, ? *Aug*.

No, I don't mind anything said about my books, they are given to the world. I don't like to [be] written about myself personally, but don't mind anything that is said of my books.

To S. C. C. S.   HOMESTEAD, KIMBERLEY, 8*th Sept*.

The little monkey is so sweet. This evening when he got cold and sleepy, he called and called to me, and when I took him he just cuddled up and wanted to go to sleep on my arm. . . . Goodbye, your strop-soet-sager-pecklesackje-Olive. [The spelling of the Afrikaans words is wrong and I do not know what peckle means ; the crude, literal English would be syrup-sweet-sugar-peckle-little-bag.]

To J. T. LLOYD.   THE HOMESTEAD, KIMBERLEY, 14*th Dec*.

I am sorry to leave this dear little house even for a year. [We went to England in January 1897.] Life has never been so beautiful to me anywhere as here, in spite of the one great desolating sorrow which has visited me here [the baby's death] and of which I cannot yet even think or speak calmly.

The book I have written [*Peter Halket*] has cost me more than anything I ever wrote, and I am broadening my back already for the Chartered Company attacks. I do not think I feel anything so much as the attacks from members of my own family.

To J. T. Lloyd.   KIMBERLEY, *Dec.*

I am copying out that book on South Africa [*Stray Thoughts*]—but really on everything in heaven and earth ! Sex, woman, the relations of superior to inferior races, the future of the human race, etc., etc. ! And often a feeling comes to me, " It has come straight from my heart. But will anyone else understand it from my standpoint? Put it away in the box with the other MSS. ! " That's my temptation, and you don't know how helpful sympathy with my past work is, to help me to overcome that reluctance to publish anything.

1897

To Miss ADELA VILLIERS (*later* Mrs. FRANCIS SMITH).
        MORLEY'S HOTEL, TRAFALGAR SQUARE, 12*th July.*

. . . The only point in which I don't quite agree with her [Mrs. Earle, Mrs. Smith's aunt] is where she says you can't judge of a child's character before 12. When I look back to my early childhood I can see how exactly I and my brothers and sisters were, as little children, what we are to-day. What I *do* think is that, from about 12 to twenty-two or three or even twenty-eight, a certain deflection takes place ; but *as one fully develops one returns to what one was as a little child.* I know that I am to-day far more like what I was at 7 years old than what I was at 16. The child is father of the man, not of the youth.

Of course, you must be keen enough to read the child's character ! Children are such mysterious things that few grown up people, even those who are keen readers of adult character, *can* understand them.

To W. T. STEAD.   LONDON, *July.*

You are quite mistaken as to my ever having had an unkind feeling to Rhodes ; if he would only leave South Africa alone and come back to England and live in a palace and enjoy life on the money he has made out of us and our country—it's the worst I wish him !

To W. T. STEAD.   CAPE TOWN.   (*No date.*   ? 1897.)

My antipathy to the physical act of writing gets stronger and stronger.

1898

To S. C. C. S.   KIMBERLEY, 8*th June.*

Intuitions are strange things on the surface, but really there is nothing wonderful about them.   They are simply *based on a knowledge of* the particular character you have to deal with, and in a lesser degree on human nature in general, but mainly on an exact knowledge of one's character, and its *desires* and modes of thought, and moral principles !   Of course, the thing flashes on you instantaneously—you *see* it.   But that doesn't mean that what you see is not based on knowledge previously stored in the brain, any more than when a savage sees a gun pointed at a bird and sees the bird fall dead, apparently at the same instant, there is nothing super-human—as he fancies !—the bullet has really travelled [through] the air and hit the bird exactly as his own stone does, only so *quickly* it can't be seen by the eye, *even of the man who shoots ! !*   The thing why " intuitions " are generally experienced about the great, especially the *intense,* the mean and the wicked or the noble and heroic actions of life, lies not in the fact that under certain conditions one couldn't arrive at the same " certain knowledge of perception," as with regard to great or evil things, but simply from this, I think—that certain knowledge with regard to actions we have not physically witnessed can only be based on a knowledge of the *intense unchanging passions* of some character ; on its heroism, its greed, its lust, its selfishness, its ambition, its power of pity, etc., etc.   When I had the intuition, absolute and unshakable, that Rhodes was at the bottom of the Transvaal rising (I have the same absolute unshakable knowledge that he is backing the Swazies now !), it was based entirely on my knowledge of Rhodes' character and his master passions of ambition and greed, unrestrained by conscious [? conscience]. Intuition is really based on one great fact—*that character is persistent*. The Trade Winds, the movements of the stars, are not really so inevitable as the action of character when once fully developed. What men of old used to call prophets, and the men who really thought themselves so, were only men with a power of reading certain characters under certain conditions ! . . . I am running on so about intuitions because I've been thinking so much about them lately, and what they really mean, and how they rise : why some men have them and some men have them not. It's very curious.

To S. C. C. S.   JOHANNESBURG, 15*th Oct.*

It is two weeks to-morrow since I came here. I have proved now that I can exist here at least as well as in Kimberley.

To S. C. C. S.   JOHANNESBURG, 16*th Oct.*

Between the artist soul and God alone can ever lie the awful answer to that question, Is my work complete, is it the expression of the truth as I know it ? . . . I have unlimited faith in your powers of doing *anything* you set your mind to.

To S. C. C. S.   JOHANNESBURG, 18*th Oct.*

When you look at my hand when I am dead, you will be able to think that that hand never set one dot or one stroke on paper for the sake of money, and that, of all I have given to the world (poor as it is), there is not one word that stands there, which, if it had been in my power to better it, would not have been bettered. If I feel I have not expressed the exact truth that is in me in any line or sentence or book, it shall be destroyed, I will not give it out.

1899

To Havelock Ellis.   Johannesburg, 25th *July*.

The wise and the full life is that which lives in past, present and future, in the life of the intellect, of the emotions, of actual present labour.   I quite understand that it is right a man should say, " *I* cannot live all my life ; I can only live part, and I select the past, or a life of pure reflection, or the life of practical labour alone ; if I try to live more, *I* shall not live at all."   I quite understand that a man should choose some tiny section of life and make that his all, and he may be quite wise and right in doing it.   But that any intelligent man should not *see* the countless sides of life, should not *wish* he could live all, and should not know that other men who have taken exactly the opposite part for their share are just as right, that I can't understand.   If I had twelve lives, one life I should be a mother devoting myself entirely to the joy of bearing, rearing, and suckling my children, one life I might devote to study of the past, one to labouring in the present for the future, one mainly to science, another mainly to travel, and so on.   Now I've only one life, and try to satisfy that illimitable craving to live all lives I have always had ever since I could remember by, as far as I can in a small way, living all round.   I am not so narrow as to think other men must do it because I do.   Darwin, sacrificing all life and its possibilities to live in one narrow direction was right, so was Goethe right living all, so was Plato when he fought, governed, wrote, thought, and dreamed ; so Jesus, when he preached his one living doctrine of love, and Buddha when he dreamed under his Bo tree.   There is one glory of the moon, and another of the stars, and each star differeth from another in glory.   What a man may do, each soul, is to exert a tiny influence in the direction good and beautiful to him ; and then he dies peaceful, having attained his end, whether it be making fairer one soul, waking one impulse of tenderness and love in another soul, painting a picture, discovering a beautiful sequence in events, and realising the *reason* in the nature of the universe, and showing it to others as all true scientific discoverers do. I shall never be a mathematician, nor a man of science making vast discoveries, nor a great leader of the people bound to them in love and sympathy and giving them voices ; I shall never be the mother of ten children, creating them and feeling their dear, soft hands on me ; I shall never find out if I have the power for music I have always felt I have, shall never know if that craving to paint I have had since I was a little child was the craving of power ; in my poor little handful of life which consists now mainly of cooking and house-cleaning I shall know few things ; I am only a broken and untried possibility,—but this I have, that I can sympathise with all the lives, with all the endeavours, with all the accomplished work, even with all the work attempted and not accomplished, of other men. I love Nature and I love men ; I love music and I love science ; I love poetry and I love practical labour ; I like to make a good pudding and see people eating it ; and I like to write a book that makes their lives fuller. I can do very little, and have never been so situated that I could do my best—but I can live all lives in my love and sympathy ! All that is sad is that life is short and one can live so little of its beauty oneself. . . . Please tell me just what Edith's heart-exercises are. If you can, send me a cheap book explaining them please, or if you have one you could lend me I will return it. . . . It's a curious solitary life I live here, seldom speaking to or seeing a human being. Cron goes at eight in the morning, and when he comes back at seven he sits and reads after dinner. I have never led such a solitary life, because when I was a girl I had Nature and in Europe I had friends.

To HAVELOCK ELLIS.

KARREE KLOOF (HOPE TOWN), *30th Sept.*

Well, I have travelled a bit about the world. I have lived in South Africa thirty out of forty odd years of my life, and still the noblest, dearest and most beloved humans I have met remain Englishmen in the main. Not only you and Carpenter and all the others I personally admire but such men as dear old General Sir William Butler, who threw up his post here and has gone home because, he said, the war would be a gross immorality, are to me as fine

representatives of the race human as any I am likely to
see. And this is not taking into view the great army of
the dead, from Shakespeare and Milton to Shelley, Darwin,
George Eliot and Browning. An Englishman is like
a Jew ; he seems to be either Christ or Judas ; but on the
whole, much as I love *all* races of men I have yet been
thrown into contact with, I think we do pretty well ; not
better than other races, but we have our peculiar virtues
as we have our vices. The worst type of English man or
woman is the most canting hypocrite that ever lived, and
I suppose earth produces nothing lower. But—I may
be mistaken, but, after life-long study I believe there is
in some corner of the best English natures a curious power
for sacrificing all for humanity, a curious power of obliter-
ating selfish interests, that is rare, rare indeed. Take the
present Transvaal business : beside the Rhodeses and
scoundrels, there are even in this country a number of purely
English men and women who love England passionately,
but are throwing all from them, self-interest, national feeling,
and are willing to spend all they have in the Transvaal Cause,
simply because they believe in the cause of Justice. One
could never speak slightingly of a race which had produced
even one Sir George Grey or William Butler. Of course,
the bulk of *all* nations are ignorant and brutal, you take
that for granted if a cultured person with any knowledge of
human nature ! An old Boer woman I once knew, after
for half-an-hour running down the English for their pride
and selfishness and cruelty, said : " And yet, when you do
get an Englishman good, he's the [? best] thing on earth."
However, I've written a whole long article, almost a book,
on the Englishman in Africa which will explain my views.
[" The Englishman " in *Thoughts on South Africa*.]

To Miss ADELA VILLIERS (*later* Mrs. FRANCIS SMITH).
                    NEWLANDS, CAPE TOWN, 10*th Dec.*

    . . . Oh, this is a wicked wicked war [the Boer War].
When I see our bonny English boys falling and know how
many hundreds have yet to fall, and our own brave South
African lads dying while the . . . who worked up the
thing go to their garden parties and lounge about with

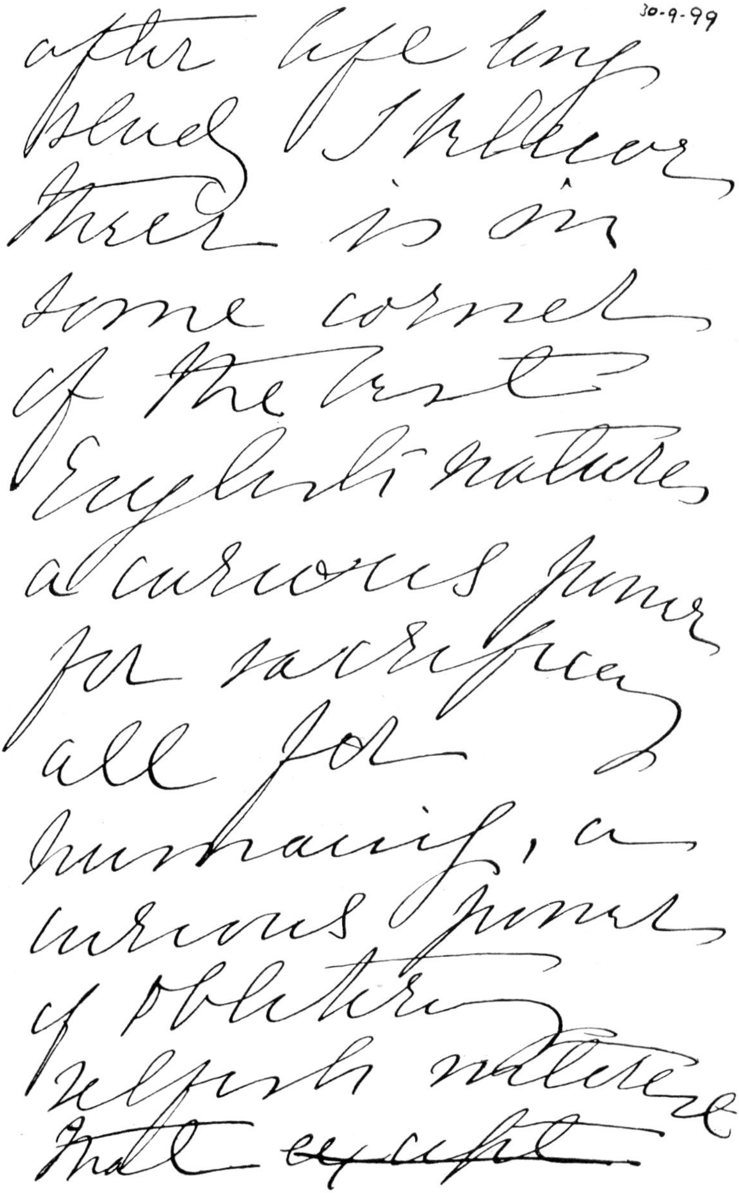

30-9-99

after life long
belief I believe
there is in
some corner
of the best
English natures
a curious power
for sacrifice
all for
humanity, a
curious power
of obliteration
selfish nature
that ~~except~~

FACSIMILE OF OLIVE SCHREINER'S CHARACTERISTIC HANDWRITING,
30TH SEPTEMBER, 1899.

(See p. 146 of "The Life of Olive Schreiner," footnote.)

To face p. 228.

their cigars and champagne, a bitterness rises in my heart that I never thought could. It is strange what a kindly feeling the Boers have for the soldiers ; an old Boer woman said to me the other day with tears, telling me of her sons fighting in the Free State (one of her nephews is already shot), " and these poor English soldiers, why should they come out to die ? We have nothing against them ; they have nothing against us. Why, why, should we have to shoot them ? the poor boys." It's all so ghastly that I can't write.

To EDWARD CARPENTER.   CAPE TOWN, 24*th Dec*.

This Hellish [Anglo-Boer] War is still going on, but the Capitalists are finding the African Boer a little tougher to swallow than they thought.

1900

To Mrs. MARY KING ROBERTS.

NEWLANDS, CAPE TOWN, 8*th Jan*.

My husband, Cronwright Schreiner, is going home to England by this mail. He is going home to try to enlighten English people a little as to the condition of affairs in this country. He will be staying with John A. Hobson, Elmstead, Limpsfield, Surrey. If you sympathise with the movement in this country in favour of peace and you and Dr. Roberts think he could do anything good by coming up to Cambridge, would you let him know. His [Cron's] opinion will have this value, that he is a pure Englishman without a drop of any un-British blood, and that he has lived for a year as a Uitlander in Johannesburg and knows all about the falsely called " grievances " there. Of course, you *may* be on the war side, but it seems to me hardly likely. It will be nice to hear all about you from Cron if he should see you.

To S. C. C. S.   BEAUFORT WEST, 14*th Sept*.

The pastor [at Fellbach] has spent months, he says, searching all the old registers and Burgomasters' books which they have had in the village for hundreds of years. My ancestors seem always to have lived in that same tiny little German village for centuries. The population in that part has not shifted much since the first centuries of the Christian era when the Alamani settled there, according to Gibbon ; no wonder I don't like towns when all my ancestors for countless generations have been peasants, labouring in the open in their own little vineyards and gardens. I feel so at home with the earth and animals.

To S. C. C. S.   HANOVER, 19*th Sept.*

You know it's my curious *horror* of uncertainty that makes me hate all games of chance, all things in which there is suspense and doubt, just as some people love it. It seems to hold the working power of the particles of my brain in such suspense that it becomes acute pain. . . .

To MRS. ANNA PURCELL (*wife of* DR. W. F. PURCELL).
HANOVER, 19*th Oct.*

Did you think my speech to the Somerset East women too strong ?   [See Appendix C.]   I fear some of the politicians will never speak the simple truth ; always play the game is the politician's rule. I believe it is never worth speaking or writing at all unless it is the simple truth as it shows itself to you in your heart. It never pays the man who speaks the truth, but it pays humanity that it should be spoken. It is the only thing that really matters.

I sympathise with Buddhism more than any form of religion. It is so beautiful that they [Prof. and Mrs. Rhys Davids] can share each other's work ; that's to me the highest ideal of marriage, at least to be able to help each other in reaching the most important things of life.

To EDWARD CARPENTER.   HANOVER, 22*nd Oct.*

I am living here in such a sweet ideal little karroo village nearly 5,000 feet above the sea, and am much better, the air is so pure and clear. How you would love this place.

Photo by]   [Elliott & Fry.

S. C. CRONWRIGHT-SCHREINER, 1900.

To face p. 230.

To EDWARD CARPENTER.   HANOVER, 2*nd Nov.*

They are a funny people, the jingoes. Eyes have they but they see not, ears have they but they hear not.

1901

To S. C. C. S.   HANOVER, 2*nd Feb.*

Yes, George Sand was an infinitely *greater* woman than George Eliot, but not so finished an artist. Just as I think Michael Angelo immensely greater than Raphael, but his work is not so finished. But George Sand was a colossal human soul. . . . She was infinitely greater than all her work. It is when you read her letters and life that the size and width and grasp of the woman reach you :—

Thou large-brained woman and large-hearted man,

as Mrs. Browning calls her. To my mind she stands easily first among the women of whom history leaves any record. A great lover of science, of art, of music, an artist, a newspaper writer, a politician of the noblest kind, a great mother : a complete human creature. There is no life of her by anyone who understands her, but if you get from the Library in Cape Town the two volumes of her own letters and read her novels you can make her life for yourself. Her Memoirs also are fine. . . . Her French is the easiest of all to read. It's like the English of the English Bible. She was a master of speech.

To S. C. C. S.   HANOVER, 3*rd Feb.*

I think a wise woman is the greatest thing on earth (except perhaps a little child).

1902

To W. T. STEAD.   HANOVER, 10*th Jan.*

Lately I have read the most beautiful book that has ever fallen into my hands through a long life. It's called *The Soul of a People*, by H. Fielding Hall. I've read it and read it till I almost know it by heart.

To Mrs. ANNA PURCELL.   HANOVER, 29*th Mar.*

A boy brought a small snake to Cron yesterday in a tin box, alive and wriggling and sticking out its tongue. Cron put the box on the dressing table before the glass ; but said nothing to me about it. [It appears that our little Kaffir boy, Chomanie,[1] out of curiosity apparently, opened the box and the snake escaped into the house.] I found Chomanie poking about the room with a candle. I asked him what he was looking for. He said he was looking for the snake which had got out of the box while we were at supper. We couldn't find it, so now we have the pleasure of knowing we are living in a room with a live snake, I rather fancy a night adder ! ! Cron consoled me by saying, " Well, I don't think it matters much if only you are careful not to get out of bed with your bare feet ; always put your slippers on." Which is truly consoling.

To S. C. C. S.   BEAUFORT WEST, 30*th June.*

I put the little mierkats in the little food basket and took them out for a walk on to a little koppie near the town this

[1] Chomanie was a little Kaffir boy Olive got from the Reformatory, near Cape Town (Tokai, I think), to train for household work. She was very fond of the youngster at first, idealised him and vested him with all the qualities a good child *ought* to have ! It was part of the tragedy of her life that she did this, on first impressions, with regard to almost all people she liked. Of course, no one could possibly be what Olive imagined ; gradually she began to feel that she had been " deceived " ; she was much hurt and highly indignant at such " deception," and then became very angry and condemned the unfortunate person (to me !) with all her tornado force ! Chomanie was no exception. He was a real " bad lot " and the Reformatory had only made him worse. I sometimes think these Reformatories should be spelt with a D. The Coloured and Native Boys of various ages, who have committed some crime, are all herded together and seem to get much worse. There were some dreadful revelations about Tokai a year or two ago. Olive on Chomanie and the " moral standard " of the place used to be very funny. She would tell of her talks with Chomanie, from which it appeared that the boy that had committed the worst, the biggest, crime was the great hero there ! She used to tell, with the most infectious laughter, how Chomanie spoke of them. On one occasion, speaking in Afrikaans, he said with reference to a certain boy (I put it into English, though it cannot be properly conveyed outside the language he used) : " He was a big boy and we thought greatly of him ; he told us how he had stolen cattle and how many, and we who had not done such great things felt what a man he was. But it came out afterwards that all he stole was a fowl ! " (This with the most scornful contempt.) " Only an old fowl ! And he had bragged so. What is a fowl ? Anybody can steal a fowl ! But he said he had stolen cattle. He lied ! He was only a fowl-stealer ! and we never took any notice of him afterwards. Only a poor old fowl ! " and Chomanie laughed with bitter contempt and scorn.

afternoon. It's the only breathing space one can get within an hour's walk. . . . They were so happy up there, poor little things. Their little spirits were quite broken with being shut up. . . . I've often thought since I was here how nice was the old Norse idea, that, when you'd lived long enough and had nothing more to live for, you made a funeral pyre for yourself and mounted it and had your favourite animals killed to go with you—then no one could be unkind to them.

To S. C. C. S.   JOHANNESBURG, 26*th Aug.*

[The British soldiers had looted our house during the Boer War. She had now gone up to get our things; she worked all the 25th at packing them, with two Kaffir men to help ; on the 26th she got two Jews to help. See p. 358 of the *Life.*]   Your bedstead is smashed and the two side bars gone.   Your old desk that you gave me has evidently been smashed open with a crow-bar. . . . The way they have smashed and burnt and broken is something wonderful, there is *one* spoon left and *one* cup, not a sign of clothes, table linen, etc., etc.   All burnt.   There is not even a bit of your father's writing table, etc.   I leave this for Pretoria to-morrow morning, will go *straight from there* not returning here.

[J. C. Smuts, with whom Olive stayed on the visit to Pretoria, wrote to me on the 1st Sept., 1902, saying how glad he and his wife were to have had Olive with them and how he hoped she would come back again to them for at least a few months, adding : " She is a national possession to all South Africa, and the more one knows her the more one reverences her.   Her health, however, disquiets me somewhat."]

To Mrs. ANNA PURCELL.   HANOVER, 30*th Sept.*

Why is it that beautiful things make one cry, and terrible things only turn one hard cold ?   The day in the Market square here when they were sentencing our Hanover men to death, one felt as if one must burst into a loud hoarse laugh.   [I do not know Olive was actually present.]   What a truly magnificent thing that poem of Bertrand Shadwell's on De Wet is ! [" De Wet," in *Songs of the Veld*.] The finest thing, viewed merely from the artistic standpoint, that has been written in the English language for over 20 years. When I read it the first time I began to cry at the second verse.

To S. C. C. S.   CAPE TOWN, 11*th Nov.*

It has been a bitter disappointment to me that I could not leave on Friday [the dentist detained her.] I don't get any more good by staying longer and I want to see you. I've never longed for you so much when I've been away from you before. If you were here I would be so happy. How is my Neta-Nila ? [Her dog.] I long to feel her by me. Her eyes always look at me in my thought like those of a human creature who loves me ; and all love given to me is so precious, the most real and valuable thing in life except the love one gives. As long as the heart continues to secrete love, it has never grown old. Death would be [It would be death] if one got so embittered one couldn't [love] any more.

To Mrs. ANNA PURCELL.   HANOVER, 29*th Nov.*

Did I tell you that we met General De Wet at Coles-berg Junction and had ten minutes' chat in the train with him ? He is just as I expected him, a man of great strength and truth, the very best type of Boer. But (is it prejudice ?) General Malan [see pp. 336, 337 of the *Life*] strikes me as a much more exceptional man, not a better man, but a man of *genius*; I wonder if I overrate Malan ; there is something that appeals to me greatly in him ; he strikes me as all men of genius strike one, as being of no nationality ; he is not a Boer ; he is not an Englishman ; he is not a Frenchman he is Malan ! They say genius has no sex, but I say it has no nationality either.

To EDWARD CARPENTER.   HANOVER, 20*th Dec.*

Have you ever read a most beautiful book called *The Soul of a People*, by Fielding Hall ? To me it is the most beautiful book that has come nearest to me of all books I have read in my life. Read it and tell me what you feel towards it, and towards the writer. My heart has felt so bitter and hard of late, and it has been like a beautiful soft rain falling on hard ground to read this book. You must get it and read it, Edward, if you have not already. It's a soul something like Bob's the man shows in the book ; and it [is what he] makes one feel rather than anything he directly says that makes the book so precious.

[" Bob " is Professor Robert Muirhead of Glasgow, at one time President of the Edinburgh Mathematical Society. When I was staying on a short visit with Mr. (later Sir) William Byles and his wife at Bradford in 1900, Mrs. Byles placed *The Soul of a People* in my hands, speaking very appreciatingly of it, though not more so than I thought it deserved. I bought a copy and brought it back with me and told Olive how fine it was. It affected her very deeply ; she cried over it for about a fortnight. She was so affected by it that she wrote to the author. His reply bitterly disappointed and hurt her. In my experience of Olive no other book affected her emotionally to anything like the same extent.]

1903

To Mrs. J. H. PHILPOT.   HANOVER, 11*th Mar*.

Yes, I long greatly sometimes to see my old friends. I was thinking last night how beautiful it would be if just once I could have them all together in one room, and look at all their faces ! Like a great beautiful bunch of flowers, every one of which was dear to you.

To Miss EMILY HOBHOUSE.   HANOVER, 3*rd April*.

I have been reading your book.

Given the conditions, it seems to me you have dealt with the subject in the most admirable manner, upon which nothing could improve. Has your book been translated into Dutch ? . . . I consider you did more effective and useful work in the cause of humanity and justice in South Africa than any other individual has been able to do. You saved not hundreds but undoubtedly thousands of lives.

I fear your work must have told heavily and permanently on you. One does not pass through such a time of combat with injustice ever to be quite the same again. . . . I am glad you are not in South Africa which will enable you to escape the past and its memory as we cannot on whom the present still presses.

This is just a word to express my admiration of your book ; with its strong self-restraint and deep feeling.

To S. C. C. S.   UITKYK (BEAUFORT WEST), *9th June.*

We got here about an hour ago from Beaufort. We got to Beisjespoort on Thursday evening about 9 o'clock, as the train was very late, but it was moonlight. [General W.] Malan was there to meet us with the cart. The farm [Phesant Kraal] is a most beautiful spot away among the mountains, yet with the most lovely views of distant mountains. . . . Malan's aunt is one of the most lovable and beautiful women I have ever seen. She is about 35 but doesn't look more than 20. Strong, intelligent and unselfish. She is a widow, a Mrs. Van Heerden. . . . Malan is lovely when you see him working on his farm. How fine that close contact with nature is ! Early on Saturday morning we started before sunrise to return to Beaufort, taking Mrs. Van Heerden with us as she had not been to Beaufort for three years. All through the war she has been on the farm without servants, cooking and washing and ironing for her father [Pienaar] and all Malan's young brothers and sisters who were with her through the war. . . . There was also at our boarding house a very fine woman, a Mrs. Minnaar of Slangfontein, English by descent but a real Boer of the strongest type, with a large mother's heart. How poor and small and artificial the English 19th century decadent woman looks beside the South African woman. . . .

(Wednesday morning.)

I am sitting on the stoep at Uitkyk. Such a wide open sky and earth. A curious solitary unbroken veld but I like it. I hope I won't get asthma here and be able to write a little. . . . I took the mierkats out for a walk this morning. They did enjoy it so much. They tell me mierkats always die in 9 or 10 days if kept in cages, so it is wonderful ours have lived so long.

To S. C. C. S.   Uitkyk, *4th July.*

Yes, you are very tired in body, my beloved, and tired a bit too in soul. I wonder sometimes if since you went to Johannesburg and especially since that terrible visit to England, you have been in something that condition in which I was from about 14 to 15 or 16, when there seemed nothing but a blind chance ruling life and no right and no wrong and no ideal ruling life. It's the only real atheism and it would be much better to die than continue to feel so. I should have killed myself soon if it had gone on. But light comes to one at last, dear heart. . . . The whole decadent world of fashionable idle London men and women live in it. . . . but they don't really live ; they are half dead, and that's why they feel no need for a nobler faith. They are so enervated they have no will and no ideal but the seeking after pleasant sensations. Therefore the faith suits them ; it formulates *their* physical and mental condition, but not that of living, loving men and women :

> Tho' much is taken, much abides ; and tho'
> We are not now that strength which in old days
> Moved earth and heaven ; that which we are, we are ;
> One equal temper of heroic hearts,
> Made weak by time and fate, *but strong in will*
> To strive to seek, to find, and not to yield.

Goodbye, my own sweetheart.

To S. C. C. S.   Uitkyk, 1*3th July.*

Ettie writes me that mother is very sinking and weak. Every note the little mother writes is about your coming and her longing for it. You know I think she feels she did not act very generously to you [see pp. 278-282 of the *Life*], so she has this curious longing before she dies to see you. Ettie says when she thought she was dying in Grahamstown she didn't talk of any of her children but only of you that night—kept saying "Do you think Cron will come too? I want to see Cron. Cron must come!" . . . The Le Roux's [the Uitkyk people] have been very kind to me too. I like them more and more.[1] I suppose with a nature like mine I could hardly live with anyone without getting to love them. Of course, there are some people with whom I *couldn't* live; I would simply run away from them; but, if you do live with people, you must get to sympathise with them.

To S. C. C. S.   UITKYK, 16*th July.*

When I said "chance" in my other letter [of the 4th] to you I should perhaps have said "fate." But either comes to the same thing. What I meant was the condition in which a human creature loses all faith in their own will and therefore almost certainly in any other will-power or wills acting through time and space—a faith which obliterates all distinction of right or wrong, and throws up all strife [? striving] after any ideal, and seeks simply after pleasure and self-gratification. It were better for that man that he had not been born. Perhaps poor old Rhodes suffered from it, Jameson to-day [suffers perhaps from it]. It doesn't matter for the ordinary London fashionable weakling man, who has nothing to do in life but spend money and amuse himself. But in men in a healthier atmosphere, who have perhaps work for others to do in the world, it is a ghastly horror when this disease grasps them. It was not in the light of such a faith that William Porter and Sir George Grey and Saul Solomon or Darwin or John Stuart Mill did their work. As vast and incomprehensible in its ultimate nature as light or time, or space, or matter generally, is that other vast reality, which we know and feel more intimately than

---

[1] One of the Le Roux little girls said to her mother: "Ek es so lief vir Mrs. Schreiner; sij's so snaaks 'n klein dingekkie!" ["I love Mrs. Schreiner so; she's such a funny little thing!"] Olive related this with great amusement.

anything else in the universe, the will within us that is not time nor space, that is not light nor heat ; incomprehensible in its ultimate essence by our puny intellects as is everything else in the universe, yet never for a moment to be ignored if we do not wish to wreck our lives and make a fool's play of our existence.   I can't express well what I mean, darling, I'm so tired, but perhaps you make out for your little wife.

To S. C. C. S.   UITKYK, *2nd Aug.*

I had pleasant women and a good little boy in my carriage, and got here yesterday afternoon, looking so well that they were all astonished.   I found the mirries [mierkats] fat and flourishing and Neta, too.   For four days after I left, 'Arriet would not come to the house to get food : when she found I was not there, she went back to her hole and ate nothing for four days.   When Mrs. Le Roux went to the hole she was sitting on a stone at the door [the entrance to the hole] but so faint that, when she tried to get off [the little mound] to go in, she fell on her side.   They brought her pail here and fed her on bread and milk and she's in splendid condition.   The Le Roux's were so glad to see me. . . . Dear one, it was so beautiful to be there [Cape Town] with you, and oh so beautiful to see you get so much better.   You have not looked young and had that bright light in your eyes once, even for a day, since you returned from England.   I think to see your face like that is to me the most beautiful sight in the world.   I am so much better for my visit to Cape Town too, I have not felt so fresh for years.   I couldn't write or think.   Happiness is very good for my intellect. Before this I had got into a state in which I woke up crying every night in my sleep, and then sleep doesn't rest you much.

To S. C. C. S.   PRINCE ALBERT, *19th Aug.*

We drove out yesterday morning, passing first through the narrow high gorge at the top of the village which opens into the heart of the Zwartberg and is the beginning of the Pass.   It is the wildest, rockiest thing I have ever seen.   We must come here some day together.   We drove up a wild

narrow valley to the left of the Pass and passed five farms
with vineyards and gardens. At the very top of the valley
we came to the farm where the orange trees grew. It is
about two and a half hours from this. We out-spanned there
and had a cup of coffee and then drove back here, calling at
two or three farms for a minute. There is a wild beauty
about these valleys with their terrific walls of rock that
is unlike anything I have ever seen anywhere in Africa.
Strange I am so wonderfully free from asthma. This is a
long, uninteresting letter, but I think you like to know all
the little things about me, because I like to know them
about you.

To HAVELOCK ELLIS.   HANOVER, 9*th Nov.*

I have been reading for the first time in my life several
French novels [translations] in succession by Daudet,
Dumas, Balzac, Maupassant, etc. Of course, Balzac is a
giant. But how strangely monotonous French novels are
when you read a number, one after the other by different
authors. Always the same types of persons, always the same
small circle of subjects, always the same kind of love-making,
with prostitutes and other men's wives, and the marriage
portions of women and marriage settlements playing such
an uncommonly large part in life and covering half the sky.
French *life* and human nature must be more complex than
that ; the only explanation is that it is a fashion to leave
out all elements in human existence but these few. Just as
in our ridiculous absurd conventional farces there is always
a mistress and nearly always a servant girl, etc. How anyone can call French novels immoral beats me ! They are
not only truthful enough in substance, but more ascetic
than any other works of art in the world. They make sex
relations in every form and shape unseductive. When
one reads even Miss Weatherall's little stories for girls, and
how Daisy broke her foot, and the doctor carried her in his
arms, and she felt as he carried her for one instant his
moustaches brush against her lip—one longs that one had
broken one's leg and been carried by the doctor, and felt
the moustache brush one's lip ! But who ever wanted any
wretched kiss that any French novelist ever painted ?—

Except George Sand of course. Possibly to men of a certain type they may appear seductive ; but to me they appear moralistic sermons of the most stern and awful kind. Poor Guy de Maupassant is said to have been one of the most sensual of men ; and yet he paints passion like an awful old prophet ! Good-night, dear. I wish so much I could see you. Shall I never see you again ?

CHAPTER IX

LETTERS WRITTEN FROM 1904 TO 1907

1904

To S. C. C. S.   HANOVER, 7*th Jan.*

You know I suppose it's because I'm weak and ill that I always seem to feel Edward Marriott about me. It's as though he always said, " I bore bravely to the end, so can you. Rest will come." It's like an actual living presence comforting me sometimes. One understands how people, who didn't know it was their imagination behind, believed it was their beloved dead *actually* with them. I can feel him.

To S. C. C. S.   HANOVER, 11*th Jan.*

I am glad all the people [the Beaufort West constituency for which I was a candidate for Parliament] like you, my dear one, I was sure they would. I'm sure you don't need Oom Jan [Cilliers] or anyone but just yourself. Why, you made *me* like you, and that was what no one had ever been able to do in the same way before. . . .

To S. C. C. S.   HANOVER, 25*th Jan.*

[Her illness] has been more a malarial kind of thing because quinine and tar water have done me such good. I am feeling better to-day than I have yet done since you left. . . . When Oom Jan came here that day, I spoke to him about the water [there was an epidemic of enteric fever] ; he burst out in the most tremendous rage, with his eyes flashing, that he was a Christian and a believer in God, and that if God sent fever to punish people for their sins, was he going to say it was the water ? Sick

Photo by]   John Trevor, Hampstead.

S. C. CRONWRIGHT-SCHREINER, JULY, 1924.

To face p. 242.

ness was a punishment from God to call us to repent.
He took up his stick and went away. . . . Mrs. ——
came to ask how I was last night.   She began at once that
that flood at Bloemfontein was caused by the wickedness
of the people who fired cannon into the air to bring rain ;
God was not going to be mocked, therefore he had brought
this punishment on them.   She and Mrs. —— sat
enlarging on this.   I suppose no soul who has never lived
through it can know how spiritually and mentally (and
therefore emotionally) alone one is in a place like Hanover.
Because people, who can't a little bit understand you, can't
love you really.   The sympathy of likeness is after all the
only basis of true endless love.

To S. C. C. S.   HANOVER, 16*th Feb*.

I wrote till twelve o'clock last night, and then read
Whitman till one.   There was a time when Browning
seemed to " express me " better than any other poet, he
is beloved of my heart still, but I think now Whitman seems
to speak my thoughts for me most.   It's to nature, it's to
the vast life of the whole, we must turn for strength.   I
love that little two-line thing so much because you quoted
it when I wrote and said one reason why we couldn't marry
was because I was older than you :—

Women sit or move to and fro, some old, some young,
The young are beautiful, but the old are more beautiful than the
        young.

This is the copy I sent you in 1893 from Matjesfontein.
Now I must get to my writing.   I wonder much what you
will think of the ending of my story. . . .   I seem so joyful
to think of seeing you again, my darling.   You seem to
have been so long gone.

To EDWARD CARPENTER.   HANOVER, 17*th June*.

It's a cold night.   I am sitting in the little front room
of our three-roomed cottage with a fire at my back.   [The
room in question was 15 by 20 feet, and the house had
five rooms and a store].   We have 16 degrees of frost here

at night often in the winter, the milk froze solid in the jug the other night, and to-day a dish of water standing in the yard which was frozen last night was not melted except at the edges this evening though the sun had been shining on it all day. I have never felt such cold anywhere in Europe except once in Geneva, when a bitter north wind was blowing.

My dear old mierkat, 'Arriet, is sleeping on my shoulder. She will sit there for hours wide awake while I write or do my work. I'm always so glad I didn't come into the world when people had killed off all the dear beautiful animals and birds.

To Havelock Ellis.   Cape Town, 13*th May.*

No, I don't agree that one wants sympathy and love less as one grows older. What I think happens is that generally, if a man or woman has ordered their life wisely, they generally *have more !* and therefore long for it less— just as a well-fed child doesn't long so much for food as a little street-Arab. He has quite as much appetite but he doesn't know it ! Ordinarily, a woman, for instance, who marries at 20 or even 30, at 40 or 50 has a family of children grown up or growing up about her, and perhaps a husband who is fond of her society. She may have even too much of close human relationship, and may never therefore be conscious of any hunger for them. So with friendships. If I, for instance, had gone on living in Europe I should now have had not only you and Bob Muirhead and Ed. Marriott,[1] and all the old friends of my youth, but I should have made many more. I should probably have found it quite a relief to get away to Italy or somewhere where I could be quite alone for a couple of months—and might fancy I didn't want love and sympathy so much as when I was young ; as after an over-full meal one fancies one doesn't care about eating at all. But it's not so. Of course merely intellectual sympathy one does perhaps care for a little less, but only because, as one grows older, personal tenderness and love seems *relatively* more important. I made Rebekah say, years

[1] Ellis remarks that he does not understand why Marriott comes in here with "old friends of my youth," and suggests it may be a lapse for Ed. Carpenter

ago when I was a young girl (and it's a curious thing as showing how instinctively one knows things one can't have experienced) that in youth, though one longs for love and sympathy, one's master passion is for the intellectual knowledge of truth and for experience ; but when one grows older, though one still loves knowledge, one's master need is for human relations of love and sympathy. The fact that perhaps this afternoon a friend of mine, one of the three only real friends I have in South Africa, will perhaps come in for a moment with her little boy as they go for their walk and ask me how I am and kiss me, seems the great and beautiful fact of the day. Twenty years ago it would have seemed to me a very little thing. Three weeks ago a girl whom I know slightly gathered a little bunch of pink flowers for me on the mountain because she heard me say I was fond of them : they are in two little vases on my mantelpiece now, quite withered. Twenty years ago I would have liked them in a way, and kept them while they were quite fresh, but as soon as they withered I would have thrown them away. You will say it was because I had so many flowers and so many friends long ago, and that of course has something to do with it, but I think, at least in my own case, one prizes all forms of human love and sympathy more as one grows older, and one longs so for sweet and gentle things because life becomes so awfully stern.

We are going back to Hanover on the 26th as Parliament is likely to break up earlier than usual this year. I am trying to get a little black boy from the Reformatory to take up with me ; then I shall have someone in the house, and he will help me with the house and work. Give my love to Edith and ask her to send her lecture on Carpenter if it is printed. Good-bye. It's been splendid to be here at this boarding-house [East Bergholt, Tamboers Kloof] with the grand old mountain before me.

To Mrs. Francis Smith.   Cape Town, 14*th May.*

. . . The week after next Parliament ends, and we return to Hanover. It has been very very beautiful to be here with the grand old mountains and the sea for three

I have three friends here, almost the only friends in South Africa, except some of the Boer generals e of the public men in the Cape (and my feeling for can hardly be called "friendship" because it is just eeling which binds people who are devoted to one common impersonal end, and whose natures may not harmonise on any other point) and it has been very beautiful to see them too. I should say perhaps I have four friends here, because the husband of one of my friends is almost as much my friend as she is, in fact she and her husband [Dr. W. F. Purcell] are so much one that you can hardly think of them apart. He is a scientific man, a rather celebrated entomologist, and she has written some rather fine little poems on the war, but the beauty of them both is the purity and simplicity of their natures. I always hate visiting anyone, but in their house I always feel as perfectly restful as if I were at home. They live close to me here and their little boy runs in every day to see my two dogs and five mierkats which I had to bring with me from Hanover as I couldn't trust anyone else to take care of them. . . . My other two friends [Miss Molteno and Miss Alice Greene] are two splendid women who have lived together for about 17 years and who are so closely united that I can never think of them apart, but as parts of one whole. They are both so noble and beautiful, each in her own way.

You say that children are "the only excuse for marriage," but I think quite otherwise. I think a close union with some human creature, permanent, bearing on all parts of the daily life and with the element of excitement and change eliminated from it as much as possible, is in itself a primary necessity in all fully developed human natures. This union may exist between a parent and child (as in the case of Buckle and his mother) or between a brother and sister or two friends of the same sex as in the case of my friends Miss Molteno and Miss Greene ; the element of sex and above all the element of physical sexual union is not necessary to it ; but I think it most naturally and fully tends to exist between a man and woman ; and that, and not the mere bringing of children into the world, is the prime excuse for marriage in fully

developed human creatures.   Of course marriage originated
for the purpose of producing children ; just as friendship
originated in animals, and afterwards man, being compelled
to unite to hunt for food and to defend themselves against
foes ; but highly developed human beings have a necessity
for each other's fellowship for very different purposes than
these.   Of course thousands of human creatures even
to-day have not the *need* for this deep calm unchanging
fellowship ; but, for those who feel, its satisfaction in
marriage is the first condition of success in marriage.
Children may make the emptiness less felt, where this
fellowship does not exist, just as lesser friendship may do.
But I believe there is, deep in human nature, a need for this
close unending relationship with one above all who shall
be as it were a part of oneself which it is the highest function
of marriage to satisfy.   But one can't explain well what
one means in a few words.   I think women have this need
much more often fully developed than men ; but among
my men friends are many in whom I know it is as strongly
developed as in any woman.   Of course the tragedy of
marriage comes in when one has the need of this fellowship
and the other has not but only of continual change and
excitement.

To Mrs. FRANCIS SMITH.

HANOVER, SOUTH AFRICA, 12*th July.*

. . . I suppose there is no man in England who understands anything about South Africa or South African
affairs except my friend J. A. Hobson—and I don't know
that he understands anything of the lay of things *now*—
though he understood wonderfully when he was here four
years ago.   It seems that the Almighty has ordained that
no Englishman, whether he be Jingo or Pro-Boer, should
ever understand any things about South Africa !   Sometimes I have an idea, that perhaps Joey [Chamberlain]
knows a little about it !   He never says anything ; it would
be madness for him to " let on " about it ; but I fancy
he saw a thing or two when he was out here—

> For Joey ain't no bloomin' fool,
> You bet that Joey sees !

Of course he can't act as if he knew anything ; he must always go on acting as if he supposed it was a great and glorious war brought to a great and glorious conclusion ; but I sometimes fancy, if he could really tell what he saw, many jaws would fall, and the party of Joe and of war would disappear as stubble before the flames of truth.

To S. C. C. S. BALFOUR, 20*th Aug.*

[Journey to her father's grave.] My husband, we left Bedford on Thursday afternoon in a strange old buck-waggon with a little tent at the back. We have a Boer and a Kaffir driver and leader, so we have plenty of folk. We have travelled through two whole nights. We have ten oxen in the wagon. . . . The heat was terrible at Bedford and Adelaide. The drought is terrible. I never saw Stockenstroom like this, yet even now it is beautiful past words. In the dim light of the morning we got here. It is strange and almost unearthly to be here again where so many of my early childish days were passed. It is so passing strange to see the old house and the old mountain, and all the old people gone. Of the people I used to know who lived here in the old days, I have seen only one, a little hunchbacked Hottentot girl called Mietje, who is now a woman of thirty. I am writing in the wagon with paper on my knee. We have outspanned on the side of the mountain just above father's grave, with the hamlet of Balfour lying below us (there are only five or six houses but no end of gardens and lands and lots of little Hottentot huts scattered about). I wish you were here, my husband. People are very kind. One lady gave me a jug of milk, wouldn't take any money for it, and when we sent to buy a fowl another lady sent it us for nothing. Ettie won't let us begin at father's grave to-day, because it is Saturday, her Sunday, and to-morrow we can't work because it's Sunday. But we shall begin early Monday with four men and shall I think get all done on Monday. On Tuesday we shall go to Katberg, from there to Philipton and Hertzog, and on to Healdtown. I think we should reach Fort Beaufort about Thursday and Bedford on Friday or Saturday, and I shall leave at once for Cookhouse and home.

To S. C. C. S.   BEDFORD, 27*th Aug.*

My darling, that morning in the dawn light, when I was looking at father's hard iron-coloured bones lying there in black earth, it came over me with such a strange realisation, how in a few years I and you would be lying so too and how beautiful we must make the little time left to one another.   I will tell you about all that happened when I come.   In the dawn light before any of the workmen had come, Ettie and I went down to the graveside where we had placed the old coffin in the new one and removed a little of the earth that had fallen in and covered it, and we saw the back of the dear dear head resting so peacefully on the earth and the arms and feet, not one bone removed, all resting embedded in the earth.   We put flowers on it and covered it all up before anyone could come, so that no one but we saw it.   But it was beautiful to me that the sun rose just then and the early morning sunlight shone so beautiful on it, the sunlight he loved so, after 28 years. The coffin rested on two big rocks and [was] surrounded by sandstone and round hard stones embedded in the sandstone and for four days we were working it out with picks at first but the last two days with hand chisels for fear of injuring anything.   It was a much greater strain than I had expected. That agonised watching each movement of the tools lest they should injure something.   When it was all over and we had the dear body safe in our waggon, a great reaction seemed to come over me, and I was a bit prostrate, but I have been wonderfully well, *no* asthma, *no* cough !   Not since the night I was in Cradock.

To S. C. C. S.   SUNNYSIDE, PRETORIA, 16*th Dec.*

I have a splendid large room [at Smuts's] and slept *splendidly* last night ; have not a touch of asthma and my heart is better than it ever is at Hanover or Johannesburg. I can feel it go quite slow and steady.   This morning at breakfast General De la Rey came in.   He's a grand old man with a noble forehead and profile.   Just after breakfast dear old John Brown turned up looking very young and sweet and good.   Ely Findlay and little George came up.

Ely looks so young and beautiful I hardly knew her. It's strange how being loved and cared for a little makes a woman beautiful ; it's that starving hungry look that makes a woman look so old. About 11 o'clock Mrs. Smuts and I and her mother Mrs. Krige drove down to see the Susanna Hall where the body [Oom Paul's] lay in state. It is one of the most superb sights I have ever in my life seen. One glitter of silvery flowers and wreaths from end to end. It's a thing to be seen to be understood. I have seen nothing like it in Europe or anywhere else. It made one feel breathless. The hall is lighted by electric light and the floor and walls from the entrance on are covered with wreaths and emblems.

To S. C. C. S.   PRETORIA, 16*th Dec.*

Everyone is so sweet and kind here. There are thousands and thousands pouring in from Johannesburg. De Wet is staying here. They say the dear old fellow quite started with joy when he heard I was here, and met me so warmly. . . . Schalk Burger sits next me at table always. . . . . De Wet does strike you as such a splendidly *true* man when you meet him, there is only one De Wet. Two of his sons are here with him. . . . I am very glad I came. . . . (Private.) I have it from one who saw the wire that the King wired specially requesting Milner to attend the funeral ; but—does he fancy the Boers want to kill him ? Why he's the best friend we have, he's ruining the British Empire faster than all the Boers in creation could.

1905

To S. C. C. S.   HANOVER, 12*th Feb.*

I've read that life of Cavour. It's exceedingly able. It greatly intensifies the feeling I have always had of him, that he was in no sense a " great " man though one of the cleverest business men the world has ever seen. One feels how right all the modern Italian liberals and republicans are in placing half of the evils from which Italy now suffers, and the breakdown of the revolution to

attain to its full end, to him.   I think you will agree with
me when you read it.   It is not wonderful that he hated
Mazzini and Garibaldi ; he hated them instinctively as
men like Rhodes hate all believers in truth and lovers of
freedom.   English people have always worshipped Cavour
because he worshipped England ; its monarchy and
Government by the aristocracy were his ideal.   Yet he
was not a small man, his intellect and his energy were
too superior for that.   We must get a life of Mazzini to
read next.   He was a very little man and stout !   Didn't
care about his dress—that was all to the good, eh ?

To S. C. C. S.   HANOVER, 1 5*th Feb.*

I suppose you hadn't time to read my bit of MS. ?
It's difficult for *me* to judge of it *apart* from the whole book.
I know it as part of the whole only, and you could judge
it apart.   In the book as a whole it is the first sort of
indirect intimation of the life Rebekah is leading and her
husband's disloyalty to her, and I'm not sure whether it
does not pull it out of the artistic shape.   I couldn't write
quite a new thing on the sex question just now for many
reasons, and yet I want the £30 much.   I wrote till one
o'clock last night at my little Boer War Story [" Eighteen-
Ninety-nine," in *Stories, Dreams and Allegories*] which is
nearly ready now though Frans [my clerk] has not yet
typed the bit I gave him.

Oh it is such a heavenly day, dear.   When one looks
outside all the cares and aches of life seem to become so
little.   Even the Hanover teachers and schoolgirls seem to
sink away to nothing, and one feels so ashamed that one
ever allowed them to humiliate one and unfit one for work.
In a way I have a certain satisfaction in finishing these
Boer stories, just because Boer girls and women have treated
me as they have.   " If thine enemy hunger feed him, if
he thirst give him drink."   But you know I have no
enemy in the sense of wishing to hurt anyone or talk against
them ; only when people have hurt one too much one
just wants to creep away and never see them again.   It's
the only defence God gives some of us ; and I think we
have a right to use it.   Perhaps if I could intellectually

understand it all, it wouldn't be so hard to bear, because, to a nature like mine, as soon as I fully understand and *grasp* a thing, it is always easier to bear. I have never heard of civilised women saying and doing the things to another fellow-woman that they have done to me. And I have loved women so all my life and fought for them and defended them, and they have loved me. I could have done so much for those Hanover women and girls, I would have lived in and for the Hanover people if they would have let me. But perhaps it is better so, that I should be forced to throw my life and thought in other directions,

> Heartily know, when half Gods go,
> The whole Gods come !

We are so determined to love this or that, and perhaps it is what we ought not to love.

I want you to read my little war story. I love the last part. The first may seem a little uninteresting, and yet the last could not be without it.

To Miss DORA CAWOOD. CAPE TOWN, 20*th April.*

I have just seen the notice in the paper that my dearly loved old friend [Mrs. Cawood] has gone from us. I don't think you can understand all I feel. Will you please write and tell me about her last illness ? Did she suffer much ? Were you all about her ? Have you put her to rest by Elsie ? It is a beautiful thought to me that when I die I shall sleep on the top of the old mountain and my dear old friend be down in the valley below.

To Mrs. E. J. STANLEY (CLIFFORD CAWOOD).

[Later in the same year she writes to Clifford Cawood— Mrs. E. J. Stanley] : Isn't it sad at Ganna Hoek now the dear wonderful spirit that seemed its life has gone. I hope all goes well with the dear ones there. Isn't Ossie's wife sweet ? I long to see their little boy. I am so glad you are so happy, dear [in her marriage presumably], and wish I could see you and yours.

To S. C. C. S.   C. TOWN, 1*st May*.

I was very glad to get your letter and it was such a surprise too, I wasn't expecting it. I'm glad you liked the little story [" 1899 "]. I wonder how much it is because it is South Africa. But you have such a good artistic taste that I think you would not be misled. . . . I am trying to write my article on the Taal to-day.

1906

To HAVELOCK ELLIS.   HANOVER, 19*th Jan*.

It's curious how bad I feel when I think of you being ill even for a day. One has so many different ways of loving, but the idea of your illness or physical suffering or death is perfectly *intolerable* to me. I believe if I heard you were dangerously ill I should start off to England at once, if I had to borrow the money and knew I should likely die on the way. . . . Of course the woman's *ideal* of marriage [with reference to a story sent to her] is never motherhood and infinite forgiveness and endurance ! The woman's ideal is of something strong and great and tender to *look up* to. When that fails, and it seems as if her love must die in anguish, then a wave of motherhood rises and takes its place. . . .

To S. C. C. S.   HANOVER, 4*th April*.

" Ollie " [my dog] cried for you in the most extra-ordinary way last night, all the evening she kept running about and whining : I fed her and at last wrapped her up in my big dressing gown and put her on my bed. . . . There will be " a light in the window for you " when you return on Thursday night. Poor little " Ollie," how can one leave her with strangers ? No ordinary person will understand her sensitive little nature. Good-bye, take care of *my* husband, remember he's not your husband but mine and you have to look after him.

To S. C. C. S.   HANOVER, 9*th May*.

All my real interest has gone from the Boer questions for the present. They are more than able to take care of themselves.   But the Natives are always with me.   As soon as I know people or causes have no *need* of me, it's wonderful how my heart can loosen itself from them :—

> Because *she* hath no need of me :
> *I* have no need of her.

That line of Mrs. Browning's poem explains a lot of my life and is often in my thoughts. . . .   I know the Boers don't need me any more !

To HAVELOCK ELLIS.   HANOVER, 1906.

One thing is beautiful to me, that though my personal life has become crushed and indifferent to me, I have not lost one little grain of my faith in the possible beauty and greatness of human nature, the divine beauty of perfect love, and of truth.   I am so absolutely certain that the dream of the ideal of beauty and goodness is that towards which human nature is slowly moving.   And life has been very, very beautiful.   Even the power to bear and repress oneself is beautiful if there is nothing else.   And one's joy in nature and in knowing and trying to under-stand has been glorious ; and I have had better and more beautiful friends than anyone in the world.   Tell me a little about yourself, not in the " damned fine horse " style —really.

To MRS. FRANCIS SMITH.   HANOVER, 10*th Sept.*

. . . Many people have been surprised that I said Heine's grave was the most sacred spot to me in Europe. I don't say he was the greatest man ; he has never helped me or modified my life as Mill did.   But that seven years on the mattress-grave, that beautiful bright joy-loving soul dying away by inches and fighting to the end.   If only I could have been that woman who went to him at the end and cheered and comforted him.   The very name of the Rue d'Amsterdam is to me sacred because he lay there.   I know that other men have suffered but not just so, because he was in a way alone to the end.   If anyone showed me a lock of hair and said " That is Wordsworth's," I should look at it and pass on ; if they said it is Shakespeare's or

Shelley's I should stroke it and if it was Shelley's kiss it, but I should lock it up in a drawer ; but if it was Heine's I should carry it about with me wherever I went.   I don't know why I love him so.

To Mrs. Francis Smith.   De Aar, 11*th Sept.*

. . . I am now at De Aar in a strange sort of place they call an Hotel.   It was built for the officers just after the war, or during it.   This was I believe the largest military centre in South Africa ; for miles the ground is all trodden bare, not a bush will grow ; they have been killed at the roots ; grey sand flies about everywhere and the earth is full of broken whiskey bottles [and] empty tins ; if you kick at something in the sand it turns out to be an old soldier's jacket or boot thrown away here.   They had a vast prisoners' camp here too, where the prisoners died ; and horse camps where horses died ; so the dust is pretty organic.   Now there are only a few railway men and Jews, living for the most part in tin houses (a few have little red brick cottages), and the remains of the location of camp followers the military drew here, Hottentots and other coloured half-castes of the lowest class, the women mainly or almost entirely prostitutes, so eaten up by horrible diseases that one is afraid to have them to do one's washing. It is like a more sordid edition of *Poker Flat.*   Do you know Bret Harte's little story ?

There is so little water here that the woman who manages this place asked me to use as little as possible in washing.   I am going to look for a little coloured boy this afternoon and hire him to bring me bath water every day. I tell you this that you may picture the queer sort of life it is here !   The only white woman in this house is a red fat-faced sort of barmaid with staring blue eyes, who calls herself the housekeeper.

To S. C. C. S.   Matjesfontein, 19*th Oct.*

You know I have got the feeling here that I'd like to live hundreds and hundreds of years in this world, and yet also the feeling it would be a beautiful thing to die.   The two feelings seem contrary, but they are really not.

To HAVELOCK ELLIS. MATJESFONTEIN, 30*th Oct.*

I've got the photograph of the drawing. I agree with Edith it's quite terrible. The only thing as bad I've ever seen was a picture painted of Cron by a young lady in England who called herself an artist. Of course, in a way, neither of them are absolutely unlike, though they are nightmares just because in both cases something that is in you both has been taken out and painted alone and exaggerated till it's awful. There *is* in you a certain cold, bloodless, examining element ; where Edith or I would say of a thing how beautiful or how hideous, or how hateful or how loveable, you would say : "*How interesting!*" There is, *besides*, in your nature an infinity of tenderness, of love of truth, even of passion and ideality, that your face does always show. I have never in my long life seen any face so transfused with beautiful and ennobling and intense emotions as I have seen yours, till it was almost angelic. Now why couldn't the man have painted something of this instead of the cold, bloodless, neckless, even mouthless man (and God knows you've got mouth enough anyhow !) ? If you really looked like that no one would ever have loved you since you came into the world. It looks like old Mr. Casaubon in *Middlemarch*. I tore it up. I hope Edith tore up hers. I don't want after you are dead for people to get hold of such a thing. . . . I've been so glad of the book you sent because my heart compels me to lie quite still on my bed or on the bench on the balcony all day, and I've nothing to read, so it was a God-send. It's very German certainly. It reminds me of the way my father would ramble on when he was talking of his school-days and the friends he knew in his youth, what this one and that one had felt and said. . . .

To S. C. C. S. MATJESFONTEIN, 1*st Nov.*

It always seems to me more and more that the only thing that really matters in life is not wealth or poverty, pleasure or hardship, but the nature of the human beings with whom one is thrown into contact and one's relation to them. One's real deathless wealth is all the beautiful noble souls one has seen and spiritually touched.

To S. C. C. S.   MATJESFONTEIN, 24*th Nov.*

I don't know when I've ever for years been so well as to-day. I've worked and written from this morning till now, 10.30 p.m. [She encloses a letter from my mother to her from Avonmore, Rondebosch, my sister Louie's house, which contains this, which I wish to keep for my dear mother's sake : " Louie went to see your friend, Mrs. [John] Brown, yesterday, and, if she were not so devoted to you, I think you would be jealous, for she thinks our dear old boy the finest man, every way, she has ever known ; *sensible woman*, don't you think ? I cannot tell you of all the good things she said of him, but *we know*, good and brave above most men."]

To S. C. C. S.   MATJESFONTEIN, 30*th Nov.*

I hope Old Party ['Arriet, the old mierkat] will be alive when I go back. You know I think we shall just some day find her sitting in the sun dead—died of old age. I don't know how it is ; just as some people have a quite curious tenderness over youth and young infancy, so I have always felt a quite curious tenderness over age. An old person or animal touches the very core of my heart, and did so when I was a little child, and very old people always love me, I think they *feel* how I feel for them.

To S. C. C. S.   MATJESFONTEIN, 1*st Dec.*

Did I tell you that a curious thing happened to me up there [at " my tree "] one day. I went up and was quite quiet and happy under my tree. It was a glorious day with a fresh breeze blowing. I was just beginning to walk down the slope when suddenly, in an instant, I found myself crying aloud in my very loudest voice till the hills all round rang again — " My youth, my youth !—give back my youth to me !—give back my youth ! " I never would have thought I could have cried in so loud and deep a voice, it was as if they would have heard me at Matjesfontein ; and the curious thing was that I had no control of it—that it was something beyond myself. I'd been so peaceful and well in hand a minute before. It wasn't my physical youth I was crying for, it [was] the hope, the faith, the

18

looking forward of youth ! In a moment or two I got myself in hand, and felt astonished. It was as if my whole soul and body were rending me with the cry. Funny wasn't it ? And yet you know I felt more peaceful afterwards ; as if that just once for a moment absolutely letting one's self go relieved one.

There is no reason why one ever should let one's hope and faith go, even about one's own poor little life one should keep it to the end : and one's hope and joy in the great life of the Universe beyond one that can never die, should grow. (A few more flakes have fallen. I expect it is snowing on Hex River to-day.)

To S. C. C. S.   MATJESFONTEIN, *5th Dec.*

It's a curious day with a thick Scotch mist over the mountains. I'd like to go out and play golf. It's the first time I've had a wish to since you left. "Oh call my chummie back to me, I cannot play alone !" Yes, I think Tennyson was a poet and a true poet ; but not a very *great* one. A one carat diamond is a diamond and a true diamond, but not a large one, and doesn't equal one of the *same water* which is 50 carats. I think some of his little lyrics will live as long as the English language lasts, "Tears, idle tears," for instance, is immortal. He was not a man with a great intellect, and therefore the range of matter over which he could be a poet and seer was small. He was a poet of pensive sweetness, moods of human life and expression like all others, by the poet who supremely *feels* them, but there is no new note of intensity, of reckless force, of passion, in all his works. "Come into the garden, Maud " is infinitely sweet and tender, but it has no breath of fierce passion. Browning, who had felt what the hunger for truth and knowledge was, could write the " Grammarian's Funeral," pouring into human speech for all time the pure deep longing of the noblest human intellects for truth and knowledge ; Tennyson couldn't, because he hadn't the intellect to hunger for them, but he *could* write a poem, a true poem, about an old uneducated grandmother thinking over the days of her youth. That's what I think.

To S. C. C. S.   MATJESFONTEIN, 18*th Dec.*

I have just been reading a story that rather interested me as reminding me of the Boers of the lower type in this country.   I'd send it you only you've no time to read.

A young London man poet, artist and thinker, wants to get away from the noise and stir of London life with all its problems for a time and study simple country life and do his painting and write his poetry.   He goes to a most out of the [way] part of the country in England, finds a primitive farm house, with a very plain scraggie common-looking farmer's wife and a husband and a lot of children. Here he determines to board, and all goes well for a time. He finds the plain country people so nice and restful to *paint* and look at.   One day the landlady, who has always gone about in a print dress with a white apron and a cotton sunbonnet, is going to a fair or show and appears to his horror dressed in a black silk with a mantle covered with black beads and a gorgeous velvet hat with three ostrich feathers in it.   She looks so surprisingly hideous and terrible in this fashionable dress that before he thinks he cries out, " Oh Mrs. Smith, you oughtn't to wear those things !   If you only knew how much more beautiful you looked in the clothes you wear every day ! "   Instead of the woman's being frightfully angry, as he expected, she lifts up her head and chats with him and seems quite unoffended.   From that time she begins to take great care of her personal appearance, is always starching and ironing her things and standing before the glass and doing up her hair.   All her life she has been told she was plain and ugly, even her husband when he was courting her never once said she was beautiful, he only praised her puddings, and here was this handsome fashionable man from London taking notice of her appearance and saying she looked beautiful in her cappje !   Often as the young man passes through the kitchen, when her husband is out he stops to talk with her, as he is interested in country life and people, and sometimes when she goes out to feed the pigs he goes to the pigsty to watch the pigs being fed, and stands talking to her.   Her good old husband notices nothing, except that she is always doing herself up, and looks at her face in the bit of glass on the kitchen wall ; he thinks she must be going daft, for, as he says to himself, " She's a good wife, and she makes the finest puddings in the country ; but there's not much she can see when she looks in the glass ! " But the neighbours are sharper, they have noticed how she does herself up, and they have seen her talking with him at the pigsty, and in the kitchen when her husband was out ; and at last one old woman comes over and accuses her of " carrying on " with the stranger and caring for him. Instead of denying it (for of course she really only cares for her husband and is only flattered by the young man's supposed attentions) she tosses her head, her vanity is touched, and she says it's no business of theirs if the young man *does* admire her ! Of course the old woman rushes out to tell the village ; but unfortunately the good old husband has come home from his work and is in the front kitchen and hears all. He comes in and implores his wife to tell him there is no truth in what the old woman suggested ; but her vanity is roused, and she turns on her old husband and says, " Do you think because you never saw anything to admire in me that no one else can see that I'm beautiful and like me," &c., &c. The poor old husband then implores her to give the young man notice and send him away and have nothing more to do with him. She refuses, and he goes silently out of the house. He has to go to the next village. He's a man who never drinks, but in his despair he turns in at a public house and drinks himself drunk. In this state he is knocked down by a waggon and killed. The next morning his body is brought home and all the neighbours rush in. The wife who really loved her husband very much is nearly frantic. The young man who is in the garden painting rushes into the kitchen and puts his hand on her arm to tell her how sorry he is. She flings it off. " You, you killed him ! " she cries, " it is all your fault ! " The poor young man stands flabbergasted. " Yes," she cries, " You, you led me on to it ! You flattered me, you told me I was beautiful. You tried to make me love you, you broke his heart ! " Then the women break in. Yes they have seen him standing at the pigsty talking to her, &c., &c., he is a vile seducer

breaking up the peace of other people's home, &c., &c.
They say he ought to support her and her children for the
rest of her life ; and there is of course nothing for the
young man but to pack up his things as quickly as he can
and go back to London, quite disillusioned with the purity
and sweetness of simple country life and folk !

It seems silly, told as I'm telling it, but it's written
by someone who evidently knows country life and country
people well and it's quite *real* as told.   There is something
even pathetic in the distress of the simple old husband ;
and even in the poor woman's delight in being, as she
thinks, for the first time in her life, flattered and praised !

I was reading the book all night and it reminded me
so curiously of Hanover.   When I first came there, there
was a family living in the corner shop where Levinkind
now is.   All the Dutch women in Hanover told me the
wife was not a woman whose call I ought to return, that
they never called on her, and implied she was a bad
character.   When I asked Mrs. ——— what exactly there
was against her I found out that twice she had been
seen walking in the plantation with her husband's clerk,
and once had the effrontery to come walking openly back
into the village with him.   I heard *exactly* the same story
everywhere, nothing else against her ; and when I suggested
she might have met him there by chance, or gone for a
walk with him with her husband's consent, they would
not hear of it, they said a " respectable married woman
does not go out walking with a man who is not her
husband."

I am quite sure if I invited v. Z——— [a friend of
ours] to have tea with me and went out afterwards for a
walk to the kopjes with him, no woman in the place would
speak to me again, and they might even bring it up before
the Kerkraad ; and if I were twice found walking in the
plantation with young K——— or young d. T———, my
character would be gone for ever !   It does not matter how
pure, or how beautiful, or how noble, your feeling is, people
of another race and class will misunderstand you, if your
conduct does not coincide with their little sexual standard.
I would never have been able to live my five years as
governess among the Boers, if I had not always clearly

recognised their sexual standard was *not* mine. If Mrs. Fouche and the girls went out of a room, and I were left alone with any man, I would at once make an excuse for going out also. I think that is why I was the only girl I ever heard of as living five years as governess among the Boers without getting into some sort of sexual trouble. The beautiful " camaradery " which I can have with such men as Ellis or Purcell, or Sir William Butler, or Carpenter, would be as impossible with a man like [two local Afrikanders], as that they should understand my view of religion or philosophy ! Such people may not be in any way worse than we are, but they simply have another standard of life in sexual matters as well as in religion, and they cannot understand our acts and motives unless we are always carefully apportioning them to *their* understanding. I think this little book is the best illustration I have ever read of the tragedy which may result when people of different classes are thrown together into a kind of intimacy. It was just because that young man *was* so pure and good that he couldn't dream of what those women were thinking.

1907

To S. C. C. S.   HANOVER, 20*th Jan*.

What a wonderful book I could write if one dared to write truly of such a place [as Hanover]. The noble, the heroic, the mean and vulgar all here. I always feel that sexual instinct pure and simple is much maligned ; that the worst and meanest vices of life do *not* arise from sexual passion pure and simple but rather from a petty vanity and love of admiration. The man likes to think he is admired and makes a great impression, the lower type of woman that she attracts the man and can count him among her " followers." The envy of other people, the desire to be first in the world's eye (not in virtue or real greatness) lie at the root of half the tragedies in life. . . . I am really keeping so splendidly well : I don't need more than the little [servant] girl. Emotional companionship, someone who loved me tenderly and whom I loved, I do need ;

but it is useless to try to find that in the ordinary coloured girl.   If I could have a little wild Kaffir boy or girl—yes ! I'm really getting on splendidly.

To Mrs. FRANCIS SMITH.   HANOVER, 1*st Feb.*

    . . . My friend Havelock Ellis, between whom and myself exists an absolutely unbroken friendship of 26 years, has had it [influenza] very badly and is weak and his heart bad.   It made my heart dumb to think what I would feel if he died ever, there has been such an unbroken brother and sisterhood of mental comradeship between us since our youth.   His wife is such a splendid, noble little woman, with such great intellectual gifts.   It's so beautiful when the people you have loved marry and you can feel to the one they marry as you do to them.

To S. C. C. S.   HANOVER, 16*th Feb.*

    Those dear [franchise] women in London.   It's the finest stand women have made anywhere in the world yet ; because only a woman knows how hard it is for a woman to fight or seem to fight for herself.   Because deep in our nature is something that makes us feel as if we should always fight for others.

To S. C. C. S.   HANOVER, 25*th Feb.*

    [Comparing a Swedish novel with *From Man to Man* and commenting how the writer, on certain points, expresses himself almost in her own words] : It is interesting because I am a woman and he is a man. It's very curious.   If my book hadn't been written years ago, and this part not even re-written of late, one would really say, " Well, one must be copying from the other." Of course the stories are quite different.   After all, if a thing be *true*, it must come to thousands of minds, it must live in millions of hearts ; and that makes the use of a writer : not that he expresses what no one else thinks and feels, but that he is the voice of what others feel and can't say.   If only the powers that shape existence give me the strength to finish this book, I shall not have that agonised feeling over my life that I have over the last ten years, that I have done nothing of good for any human creature. I am not sure of the book's artistic worth : to judge of that from the purely intellectual standpoint one must stand at a distance from one's own or anyone else's work. But I know it gives a voice to what exists in the hearts of many women and some men, I know I have only tried to give expression to what was absolutely forced on me, that I have not made up one line for the sake of making it up.

To S. C. C. S.   HANOVER, *5th Mar*.

I am so absorbed and interested in my book I don't like to think of anything else. I suppose to-night will see you back in De Aar. No, I *don't* like obese people, or flabby people. Muscle I admire beyond anything in man or woman : it's sinew and *bone* I don't like to see. [She likes] rounded muscle . . . like catching hold of hard india-rubber ; your hand comes off with a *bound*. I used to be like that till I had measles [at Matjesfontein]. Even now the people who massage me are astonished at my muscles. If my chest was all right, I would even still be very strong ! ! It's this curious muscular strength that has kept me alive the last years. . . . (Evening.) I've been lying down most of the day and quite forgot the mierkats at six, which is their time. At a quarter past seven I looked out at the pantry window and there they all were in a terrible state of mind at the kitchen door, trying to get in ! It was almost dark and they were running about and scratching at the door in a desperate way ; they couldn't think what was the matter. So I let them in and gave them a big feed and they all jumped into the box and went to sleep. I give them the one big feed of the day when they go to bed and that makes them very punctual in turning up. "Old Party" is more than tame. She never will leave me. To-day when I was lying on the bed she would come and sleep on my shoulder. Every time I carried her back to the study armchair or put her outside, I would hear a little trot, and she would climb up again and tuck her head into my neck—so I had to give in.

To S. C. C. S.   HANOVER, 14*th Mar.*

I have painted my baby's little inner coffin, the shell, a beautiful pure white with Aspinal's Enamel and written on it for her birthday on the 30th April. It is so nice to think it will lie close beside me in my coffin. You must take it out of the outer case and put the little white shell in by my side, not at my feet dear. . . .

To S. C. C. S.   HANOVER, 20*th Mar.*

I have got a letter from Mrs. —— asking me to be one of the vice-presidents of the Woman's Suffrage League they are starting in Cape Town. She also sends me some papers on the C. D. Acts which I'll show you when you come . . . To me there is nothing else in the world that touches me in the same way. You will see that if you read my novel [*From Man to Man*] all other matters seem to me small compared to matters of sex, and prostitution is its most agonising central point. Prostitution, especially the prostitution of men of themselves to their most brutal level, can't really be touched till man not only says but feels woman is his equal, his brother human to whom he must give as much as he takes ; and the franchise is one step towards bringing that about.

To S. C. C. S.   HANOVER, 22*nd Mar.*

The older I grow the more intensely it seems to me that there's nothing worth living for but love and tenderness between human beings.

To S. C. C. S.   HANOVER, 5*th and* 6*th April.*

. . . It's strange how that ideal of an absolute love and sympathy with your man companion haunts all " new women." The old sort never care half as much, if their husband provides them with a comfortable home and is liberal in money matters. It is the most ignorant thing to say woman's aspiration for freedom makes her indifferent to sex emotion. We only lay down our sex-love and fellowship when death comes ; just as we desire to have

[a] child and mother it, *more* than the old woman, not less.   The old woman cared mainly for having a baby ; the new [woman] dreams of her grown-up son or daughter. Good-bye.   Your pal, Olive.

To Mrs. Francis Smith.   Hanover, 19*th April.*

. . . I hope next month to get away for a few days and go to see a Mission Station called Heald Town, where I spent my childhood from six to nine years old.   The little sister [Ellie] whom I loved so is buried there in the garden, and I love the whole place so ; it is sacred ground to me.   It is such a pity that travelling is so expensive in this country and the distances so immense.   My childhood was so very bitter and dark, but I cling to the memories of it and especially the places I lived at, they were so unutterably lovely and it was in nature I found all the joy and help I had in those lonely years.

To S. C. C. S.   Hanover, 5*th May.*

Weary, dreary, mizzle and wind.   A dark grey sky from which thunder and lightning sometimes comes.   I have got another letter asking me to go to England to lecture for the Socialists on the Woman Question.   Well, I haven't got my marching orders yet.   The day *may* come when I shall.   There is something rises in me, not a guide to anyone else, but for myself, which, when it says " Go," I go ; but, when it doesn't speak, I *wait.*   That must have been what Socrates meant by his Demon, and what Christians mean by the voice of God in answer to prayer : what it really is, I suppose, is the result of long unconscious balancing in the mind suddenly coming to a result and that result flashing out on the conscious reason, or perhaps, rather, being flashed on by it. . . .

To S. C. C. S.   Hanover, 8*th May.*

. . . 'Arriet is very tame and she *understands* more than the others.   I think with animals as with savage nations, the old are *much* wiser than the young.   Where there are no books and no artificial education, the being learns pretty much only what experience teaches, and therefore, other things equal, a savage man's or an animal's wisdom may be measured by its years.   Ollie is getting much much cleverer than she was.   The way she asked me to-day if she might have some of 'Arriet's bread and milk was quite wonderful.   I am so much, much better to-day.   Oh, if the weather could stay like this a little. . . . I used to think only women passed through that time of anguish when they first felt youth going ; but now I think men feel it too.   It is the kind of sorrow one's pride makes one bury deep in one's heart ; that I suppose is why so little is said on it in art or in books.   If one's heart grows wider and wider and one ripens into a broad, tender, sympathetic age, it's the most beautiful thing in life.

To S. C. C. S.   HANOVER, 9*th May*.

Con. Lytton [Lady Constance] went to see Miss Molteno, who is very much impressed with her, says she's like a goddess and " makes one realise anew the wonder of womanhood."   That's how she always makes me feel : " What a grand thing womanhood can be."   Oh I am so well to-day.

To S. C. C. S.   HANOVER, 13*th and* 14*th May*.

I hear from Miss Viljoen that a *lion* killed a man at Oppermans Kraal [a neighbouring farm] yesterday ;   a Kaffir herd [herdsman].   His head and his legs have been found.   I'm going to hear the truth from [Dr.] Wilson to-morrow.   The man who was walking with the man who was eaten says the lion had a bit of chain round its neck, so he has evidently escaped from somewhere.   He says the lion kept roaring after him as long as he was in sight.   It's a curious story.   Oppermans Kraal adjoins the Commonage I believe.   Fortunate the lion didn't turn his walk this way yesterday afternoon and find you and me among the kopjies. . . .   I went over to Mr. Burger's to hear if the lion story was true.   It turns out that two men *said* they *saw* a lion ; there's no one dead.   [No lions had been in those parts for over half a century.] . . .   But there is some truly Hanoverian news. Coming out of church last night —— and —— [two grown-up unmarried women, daughters of leading people] had a stand-up fight, banging and striking each other in the face ! ! ! Some people ran away when they saw them fighting, some stayed to see the end. They say there is to be a Court case to-morrow. Don't say a *word about this at De Aar* till it gets there by other means. What terrible things these young Boer girls are. The lowest servant girls in England would hardly fall to such depths. The only persons who can really cope with them are people of their own class. The quarrel was about some man, really, I believe, but they fought about clothes at the end ! ! ! One would object in England to take women with the faces and manners, say, of the Miss —— yet here, because of *their money*, you have them calling on you ! It is this little smattering of education that ruins them, but they must pass through this phase to reach a higher. I suppose it really is because one never has to do with the same class of persons in England that they seem so terrible. I expect the costers' daughters fight just that way about their " *young men.*" But one never sees them or knows them.

To S. C. C. S.   HANOVER, 16*th May.*

So [Edmond] Garrett's gone ! Yes, how short life is. When I look back on mine nothing seems *real* and to make life worth living but the love one has given and received. What is all mere success and fame to this. We had an awful rain last night. Floods and floods ! *The Vley is like a river round the town.* The case [the fight referred to on the 14th] is to come before the Church, not the Court. They say the language used on both sides was something unspeakable, " vrieslyk om te hoor " [fearful to hear].

To S. C. C. S.   HANOVER, 23*rd May.*

Very hot and oppressive, but I have to keep the fire going to dry the air. . . . Oh, I wish I could get my book [*From Man to Man*] done before I die. It may not

be any good ; but I feel I have to do it.   I used to feel
I couldn't die till it was done ; that fate wouldn't let it
be.   Now I know that anything may be ; you trust and
hope for years but the things never come.   If one has
done one's best, that is all. . . .

To S. C. C. S.   HANOVER, 25*th and* 26*th May*.

My dear women, how they are coming on !   [Apropos
a fine article by one of them in the *Nineteenth Century*.]
You would have to know how I have loved women, and
how much they are to me, to realise how *some* women can
hurt me.   It's only the things you love can really touch
you and agonise you.   If I didn't care for women so much
I wouldn't mind.

To S. C. C. S.   HANOVER, 27*th May*.

Oh, if I could be under conditions to finish it [*From
Man to Man*].   I've set my heart so on finishing it before
the end comes.   I could do so much work now if I was
strong and could get fresh air.   My brain has never been
so clear and strong before in one way.   I tried to go for a
walk yesterday but I came staggering back and am only
now recovering from it.

To S. C. C. S.   HANOVER, 4*th June*.

I have never felt that age made any great difference
between men and women, but the happiest marriages I
know of, Mill's, Browning's and many I have known
personally, the woman is older than the man.   Women are
older for their years up to 30.   I mean a woman of 20 or
30 seems to be older than a man of the same age—after
40 the man begins to seem older than the woman of his
age, and a woman of 60 is generally younger in all ways
than a man of 50.   Perhaps it is as you said, that the
woman " type " is more flexible and childlike and therefore
tends to keep its flexibility much longer mentally and
physically.   Of course if people marry merely to produce
children, then the woman in that respect is often older
than the man.

To MRS. FRANCIS SMITH.   HANOVER, *6th June.*

. . . Yes, you are wonderfully right about my brother
Will. He is the most generous enemy who ever existed.
The more a man has injured him, the less he will injure
back. It's something he's got from my father, whom he
is physically very like, only my father was an even bigger
and a much finer built man. It is such a noted trait in his
character that, when he was Prime Minister out here, one
of his colleagues remarked that " If only Schreiner would
be half as polite and considerate to his friends as he is to
his enemies the Government would work." . . . But the
real beauty of his character comes out in his personal
relations with those dependent on him or needing his
help, his children, his servants, poor young barristers
struggling at the Bar—anyone who wants help. Except
my old father I never knew any human being so lavishly
generous, taking such a *delight* in assisting other human
beings who may be nothing to him at all. Yes, he is a
freethinker in religion, as I am ; but he always takes the
lawyer's view even of that. He was more enthusiastic
in writing about you and Con. [Lady Constance Lytton]
then he almost ever allows himself to be. I was quite
astonished. He is a man of intense passions and
emotions, always holding them down. There is something almost awful in that self-restraint in which he
habitually lives.

To HAVELOCK ELLIS.   CAPE TOWN, *6th July.*

Dear old Havelock, as to your theory about absence
being necessary to continuance in-loveness, if you mean
by in-loveness (which isn't quite clear from your letter)
anything but delusion, then I differ from you *entirely*. In
friendship of a purely intellectual kind, absence may and
does *sometimes* increase affection by removing all possibility
of those physical discords and small repulsions, which may
exist between two people who are great intellectual friends
but physically antipathetic. But " in-loveness," I take
it, has always *something* of physical not purely intellectual
elements in it, and here physical presence and nearness is

all-important to its continuance as to its beginning.   I
hold it a rule with no exception that, if a man and woman
are " in love " with each other, the only *possible* way of
ending it is to separate and never to see each other and the
wider the separation the more successful.   When a man
or woman finds they cannot return the love given it is
better to leave them and never if possible allow them to
see them.   If I, for instance, had insisted on —— never
meeting me or speaking to me, he might have been
happy and married before, and if I had not at last *insisted*
I believe he would never have married anyone else and
kept on loving me till to-day.   I believe, and I *know*, that
there are hundreds of husbands and wives who would have
lived all their lives tenderly and passionately in love with
one another if they had never separated for a day ; who,
if separated for six months or a year, drift away from each
other at once and never come near again.   I believe physical
absence is fatal to " in-loveness," except where there is a
deep and purely intellectual sympathy.   So far from
Edward Carpenter's theory being true that separation
adds to the love between married people, I believe that for
the average man and woman there is more truth in what
I heard an old Cape Town woman say sixteen years ago
that if a woman lets her husband be separated from her
for six months she may just as well get a divorce from him,
meaning that he will have ceased to love her and care for
someone else.   I believe that the five or six months' trip
to Europe, that so many men in South Africa take, has
ended more love and done more to darken homes and lives
by making life henceforward loveless, than any other
cause.   The terrible problem seems to be that while
multitudes of men will feel loyal and tender and passionately
drawn to a woman as long as they are unbrokenly with
her, multitudes are absolutely unable to maintain any love
as soon as separation comes.   With them it is always the
nearest woman.

   Friendship may be increased by absence.   Whenever
I didn't see —— and thought only of his work and the
terrible incurable disease he had told me he was dying of
I loved him with a strange intensity ; but the moment I
saw him or came near him, a kind of constitutional antipathy

seemed to put him far from me.   With ——, on the other hand, as soon as he was away from me, great as was my friendship for him and my admiration for his noble character, it was easy for me to pass days without ever remembering him ; but as soon as I met him the deep still joy and delight and satisfaction which his presence gave me came back, and I am quite sure that, if ever I had been compelled to live in the same house with him for six months or a year, it would have ended in my loving him so desperately I would have been obliged to marry him. There is *no* cure for " in-loveness " but absence.

My father was madly, intensely, passionately in love with my mother all his life ; he worshipped her when he died, an old man of 64 [61], yet more than when he married her, a young man of 21 [23] ; but if it had ever been necessary for him to leave her for six months, or a year, or two years, would it have survived the separation ?   The statement that absence is necessary to the continuance of love and passion seems to me the most at variance with fact of anything I ever heard !

Of course in the case of a fantastic intellectual delusion like Dante's, no doubt, if he had ever known Beatrice, if he had spent a week with her, he would most likely have called her a horrid vain, stupid little girl, and have found some other woman or object to hang his verses to.   But then such a feeling is no more being in love with a person than the feeling [? of a Christian worshipper towards an] imaginary Jesus Christ whom he conjures up out of his inner consciousness and who perhaps has never existed at all.   I believe that there is a purely vital attraction between human creatures (not only sexual in the ordinary sense) which will always awake when these two persons meet, and where that strange vital attraction is supplemented by a strong intellectual sympathy, then you have the most perfect deathless relations that can exist between two human creatures.

I am better this week and have been out several times. I went to the debate in Parliament on Woman's Suffrage. The speeches of the men on our side were magnificent, especially Sauer's and Malan's.

To Mrs. FRANCIS SMITH.   SEA POINT, *25th Aug.*

. . . Rather a beautiful little thing has happened since I was down here.   One of my old and very dear friends, an English Officer, was killed out here during the war.   His wife has come out to see his grave, etc.   I'd never met her before.   Since his death she has been reading all my old letters to him, and the way in which she, a hard, reserved, society woman, has turned to me and almost clung to me is very beautiful.   It's one of the things I value most in my life, that all my men-friends' wives love me almost more than the men do after they get to know me and never wish to end our friendship.

In [the] little box where I keep my greatest treasures I have a letter from the wife of my oldest and dearest man friend in which she says she is sure her married life is so beautiful because of the seven years in which her husband loved me better than anything in the world, and our close unbroken friendship.   I value that letter more than anything I have I think.

Some people say friendships between married men and women are impossible.   They are, unless there is a high sense of honour on both sides—an abiding sense that you are dealing with a doubled and not a single individuality any more—you are no friend, but the greatest enemy of the man or woman, if you make marriage less easy and not more beautiful and easy for them. . . .

To S. C. C. S.   HANOVER, *3rd Oct.*

I've read the volumes of Theal [S. African historian] since I came here.   How utterly he has changed this edition since he got in tow with Rhodes and the [Africander] Bond ! He has the face to say people may wonder at the changes he has made but he has entirely changed his opinion !   A funny thing for a man to do who has been making a study of South African history all his life !   He used to be a great friend of the native ; now he even attempts to defend slavery.   It is very sickening.   There is nothing I think a man might more wisely pray every night than that he may never change and modify his view except in the search for truth. . . .   I am so well this evening, dear.

To MRS. FRANCIS SMITH. DE AAR, 22*nd Oct.*

. . . The most important event of my childhood was the birth of a little sister [Ellie], and my love for her has shaped all my life. It was her death, when I was about nine, which first made me realise the falsity of what I had been taught and made a freethinker of me. She only lived eighteen months, but for that 18 my life was entirely in and through her, and I watched her die. The novel [*From Man to Man*] I am revising now is dedicated to her, and the opening chapter [" The Prelude "] is about a little girl's feeling when her new little sister is born. I sometimes think my great love for women and girls, *not* because they are myself, but because they are *not* myself, comes from my love to her.

To HAVELOCK ELLIS. DE AAR, 6*th Nov.*

I should be glad to see your book on Spain. It will be invaluable if only it's in your simple concise style, like when you write letters to me, not one word too much, not one for show or ornament—and therefore all so ornamental. Yes, Lewes's life of Goethe is one of the two or three biographies in the world really worth reading. It's long years since I read it as a young girl before I went to Europe, but I was a passionate lover of Goethe's, and if it had not been true to the man, the *real* man of the writings, I should have felt it at once. A man *can* only write the life of a man whom he understands, and of whom he understands not only one side but all the important sides, and Lewes was particularly fitted to understand Goethe. Most people seem to think any smart writer who gets all the documents about him can write of any man. The older one gets the more one realises there can be no *absolutely true* life of anyone except written by themselves, and then only if written for the eye of God. Only after long years looking back does one really understand oneself sometimes. . . . I'm still living here in this little room in the veld, in the dust and sand and mud [*mud* at De Aar !] of this great terrible plain, and yet I'm happier than I've been anywhere for twelve years. If only I could get well a little and go on with my book !

To S. C. C. S.   HANOVER, *8th Dec.*

[Writing about the house at De Aar, she asked me to put up a small room—as I did].   I want it nicely plastered up and a tiny window at the back and a door in front with a fan-light.   I want to make it into a tiny very pretty little room to put our little coffin in.   I'll make it so pretty, dear Chummie, with flowers, and no one but you and I will know it's there.   It's so long been a dream of mine to have a little stand.   [Baby's and Nita's coffins lay in this room until I buried them in Sept. 1919 in the cement grave in my garden.   See p. 394 of the *Life.*]

CHAPTER X

LETTERS WRITTEN FROM 1908 TO 1911

1908

To EDWARD CARPENTER.   DE AAR, *March.*

It's very strange the sympathy I feel with the Japs, and have always felt. It increases with all I know of them. That love of the past men and women and of your own dead. Ever since I was a child I've always thought if I had my ideal house there would be one room set apart where I would have the pictures of my dead and put flowers before them and anything that was beautiful to me. And I could go and sit there in quiet with them every day ; it would be like a chapel—the only chapel I can think of— God, the whole life, doesn't need a chapel—the sky is his roof. And I would have remembrances of all my animals that I have loved so utterly there. Buddhism is so much more wide and satisfying than Christianity can ever be because it takes in the animal world, and *sees* that all life is one.

To S. C. C. S.   MATJESFONTEIN, 2 5*th Mar.*

Ruskin's a curious antidote to this commercial, striving, self-seeking, individualistic world. Man is not meant to live striving against his fellows, but living in an organised union with them. It is right and not wrong that we can feel no restfulness in this life ; that we ask ourselves " Is life worth living ? " and say " What do I live for ? " One never feels that if one is living with and for others, because the deep instinct for unity with our fellows is satisfied. That is why the Kaffir is happy in his tribe, [why] a poor miserable looking creature knocking about in one of our

276

ndividualistic modern towns, organically united to nothing,
[is not]. For *us* of course life in South Africa, and especially
up-country, is abnormally and horribly isolated. The Boer
has his Church, the one large impersonal interest that
unites him with his fellows and gives him an object to live
for and sacrifice himself for ; every time the church-bell
rings it is the call to a common life with his fellow men.
—— very well expressed this idea when he said how much
one lost by not being of the same religion as the mass of
people in your society because you could not weekly gather
together with those sharing your deepest convictions in an
act which was the common expression of them. I think
this deep craving for union of thought and feeling with the
mass of our fellows and this endless sense of want when we
have it not is one of the deepest elements making for growth
and advance ; but we must not seek for its satisfaction by
trying to step back to a lower level of intellectual or emotional
growth than that which we have gained, but endure the
craving, till, far in the future—or never—we find our own.

To S. C. C. S.   MATJESFONTEIN, *2nd April.*

This morning I was on the balcony [of the hotel] and
saw the train come in with two engines and smoke flying,
and all going, and I suddenly found myself singing and
dancing and clapping my hands, just as I always used to
in the old days when I saw the train at full speed—so now
I know I'm better. Life is such an awful delight to me if the
physical and mental pressure is lifted a little. I think Dot
has the same sort of feeling. " Oh, how beautiful to be
alive ! " Your mother has sent me a sweet little gold safety
pin for my birthday. I don't think I can tell you how I
prize it.

To Mrs. FRANCIS SMITH.   MATJESFONTEIN, *9th April.*

. . . It's funny to me to think of your having the little
son christened. It's to me quite as savage an institution
as a Kaffir witch-doctor weaving a spell to keep away the
evil eye : and so un-Jesus-like. But then all Christianity,
so called, is. To *me* Jesus was a poor working-man socialist
of genius, a sort of Keir Hardie !

To S. C. C. S.   MATJESFONTEIN, 4*th May*

One day, when Edward Carpenter dies, they will discover there was a great spiritual force among them.

> And did you once hear Shelley speak,
> And did you see him plain ? . . .

Do you know that poem of Browning's ?   After all, what a
little thing is fame !   To have loved and been loved and made
something happy is the whole of life.

To Mrs. FRANCIS SMITH.   MATJESFONTEIN, 7*th May.*

. . . The Cape girl is so bound to think that all
persons who are not quite young are narrow, bigoted, dull :
very good and virtuous perhaps—but utterly dull and dead.
It rises from the fact that suddenly, during the last 15 or
16 years, an entirely new type of education for women
has grown up ; the *young* Cape girl is 20th century ; her
mother and aunts are early Victorian ; quite a century old.
So there has suddenly grown up nearly the lapse of a full
century between one generation and the other ; and South
African girls must find it hard to picture a woman over 50
as young and liberal in spirit as themselves.

To S. C. C. S.   MATJESFONTEIN, 8*th May.*

It has been such a glorious wonderful day here.   Even a
bit of white wall with the sunlight falling on it, or a stone
has been beautiful, and a trail of smoke from the chimney
I see from my window has been lovely.   Anything *more*
beautiful there could not be on earth. . . .   Just as no one
who didn't live through the horror and oppression of Martial
Law in this country can dream what it was ; so, no one
who did not *live* through it can ever know the joy, and hope,
and passion of enthusiasm with which we worked in those
years in the eighties.   I was talking about it with Keir
Hardie and tears came into both our eyes when we spoke
of it.   But it was not for nothing.   The solid, stolid (call
it sordid if you will), but *real* advance in the condition of
the working classes in England is the result of that move-

ment, begun and carried on almost entirely by a small handful of men and women mostly of the " upper " classes and all of ability. It was the brilliant sunrise, without which there could not have been any day. Of course, Ed. Carpenter's book touches us in a way it can't others, just because it brings us back to that time—"All we have dreamed or hoped or willed of good shall exist."

To S. C. C. S.   MATJESFONTEIN, 18*th May.*

I wonder if you would some day perhaps have time, on a Sunday afternoon or morning, say, to do something for me ; to read over my little chapter " Fireflies in the Dark " [in *From Man to Man*], and tell me quite truthfully, without fear of hurting me, if you *find it interesting*. I am so afraid I have become so subtle in my modes of thought, I have thought so much about some impersonal things and care so much for them, that others may find them very *un*interesting. . . . I live so much alone and think so much that I am afraid sometimes I have lost touch with the intellectual artistic reader.

To MRS. FRANCIS SMITH.   DE AAR, 2*nd June.*

. . . It often has seemed to me that there is a form of danger for delicate women. I can't enter fully into the matter because from the impersonal standpoint there's so much I have to say about it I could write a book about the matter in all its aspects. I mean that when a woman is delicate, suffers *horribly* and *continually*, so that to most of those about her it is an understood thing she should always be suffering, and the mightiest love takes it as part of the thing that has to be, then the one person, who has always to interest themselves *actively* in that physical condition and try to relieve it, may become a danger. They alone seem to *enter* the life of suffering, they alone seem to understand, and the woman is apt to forget that the man has had hundreds of other patients in just that relation to themselves, that many of them make their fortunes and reputations (as many priests and parsons do) by the influence they get over women in their times of weakness and suffering. This may be

. . . I have just had a wire from dear old General Butler ; to-day he has landed in Cape Town. He is the one Englishman we South Africans really love ; I mean among public men.

To F. W. PETHICK LAWRENCE. (*Undated*.)

Did I tell you dear Keir Hardie came to see us at De Aar ? It was the most red-letter day in my life since you and your wife were at Hanover.

To MRS. FRANCIS SMITH. DE AAR, *Sept.*

. . . I have been re-reading that *Elizabeth and her German Garden* you sent me. It's very curious that I like the book so much that I've read it three or four times—it's like *Pickwick Papers*. I can read it and her other book when I can't read anything else hardly, and yet curiously enough I don't like the woman herself. I feel I should be afraid of her, as I always am of those sharp clever women, who don't mind how they hurt people. I don't think I like " clever " people very much, unless there is something much deeper behind the cleverness. I like a stupid loving person better. . . . Isn't it strange that no great artist has ever translated into the common language the meaning of continual suffering disease to the human soul. Heine did it a little in his wonderful way. You once, in a letter to me, expressed better than anyone else has ever [done] that awful solitariness and aloofness from all things existing that certain forms of intense physical anguish leave the soul in ; and it is that solitude of the soul and not the mere physical suffering that is so awful. The mental anguish of the mother who loses her child, of the lover who is betrayed—almost all forms of purely mental anguish unconnected with the individual's own body—have been expressed, or have sought to find expression, in art ; but the awful anguish of a *soul, striving against its own body*, has found no expression. Is it not because this doesn't so very often happen ? I mean in most cases, where physical pain and disease are very intense, there comes, mercifully, a deadness of the nerves and brain, a stolid absence of power to feel or desire almost. Only in a terrible exceptional case like yours, in some forms of diabetes and heart disease and asthma, etc., does the brain keep all its clearness and the nervous system seem almost sharper and keener than in health ! The time before last [that] I got violent influenza, which of course settled on my lungs, according to the doctors I was very bad—but what *we* know as suffering I didn't have at all. From the second day I just lay in bed, my head ached and I didn't want the light to shine in my eyes and I wanted poultices ; but when I look back at all the three weeks there was *no anguish !* I wasn't comfortable or happy, but then I didn't feel much of anything, and it was nice to go to sleep ! I think in the Gods' mercy much of what is called human disease and suffering is like that. But oh, it isn't all like that. I have seen such terrible things in a hospital of a soul all alone and keep fighting the fight. But I think we can comfort ourselves by thinking that such suffering is rare ; that, with great physical disorganisation, comes generally deadness and indifference to life even, only a wish for rest. It's so blessed to think this. Do you remember Heine's wonderful poem written on his mattress-grave, where he fights with that other man, and that other man is himself.

To Miss EMILY HOBHOUSE.   DE AAR, *3rd Oct.*

It seems so sad that you are really going away from Africa, and yet I feel it's best. I too would go if I could. That is, I feel I could do much more in Europe than I can here. No one needs me here now except the natives—and that is indeed hard and stern work that calls to all the bravest souls in South Africa for many years to come. . . . We shall have an uphill fight here to rouse and educate our women to their public duties. You see, we are just 60 years behind Europe in this, as in so many other matters. I wish you were coming this way on your journey home. It is a noble page of a woman work that you are closing as you go away. . . .

To Miss E. HOBHOUSE.   (*Undated.* ? DE AAR, 1908.)

. . . When my husband comes down for the long session I shall try to find some cheap quiet little place in the

Eastern Province where I can settle down and try to get on with my writing, near Healdtown, the great mission station where I loved as a child. Perhaps, if I find nice quarters, you would be interested to come for a week or two, and see a bit more of our natives.

I am so sick of Party Politics! My friend Havelock Ellis was right when he said that after the war South Africa wouldn't for fifty years be a place for a civilised man to live in. If it wasn't that I can't leave my darling husband, I would take the next steamer for Europe and not return till they brought my body back to bury it among the mountains where I was so happy as a girl. I do so fully understand how Miss Molteno and Miss Greene *can't* return to this country. I never as [? ask] them to, much as I long for them.

To Mrs. Francis Smith.   De Aar, *6th Nov.*

. . . Long ago when I was a girl of 15, a girl whom I had known very slightly all my life and who was four or five years older than I, about 19, died rather suddenly of fever. I had never liked her particularly and did not know much of her, but her death was a milestone in my life marking off what had been from what came after, so it seemed to bring me face to face with death. I think her death struck me so deeply just because she didn't seem to have much intellect or very deep feeling, but [was] so pretty, so bright, so full of the joy of life. None of the deaths of the people I loved best in the world have seemed so *deadly!* When my friend, that beautiful English officer [Capt. Marriott], died a few years ago it didn't seem to me death at all ; his wide spirit, always living out of himself and beyond himself, seemed to me simply set free, gone back to the infinite for which it had always yearned.

1909

To Mrs. Haldane Murray.   Matjesfontein, *3rd Jan.*

Miss Molteno thinks I am so wrong not to go to Europe where I am so much better and could finish my work instead of staying here in this hot climate which doesn't suit me. She doesn't realise I *can't* leave my husband and go where, if he were ill or in need of me, I couldn't get to him. . . . I don't think any woman who is not married can realise all a woman feels to her husband. I have loved my two brothers and my dear men and women friends so intensely, but yet the feeling is different. They all seem to be other persons ; he seems to be your real self for whom you would give up and sacrifice everything.

To S. C. C. S.   MATJESFONTEIN, *6th Jan*.

I have been watching a little ant this morning for more than half an hour. I think I never loved such a tiny creature so much. It was trundling along a dried ball from a mimosa tree three times in bulk as large as itself. I followed it for nearly 100 yards, being blown over and over by the wind, regaining its feet, never leaving hold of its ball, climbing over stones and sticks and through grasses till it got it to the hole. I never knew one's heart could go out in such a curious way to such a small speck of matter.

To S. C. C. S.   CAPE TOWN, *7th June*.

You know I feel to anything that is oppressed or hurt just exactly as I felt to my little baby. I was lying on the bed and thinking of her, how I held her after she was dead, and then for the first time I realised how absolutely *identical* my feeling for her was with that I feel for anything oppressed. It is a feeling deeper-seated in one's nature than all argument or self-interest. I suppose that those people who haven't got it can [? can't] understand it. I'm lonely here but dear Anna [Purcell] is coming to-morrow. She and I are going to see a bioscope and she is going to sleep with me here in your bed. Isn't that nice ? Close personal affection takes the place to me of all sports and amusements and dancing and all the things most people want. I'd rather live in a little ganger's cottage on eight pounds a month all my life with someone who loved and wanted me than in a palace with ten thousand a year and books and music and travel thrown in.

To S. C. C. S.   CAPE TOWN, 13*th June.*

That is an interesting talk of Jerome's on marriage in the *Nation* you sent me. It takes, in quite another way as to expression but still, the same the view I take. The sacrifices which both man and woman are compelled to make in marriage, in the doubling of your before free and single personality, with all the excitements and pleasure of exercising sex attractions and arranging your life and action for your single good pleasure : that—unless deeper than all this the need of the closest companionship and permanence and a delight in sacrifice for the thing you " love," as the mother feels it for her child and the true friend for the true friend—must of necessity be a failure, because *this* is what marriage has permanently to offer, as *nothing else has.* The excitement of the sexual chase and capture, the *passion* of courtship, must of necessity be always evanescent. It can no more continue than a man's desire to reach the winning post *can* continue when he has won it and gained the first prize ; and the man or woman in whom *this* is the prime necessity should never marry, or marriage must be of necessity a tragic failure, not only to the one who feels so but to the other. The tragedy of life rises because, when the desire of chase and possession is on them, man and woman will often not think : " Is my love for that creature so great that to share everything with it, to try and beautify its life, to feel that till death I can share their joy and sorrow, their sickness and health, that they and their life are *part of me,* will compensate me for what I lose ? " I believe some people, interesting and charming in many ways, are quite incapable of the " love " which alone can make married life workable. My great desire for everyone I love, man and woman, is that they should feel this love and find this companionship ; but I believe many people are absolutely incapable of it. It is not ——'s fault that his wife spends all her time dyeing her hair and painting herself in trying to attract young men, and spends all his money, which he pours out generously at her feet, in this aim. It would have been so whoever she had married. I used to think that every sad marriage was only a mistake because the wrong people had got together ; but for some people there is no right person, in the sense of being truly married; they could never love anything as well as themselves. As ——'s wife once wrote me in a wonderful letter : " It's not his fault we are not happy ; what he wants is love and companionship ; what I want is change and excitement." Even that man [not her husband] she seemed so desperately in love with she said she knew she would not love always. It's a strange world.

To Mrs. Francis Smith.   De Aar, 2 5*th July*.

. . . Before I was born my mother lost two children, a little son of five about six months before, and a little one of two years three months before I was born. My mother never cared for her children especially her daughters as soon as they were older, say eight or nine. But of her tiny babies and children she was *passionately* fond. She was almost distracted when the little one died three months before my birth, and said she found no comfort in anything but walking up and down by herself behind the church which stood near the little mission house in which I was born. It's curious, as all my life since I was almost a baby of two or three, I've always had such a passion for walking up and down. One of the first things I can remember, when I can't have been more than three, was walking up and down in a passage with cocoanut matting on the floor and making stories to myself : and I can remember the other children laughing at me and my mother telling them they were to leave me alone. Can you remember things when you were very small ? I and my sister Ettie can remember things quite well that happened when we were two, and some of my family can't remember anything before they were five, and one brother *nothing* before he was seven.

To Mrs. C. A. F. Rhys Davids.   De Aar, 20*th Aug*.

Thank you for the pamphlet ; and thank you much more for your wish to dedicate the book to me. In two ways I shall feel it an especial gift. In one, because of my strong feeling about Buddha's teaching, that it was of a higher grade in many directions than that of any other religious teacher ; in the other, because you impressed me

so much. I had two very dear friends. They became Christian Scientists and were very happy. One was always writing to me to say, if I would only let her, she could cure me entirely of my heart disease. Well last year the other dropped dead suddenly of heart disease. If they could have cured me why couldn't they have cured him? —he was not one 20th as bad as I was! If he couldn't cure himself and she couldn't cure him, how could she have cured me? When I wrote to her about it she said, O death wasn't a reality, he only seemed to be dead; and so got out of it! But she is one of the noblest and best women that ever lived and her Christian Science makes her very happy.

To Mrs. FRANCIS SMITH. CAPE TOWN, *Sunday Night, Oct.*

My darling, you've seemed so with me in thought all day. I've seemed to feel you about me. The thought of you has comforted me so. Only my friend Edward Marriott, that English officer who died about 5 years ago, ever seemed so near me when he wasn't, as you do. The strange thing was that after he was dead I had that consciousness of his pure beautiful presence more even than when he was alive. I didn't *think* of him, I felt him near me. I don't believe in a *personal* life after death, but, if there were such a thing, those who have been drawn to each other, not by circumstance or even by passion, but by a deep natural sympathy and likeness would be likely to find each other again, if any could. . . . On the other end of the table is a huge brown paper parcel which contains my novel that I love so, much of it unrevised and no good if I died. I've been sorting my papers to-day and it's made me feel so hopeless, all that mass of half finished work. All my life seems such a failure, but I've lived and I've loved many beautiful things; and had even more love than I was worthy of. . . . I am sending you the little Prelude [to *From Man to Man*]. Send it back when you've read it. I've got to revise it yet. It's just as it came to me many years ago one day on the Riviera. I *know* you'll understand it. I love it specially because it came to me in such a curious way. I wrote the rough draft of this novel years and years ago when I was quite a young girl, before I went to England [before 1881]. In England

I was too absorbed in social problems ever to read it over even.   One day, I think it was in the winter of 1888, I was on the Riviera at Alassio; I was sitting at my dear old desk writing an article on the Bushmen and giving a description of their skulls ;—when suddenly, in an instant, the whole of this little Prelude *flashed* on me.   You know those folded up views of places that one buys ; you take hold of one end and all the pictures unfold one after the other as quick as light.   That was how it *flashed* on me.   I started up and paced about the room.   I felt absolutely astonished. I hadn't thought of my novel for months, I hadn't looked at it for years.   I'd never dreamed of writing a Prelude to it. —I just sat down and wrote it out.   And do you know what I found out—after I'd written it ?—that it's a picture in small, a kind of allegory, of the life of the woman in the book ! !   It's one of the strangest things I know of.   My mind must have been working at it *unconsciously*, though I knew nothing of it—otherwise how did it come ?   Don't show the Prelude to anyone, and don't tell anyone about it.   It's only for you.   Good night, dear one.   Olive.

To Mrs. FRANCIS SMITH.   CAPE TOWN, *5th Nov.*

. . . Dear one, don't you see it's not the vote they are fighting for ?   It's *freedom* for women !   It's the fact, that, in some cause they believe to be of benefit to woman and promoting human freedom, there *are* found women ready to fight, to face ridicule, abuse, suffering and even death if necessary, that is so grand !   If *I* didn't believe in the vote being of *use*, the fight would be equally glorious to me ! If it put the vote off in England for twenty years, the freedom of action they have given an example of to all women, makes their fight of infinite value.

If a race or class is willing to dare and do and die for freedom they will ultimately be free—their *spirits are free now*.   The true freedom of woman is something that cannot be given her, that she has to work out *within herself*.

To Mrs. FRANCIS SMITH.   MUIZENBERG, *14th Dec.*

. . . Did you get my little Prelude [to *From Man to Man*] ?   Please return it, darling.   In the novel, when the little girl grows up she spends some of the most important moments of her life at Muizenberg close to this spot. It's so curious that I feel as though some great tragic events of my own life had taken place here. I walk again and again to the spot where years ago " Farmer Peck's " little thatched house used to stand, and think " Yes, here Rebekah walked." I don't think any one else can have an idea how real and how " out of oneself," something not made up by oneself but which one *simply knows*, all these people are.

1910

To S. C. C. S.   (?) MUIZENBERG, 4*th Jan.*

Oh my love, my darling, I love you so. You will always know that I have loved you like nothing else on earth—that I wanted to make life so beautiful to you when I came to you. I've never really wanted anything else in the world since I knew you. Goodbye, dear one, my own man, the self that is more to me than myself. [She was in pain and ill.]

To S. C. C. S.   (?) MUIZENBERG, 26*th Feb.*

Mrs. —— is dead. It's strange that the death of a great beautiful person never affects me so painfully as one of quite the other type [as she held this woman to be]. Great, beautiful, silent death doesn't seem to belong to them.

To MRS. RHYS DAVIDS.   DE AAR, 12*th April.*

I have been so ill for a long time I have not been able to write a real letter as I would like and tell you how much I value your book and its dedication. It is so strange how entirely modern so much of the book [is] though that is not true of all real books, they belong to no special time.

I have a strong abiding interest in all that concerns India, and a special personal interest now. We are hunting about the Indians here as if they were wild beasts and not men. I don't know if you have noted the treatment of our Indians in the Transvaal.

To Mrs. Francis Smith.   De Aar, 19*th April.*

. . . A friend of mine in England has sent me a book called *The Diary of a Lost One,* translated from the German. Have you read it ? It has interested me a great deal. It's such a terribly true picture of the soul of a woman who is by *nature* lost, lost to all that is good and beautiful in life from birth. One meets such women among so called " respectable " women of fashion. They are just as much " lost " as if they were called prostitutes. I cannot understand that it awakens sympathy in them—in me it awakens only horror and terror. It's our absolute selfishness and hypocrisy that are so terrible. It's not what people do ; it's the why and how that matters. I do not believe that all prostitutes are so terrible as that woman. From my knowledge of prostitutes I should say that *no clever* intelligent woman ever becomes one unless she is inherently selfish and bad, but weak, *stupid,* very *stupid,* women may continually become prostitutes out of sheer stupidity. When I read that book there come to my mind so many fast fashionable women I have known who are so like her. They are only not prostitutes because life has never put any pressure upon [them]. Rather than a life of grim toil and dullness they would all be prostitutes. The terrible thing is that more than half the men in the world are prostitutes, and pay no price for being so. The real reason why I want the emancipation of women is that this hideous thing may end. I meant to do so much in my life to help. I have learnt so much, and now I shall never use it.

To Mrs. Francis Smith.   De Aar, 5*th May.*

. . . Every woman who is thirty or over ought certainly to have her own " little foot of earth." People never realise as long as a woman lives at home that she is grown up, if she remains unmarried. It's only four months now, dear, and then the little one will be with you ! You will miss its closer connection with yourself, but oh the joy of having it safe in your arms. I never forget that wonderfully vivid dream of mine when you came in the green cloak and put such a beautiful baby in my arms (I was lying on the bed), and looked so radiant and full of joy. I am reading Milton a little as I've nothing else to read. I read him a great deal when I was a child aloud to my mother while she was cooking and doing needle work, and got to love him even when I couldn't understand all. I think one should always try to let children read and learn by heart the best poetry while they are quite young. One loses one's taste for inferior things if once one has known the best, and children feel so much more and understand so much more than people dream ; most people grow stupid and blunt off between eleven and eighteen. There is many a man who would have got to love and understand Milton at ten who couldn't possibly understand him, reading him for the first time at twenty. If I had a child I should mainly educate it up to ten or eleven on the best poetry.

To Mrs. Anna Purcell.　　　　　　　De Aar, *6th Aug.*

[Gilbert Murray's translation of Euripides' *Iphigenia*].
　—How strange it is that, after two thousand years, one should be able to lie on one's bed amid the wind and dust of De Aar and thrill at the touch of the thoughts that were in that Greek's head so long, long since passed away and turned to dust.

To Mrs. Anna Purcell.　　　　　　　　　　(*Undated.*)

A superb translation in verse. [Gilbert Murray's translation of Euripides' *The Trojan Women*.]
Euripides is to me much greater than Shakespeare. If one only knew Greek well enough to read him and enjoy him in Greek ! I wish I had been born in the fourth century (b.c.) in Greece, though it must be very fine to be in Europe (now ?).

To Mrs. Haldane Murray.　　　　　　De Aar, *7th Oct.*

It is very terrible this having to leave my home and husband for months every year in a country like Africa where there is no provision for people wanting change and fresh air except at the sea-side where I find it very difficult to live.

I live principally on milk, sour milk mostly, and a little sweet, so if I could buy bread I could easily do for myself. [This is not so ; far from it.]

The problem of where to go in the summer is so trying that, if it were not for my husband, I should leave South Africa for ever. My book on the Woman Question will be out in a few months' time.

To Miss LOUIE ELLIS.   DE AAR, 12*th Oct.*

. . . I wish often it were possible for me just once to visit England again so that I could see my friends and take up the threads of their lives again and understand all about them. Has Havelock changed much ? I can't bear to think of his growing old. As I grow older I cling more and more to the friends of my youth. When I was young I used to say I felt mostly that my nature needed to *give* love and help to others ; I seemed to care less than other people for receiving it ; but now I feel so grateful for every tiniest little bit of love anyone gives me.

To Mrs. FRANCIS SMITH.   DE AAR, 22*nd Oct.*

. . . We went to a Boer farm where there was a wedding (oh, such a quaint, grim wedding !) ; my husband had to go for business and said I might go with him. We drove for three hours and only once saw a house and twice a small flock of sheep till we got there. The mother and three other elderly ladies were sitting on one long sofa ; they must all have been over 200 lbs. in weight ! ! The eldest son, a huge man of 6 foot four inches in height, is dying of heart disease, he has been dying for three months, so huge, and bloated, and blue ; they have tapped him but it doesn't help. Such a wild curse against God came into my heart when I saw his anguish-stricken face fighting for breath. No creature has a right to make another suffer so. But there is no God, in the narrow, personal sense ; if there were he would be a devil ; only a great terrible mystery of which we can and do know nothing. We must fight it to the end ; it will beat us at length, but we must fight it as long as we can. When you saw that room full of strong, determined, iron-willed women, you understood all the South African war afresh, the glory of that struggle of a handful of folk against a mighty folk, and also the narrowness and hardness of South African life.

To Mrs. FRANCIS SMITH.

PORTLOCK, NEAR GRAAFF REINET, 15*th Nov.*

. . . This is a beautiful wild solitary place on the very tops of the mountains. It is bare like a Yorkshire moor just about the house, but if you walk a few hundred or a few thousand yards you come to the edge of the mountains everywhere and look down into deep "kloofs" [ravines] and over hundreds of miles of hills and valleys stretching away like the sea. I've been here five days, and have spent most of my time in sleeping to make up for the long long time when I haven't slept. Just about the house is a garden of fruit trees and roses, roses everywhere climbing into the trees and over everything. The people [the Murrays] are so sweet and kind to me. If only I can get better and work here it will be splendid. Just now I'm only trying to sleep. We are thirty miles from the nearest post-office, and twelve or fourteen miles from the nearest farms, but then we can't see them because they are over the mountains. So we just are all to ourselves. There is that strange beautiful peacefulness about this place that nothing I know on earth but a solitary African farm has. You wonder why you ever worried about anything, or why you ever minded living or why anyone should mind dying.

To Mrs. FRANCIS SMITH.

PORTLOCK, GRAAFF REINET, 20*th Nov.*

. . . Have you read Gilbert Murray's translations of Euripides' plays? They are so splendid. They are a revelation and I believe must bring one *very* close to the Greek original. A friend has just sent me his *Hippolytus*. Nothing of Shakespeare comes within a thousand miles of touching me as Euripides does. It is his outlook on life, that fierce, restrained questioning of the mystery of existence, and also his deep understanding of woman's position that touches one so.

To Mrs. FRANCIS SMITH.

PORTLOCK, GRAAFF REINET, 12*th Dec.*

. . . If ever anyone were to try and write my life the thing they would never understand would be the dominating, over-mastering *horror* I have of coming into contact with human creatures from whom I shrink and whom I feel false. Whole pages of my life would be quite incomprehensible if one didn't understand this. There is just ——, and in a lesser degree two or three men and two or three women to whom I feel this ; I just want never to see them, never to hear their names, never to speak to them, never to write to them, never to remember that God made them in this world. I left England and came out to this country the first time I came out [end of 1889] mainly to escape one woman, who would persist in coming to see me and writing to me though I *told her what I felt to her*, and returned all her letters unopened. It's not what people have done to you ; it's what you feel they *are*, you shrink from. They form a blur on the whole of humanity for you. Fortunately they are so very few, and there are so many brave and noble and true natures. I seem so fortunate in my life and to have met so many. That's why it's so nice being on this farm, the people are all so simple and open and true. There's not a person here whom I don't like, even the servants and the over-seer's wife (a Boer woman who weighs over 400 pounds !). Life isn't beautiful unless you can love and go out to every human creature about you ; it's so terrible there should be anyone you can't love and trust.

1911

To Mrs. FRANCIS SMITH.

PORTLOCK, GRAAFF REINET, 9*th Jan.*

. . . I've had a letter that's made me so glad. A man who lives on a farm [Lelie Kloof] high up in the mountains, a farm where I lived for a year and a half as a girl and was so well, has offered to let me come and board with them. I am going there soon for a month before I go back to De Aar. I have the most ridiculous feeling that if I once get there I shall be quite well and a young girl again. I shall go away by myself on the dear rocks by the little river and dance and sing and throw up my arms from fullness of life and inward joy, like I used to when I was a little Boer school-teacher living there alone and used to escape so joyfully too, when my school was over, to rejoice by myself. Of course I'm not such a fool as to *think* it can be the same ; but I *feel* as if it would be. I can't realise it ! To be at Lelie Kloof again.   That's the little farm I've always wanted to buy.

To Mrs. FRANCIS SMITH.

PORTLOCK, GRAAFF REINET, 10*th Jan.*

. . . I've just got all the proofs of my *Woman and Labour* book and am very busy revising them.

The preface is *terrible*—Will was quite right about it— I could re-write it now in a few hours and make a good thing of it ; but I fear —— may say I've been altering the book, so I won't. I'm so awfully sorry to let it go as it is. I must have been *very* ill when I wrote it—I can realise how ill when I read it.

To S. C. C. S.   PORTLOCK, GRAAFF REINET, 11*th Jan.*

[She had written from Portlock, Graaff Reinet, to the occupier of Lelie Kloof about visiting that farm, and he had replied he would board her and let her have a sitting room and a bedroom.]   Won't it be lovely to be at old Lelie Kloof again ? I *feel* as if I should be a young, young girl if I go there and dance about on the rocks in the river and throw up my arms and shout from sheer excess of life and joy like I used to in the old days ! ! Of course, I'm not such a fool as I *think* I shall, but I *feel* as if I would !

I've just been reading Shakespeare's *Measure for Measure.* How pure and beautiful and sweet he is, but *broadly human,* but with such a high sense of honour always. Never in one instance does he countenance falsehood or disloyalty between human souls.

To S. C. C. S.   PORTLOCK, 16*th Jan.*

[Enclosing a letter.] It's rather interesting about *The Hunter* being read to Herbert Spencer just before he died.

[The correspondent says, " Shortly before Mr. Herbert Spencer's death, I had the opportunity of having *The Hunter* read to him."]

To S. C. C. S.   LELIE KLOOF, *Sunday morning* [? 19*th Mar.*].

I got here last night. I got your letter in Cradock. I shall be home the end of this week. The air here is splendid, even better than I had dreamed. The place about the house has changed utterly even since we were here [Sept. 1896, see *Life*]. All the trees in the garden are gone, all the poplar bush is cut down ; only the beautiful hills and the splendid air are the same. The air is finer than I thought. The road up is almost untravellable. I'm longing so terribly to be home. I will certainly be back at the end of the week.

To Mrs. HALDANE MURRAY.   DE AAR, 2*nd April.*

Just fancy, I got a long most sympathetic letter from old John X. Merriman about my book [*Woman and Labour*]. It did astonish me ! He says it's " very fine " ! I was quite touched by it. But he says he doesn't think I'll realise my hopes, " man has always been a brute, and is a brute, and will always be a brute." I of course don't agree with him. I wish he knew some of my beautiful men friends in England as I know them. [Merriman is an unswerving opponent of female suffrage.]

I found the air at Lelie Kloof wonderful, as good as sanatogen ; but I couldn't stay there under present conditions ; one would have to build a new house, etc. The man will have to sell the farm some day, he'll farm himself out.

To Mrs. PETHICK LAWRENCE.   DE AAR, 29*th April.*

I am a very mild woman, but I would scalp my dearest friend if they tried to alter two lines in any book I had written. I would forgive them if they tried to cut off my head or my nose, but I draw the line at that. [Some woman wanted her book (*Woman and Labour*) altered.]

To Mrs. HALDANE MURRAY.   DE AAR, 28*th April.*

I went to the Station [De Aar] yesterday to meet my old friend Mrs. Drew, old Gladstone's daughter. She looks very sad and tired. She is coming to spend a few days with me here. . . . The Governor [Herbert Gladstone] and his wife were there too. She's a very nice little woman, so girlish looking ; but whenever I looked at him I thought of Con Lytton and the forced feeling ! He invited me to go and stay with them at Pretoria, but I told him Pretoria didn't suit my health, which is quite true.

To Mrs. HALDANE MURRAY.   DE AAR, 31*st May.*

I am going to the Victoria Falls on the 2nd June with my brother Will's wife, the two girls and Oliver. My sweet old brother Will has invited me and is paying for my ticket that I may have the chance of being with the children before they go [to England]. I am looking forward to it so greatly, if I can only keep well.

To S. C. C. S.   ZAMBESI FALLS, 5*th June.*

We got here this morning, dear. The journey was delightful. You know how I love the train. The Kalahari is the most beautiful part of the journey, wide wide spreads of lower bush with tall camelthorn and other trees just here and there. The trees are so glorious all the way from Bulawayo, not dense dark forest, but beautiful park-like scenery. We could see the mist [the " smoke " of the Falls] from far, miles away. The Hotel is a curious pretty place, the separate houses built on poles to keep them from the damp. There is only one post a week here.

To S. C. C. S.   ZAMBESI FALLS, 6*th June.*

We saw the Falls yesterday. I walked all through the Rain Forest and past the Danger Point. Oh, Cron, no words can describe it, can give the faintest idea of it. I was glad the wet rain [from the spray ?] was falling on my face that no one could see I was crying. You must see it, dear one. There is nothing like it on earth. We have just had break-

fast and are now starting in a steam launch to go to Kanda-
har [Island] *up* the stream. We shall be back at one to
lunch. This afternoon I am going *quite* alone through the
Rain Forest to see it all.

To S. C. C. S.   ZAMBESI FALLS, *7th June.*

We went up in a motor boat on Tuesday morning, a
small motor boat with 15 people in it beside the man who
worked it and a native boy. When we were returning,
about half a mile above the Falls, the motor broke down and
we began drifting to the Falls. We must all have gone over
if a canoe had not come down the river. They saw our
state and the natives rowed hard and came back with 6 large
rowing boats and got us off and towed the steamer [motor
boat] back to shore. . . . We went up in a canoe to-day.
. . . No one will go in the motor boats any more. We went
to see a hippopotamus that was shot yesterday, a huge
beast ; all the natives were skinning it.

To HAVELOCK ELLIS. VICTORIA FALLS HOTEL, ZAMBESI, *June.*

Dear Havelock boy, we leave to-morrow this most
lovely and beautiful and wonderful of earthly sights. No
pictures, nothing that has ever been said of it, gives the
faintest conception of what this is, the vast " spirit of the
waters." A mile and a quarter of water leaping down
into the almighty chasm with the roar of thunder that sounds
for eighteen miles, and which as it falls leaps up again into
clouds of white and rainbow-tinted mists four thousand
feet high. The colours, the wild spirits of the mist, it
is that overpowers one, and *fills one with joy.* One cries
but only from happiness.

We were nearly all drowned on Wednesday. The
motor boat we were in broke down and we were drifting
down on to the Falls. We were only saved by a canoe
coming past and going for help to the landing, and calling
six more canoes which took us all out and towed the boat to
land. The pluck of all the women and girls, except one
miserable old Christian, was wonderful. I must tell you all
about it some day. The curious thing is that, having been

so near death in its arms, instead of making one feel horror of it, seems to draw me much nearer to it—my Falls that I was nearly part of ! I have never loved any natural phenomenon so.

To Mrs. HALDANE MURRAY.   DE AAR, 27*th June.*

[A profession for women] does not stand in the way of marriage ; it helps towards a wise and happy marriage.

To HAVELOCK ELLIS.   DE AAR (? *June*).

No, dear, I *don't* think it's because Ibsen wrote in a small country, or amid a simple life, that his plays lack *something*. It's because his persons are so often *types*, not *individuals* ; they are not *real*. The woman in *Ghosts* is the most real. I think that's what one feels the want of, just as in much of Sir Walter Scott's writing—they are types ; though Eardly Hendry [?] and his old mother and many other of the poor persons are persons and no types, and so splendid. I don't think Ibsen ever *loved* any of his characters really, so you don't love them ; they were only pegs on which to hang actions and ideas, they weren't real men and women to him. Like Bernard Shaw's uninteresting men and women, you wouldn't care at any moment if the whole lot were drowned. Shakespeare felt his characters—they *lived* for him, and so did Euripides.

To EDWARD CARPENTER.   DE AAR, 4*th July.*

Where he [Gibbon] is valuable is in his dissection of the rise of Christianity, but above all he, and he only, paints vividly and clearly the causes which have led to the division of Europe into its present form of nations. Mommsen's *Rome*, now, teems with interesting information with regard to woman ; and all the old Greek plays and Homer, and even dear old Herodotus, pour light on the question of woman and her position in ancient times. . . . It always seemed strange to me that Gibbon seems almost to ignore the existence of woman, and certainly never touches on any problem of sex.

To EDWARD CARPENTER.   DE AAR, 16*th Sept.*

The Greeks were so wise in making the learning of poetry one of the great methods of educating young children.

To HAVELOCK ELLIS.   CAPE TOWN, *Dec.*

I believe the only remedy for the agony and suffering sex inflicts is absolute truthfulness and openness—not *after* the new relationship is formed but *before*. I do not believe a man or woman ever enters on a real sex relation with another, without knowing they are sexually attracted to one another. If it is only a few hours before there is time to tell the person whose sexual life you have for ever bound with yours what you were *feeling*. Oh, I do wish the part of my book on sex relations was not destroyed ; I can never write it again. Here is my friend ——, the one who wrote to Edith about Hinton, who thinks it's wrong for people, even if married, to have any sex relations with each other except just when they want to make a child. She says her husband feels just the same ! I would base all my sex teaching to children and young people on the beauty and sacredness and importance of sex. Sex intercourse is the great sacrament of life—he that eateth and drinketh unworthily eateth and drinketh damnation to himself ; but it may be the most beautiful sacrament between two souls without any thought of children.

orthodox Christianity that made my childhood and youth so bitter *is* fading, but in its place many other superstitions seem to spring up. They have their root on that side of human nature which wants not truth, but ease.

To Mrs. FRANCIS SMITH.   DE AAR, 13*th May.*

. . . Something interesting happened to me in Cape Town bearing on the question of teaching children Christianity. A splendid girl of about 22 was talking to me. She has studied and thought and so of course is a freethinker. She spoke with so much bitterness about her father, whom she otherwise loves passionately, because he himself, an enlightened freethinker, had allowed her to [be] brought up a Christian. She said, " I cannot, I cannot, understand how he, who loves me so and has otherwise been so tender to me, *could* let me be taught what he knew to be false and did *not believe himself*, and never hinted to me that he did not." She said how he could have saved her years of struggle and anguish, which might have ended in her moral death, if he had spoken a few words to her when she was a child. I showed her his difficulty, that, while the mother was an ordinary Christian who could have insisted on teaching them prayers and taking them to church, it was hard for *him* to speak. But I think he might even so have told them what *he* thought. Where both parents are enlightened there is of course not this difficulty. Why should a human being spend years of their life in learning what later they will have to unlearn. I agree with Havelock Ellis, that the more one teaches children morality and right doing and love for all animals and people in the world, *without* fastening it on to any system of theology, Mohammedan, Christian, Buddhist or any other, *the safer will its roots be*. I would teach children the history of all religions carefully as they grow older. Show them how all savage and primitive peoples have formed theories of the unknown, and that the priestcraft have forced them on the people, so that a man as a rule accepts the religion of his country without any thought for himself. The Greeks killed Socrates for not believing what *they* believed in, Zeus and Venus, &c. ; and the Christians killed people for not

believing Jesus was a God ; and the Catholic people [
killed people for not believing Mary was a Goddes
Show them how right it is to let everyone think what the
like where no one knows anything *sure*.   I would leave
a child quite free to choose its own theory of the unknown
when it came to ripe years.   Surely of all matters in which
an infant mind should not be forced in any direction [?this
is the one.]   Christianity, with its horrible doctrine of
a man as *God* ! ! and of vicarious atonement, darkened and
embittered my childhood, in a way perhaps a simple noble
religion like the Jewish, with its simple faith in one God,
could not do.

To HAVELOCK ELLIS.   DE AAR, *May.*

. . . My father was infinitely tenderer to us as children
and had a much greater heart than my mother.   A woman
loves her own *little* babies with a selfish animal instinct, but
as children grow up it is continually the father who gives
the widest, most sympathetic love.   And as for other
people's children, are not the words *step-mother* and *mother-
in-law* the two bitterest words in the world ?   Who farm
little babies and starve them to death ?   Women in most
cases and not men.   Who keep brothels and betray young
children and girls into a life which means disease and
generally early death, without motherhood or wifehood or
love ? Women ! . . .   I don't for one moment believe in
the moral superiority of women.   Perhaps the noblest,
most unselfish, tender woman-soul I know is Con Lytton
—but Bob Muirhead is just as good and rare in gifts
of heart.

To MRS. FRANCIS SMITH.

NEWLANDS, CAPE TOWN, 11th *June.*

Darling, I am here at Will's ; I came down last
Wednesday.   On Thursday I went out to Blauberg, that
sad wonderful place where my sister [Ettie] died, and saw
the beloved face for the last time lying in the little room
where she went through her 7 months of mortal agony, with
its two windows looking out on the wild sea she loved so.

Adela, you know what is so strange is that, since she has died, even the memory of the sad agonised woman has passed from me, and I live always in thought with my beautiful little girl sister whom I worshipped with that peculiar worship a younger sister sometimes gives to an older. I see her often as a radiant girl of 18, with her long golden hair and passionate life and activity. It's been a wonderful life of labour and self-sacrifice, and of marvellous intellectual gifts left undeveloped. Your face always reminded me of her. Dear, the lines of agony were so terrible in the dead face ; but it was so superbly grand !

Last Sunday we buried her. We had had four days of unbroken rain and wind, but Sunday rose one of those superb days we only have at the Cape when there has been rain. All the world was green and glittering and the sky and sea intense blue. Will and I and Lyndall and his eldest son Will motored out at 11 to a place called Milnerton about 8 miles from here. There we met the dear body coming from Blauberg on an old open African ox-wagon, such as she and I always loved. All the family gathered there, and we put it on the hearse and drove after it in carriages to a place called Salt River through the beautiful green fields and sunshine. At Salt River all the wonderful crowd of the people she had helped and befriended, and thousands of the poor coloured people she had loved so and worked among, met us. There were about 10 thousand in the procession, and we travelled slowly the mile and a half to the cemetery at Maitland through green trees and fields. There were old men who could hardly walk, and parents had brought their young children that when they grew up they might say they had walked behind her.

It was her wish no one should wear mourning for her, and nearly all the women and girls were in white, many carrying little bunches of flowers. The most touching thing to me was when the poor coloured people filed past the grave each dropping in their little poor bunches of flowers till the coffin was deep buried. The whole took so long we did not get back till seven in the evening. It was strangely beautiful : quite different from other funerals, with their terrible black and sadness. At the very time she was being buried, my husband's mother, who died here on Saturday, was being buried in another graveyard [at Muizenberg].

To Mrs. Francis Smith.   De Aar (? *July*).

. . . I feel that the woman's movement is so vast that we all have quite distinct work to do in it. I induced my niece Lyndall Schreiner to give up being secretary to the Woman's Enfranchisement League in Cape Town, which took nearly all her time, and study law. If she passes her law exams well and gets admitted to the bar here, and still more if she becomes a great lawyer and one day, perhaps, a judge, she will be doing far more to raise the standing of women in South Africa than if she led the franchise clubs. I feel that I could do 20 or even 50 times as much for woman's freedom by writing if I were well enough than by joining any societies. A friend of mine here who is saving and economising and working hard on her farm that she may give her daughters a good education and send them to Europe to study for profession is doing more to free women in Africa than any other woman I know here. If I, personally, had to devote myself to working for woman's emancipation in some special branch, I should devote myself to aiding women to enter professions and business, and to reform in dress. But that is not to say that the vote and dozens of other things are not as important and more so. I sympathise with all the women of earth, in whatever direction they are working, who are helping to do away with artificial distinctions of sex. I hate prize fighting, but I would I think be quite willing to cut off my left hand, if by doing so some woman would be made a great champion prize fighter. What we have to do, from my standpoint, is to break down all the *artificial* differences of sex, to leave each woman as free to develop along the line she feels her nature best fits her for. It would be a very wicked thing if a man who had the genius to become a great cook, a great artistic dressmaker, a great tailor, were by law prevented, because needlework and cooking are supposed to be the works for which nature has fitted women. So I feel it is a great crime if the woman who is perhaps the person in a whole country best fitted to be Prime Minister or Chief Justice, or great shop-builder is not allowed to become one. *I* would not care to be a politician or lawyer ; *I* would prefer to be an architect—but Lyndall for instance and my friend Minnie de Villiers are splendidly fitted to be lawyers and not at all to be architects.

To Miss E. Hobhouse.   De Aar, 22*nd July.*

It is with such distress that I have just heard from Mrs. Murray that you are in England, that the journey has been too much for you and you are very ill there. I was feeling so happy about you thinking you were much stronger and better. Dear, I know what this long stretch of unbroken physical suffering is—no one knows or can understand who has not lived through and is living through it. When I think of you so beautiful and strong and stately as I first saw you in Cape Town, and then even as you were when you spent that time at De Aar with me, my heart aches. Are you still able to walk about ? Have you dear sympathetic friends about you ? That is all, that is all that could comfort one, when one comes where you and I are. And oh, dear, remember all you did in the cause of justice and mercy in South Africa. You have not lived for nothing. You were the only one who really succeeded in saving thousands from just that terrible physical suffering which has you now in its grasp. Let that thought comfort you in all your terrible pain and weakness, dear brave woman. . . .

In the summer I was down in Cape Town for nearly three months to be near my favourite sister Ettie who was dying of the same form of heart disease I have. She had been dying for two years, but during the last 7 months her sufferings were too awful for any human words to describe it. She could never lie down, and someone had to hold up her head. Her dear body was so swollen no one could touch her without giving her agony, and, if they wanted to move her only a few inches, two people had to stand on the bed and raise her with a sheet. One could only pray for the end, and oh one was so grateful when it came. The day after the funeral I drove to the graveyard and it was so beautiful to see my darling sister whom I had played with and loved so when I was a little child resting under the great heap of flowers. I know some people don't feel so, but it is so beautiful to me to think she is having an everlasting sleep. I couldn't bear to think she was in another world where she might be made to suffer as cruelly as she was in this. It was such a beautiful funeral, there were ten thousand people in the procession ; what was so [? beautiful] was that they were most of them poor people, many coloured and black, whom she had loved and helped who had come from all parts of the country to follow her. She had asked no one to wear mourning, so nearly all the women and girls were in white. As they filed past the grave many dropped a poor little flower or a bit of green in till the grave was almost quite full. Oh it is so sweet to think she's at rest.

. . . Thank you, dear, so much, so very much for the sweet loving thought of me that lay behind your kind wish that I should try that man in Florence. . . . You don't know what it meant to me that there were any people in the world who could feel so kindly to me that they wanted to help me to get better. It has taken away so much of the loneliness of this year. I had always thought the sadness of living to be very old, say seventy or eighty, would be that you had so outlived your world, and your human relations—I never realised one could be comparatively young and yet be so severed from your fellow humans and human life. The great joy of my life is now the Thursday's mail from England and the letters from my dear friends there, some of whom are so good in writing to me whether I write or not, and though they have not seen me for 16 years. A great man friend of mine in England says he finds that as he grows older he cares less for human love and sympathy than when he was young. With me it is just the other way about. When I was young and lived in England I was so surrounded by dear friends and sympathisers that I was like a millionaire who thinks nothing of money ; but now I feel that every little bit of human love is like a precious bit of gold, to be picked up and treasured carefully.

Conservative Party where they truly belong. I am not so anxious for women to get the vote as that they should keep on fighting for it—it is the struggle that *educates*. A degraded and subject class or race gains much more by a fight for freedom than by having it given them. The great thing one wants for women after their long ages of subjection is that they should be *mentally* and spiritually free, and hold freedom the dearest thing on Earth. *Giving* them the franchise is of value because it will educate them to demand freedom in all things : but the fact that they fight for it and win it shows at least that body of women are free ! I am so glad to see the women are taking a strong part in the American elections.

To Mrs. Francis Smith.   De Aar, *Aug.*

. . . Oh Adela, I have had such a lovely time. Will [her brother] and his son Oliver came on Friday morning and stayed till this morning four whole days and a night. It *was* lovely. I wish you really knew Oliver, but young men of 22 are so difficult to get to know ; older men are much easier. He has one of the most beautiful natures I have ever known. With all his really remarkable intellectual gifts, he is like a little child in his tender loving-ness. He [is] so deeply interested in the problems of life. I always think of him together with you and Con. and my beautiful friend Bob [Muirhead]. It isn't a bit because he's my nephew ; I've heaps of other nephews and nieces that I think nothing more than the most ordinary. It's wonderful combination of intellect with tenderness of heart that's so beautiful in him. The last thing he said to me when he held my hand as he sat in the cart to drive away was that he would never miss writing to me every week while he was in England. How few young men at Cambridge would trouble to write to a little old aunt every week. I hardly think one. My old Will was as beautiful and sweet as only he can be. He said he had such a happy happy time here, and rested so. He looked quite different when he went away from what he looked when he came. Oliver is a great joy to him ; you would love to see his tenderness to his father and his admiration for him. He

[Oliver] said it had been an important part of his legal education to go up with him now to Kimberley and watch him conduct a great diamond and will case he has just had.

I'm telling you all this dear because I know how your beautiful nature loves to share your friends' joys with them as much as their sorrows. Will and I talked often of you.

To Mrs. Francis Smith.   De Aar, 27*th Aug.*

. . . I'll write about the suffragettes another day. I can understand your position if you condemn *all* force—all fighting for freedom and justice and right—Washington and the Americans who fought *because they would not be taxed but by their own representatives*—Oliver Cromwell and Pym and Hampden—the Greeks who died at Thermopylæ. If you say no wrong, no wickedness, no injustice must be opposed by force, in that case the Boers were wicked in fighting for freedom to save their little Republics, William the Silent and the Dutch of Holland were wicked to fight against Philip of Spain, Garibaldi, Cavour and the Italians when they fought against the Austrians, &c. &c. &c. ! If you really hold this principle, if you feel that if a Russian army was landed in England to-morrow it would be the duty of English people to sit quite still and let them burn down houses, kill people, and take possession of and rule England—and that to use force to expel them was wrong—then you are *quite* justified in thinking the militants wrong. But those people who think of Washington and Pym and Hampden and William the Silent and the Dutch who fought with him as heroes, who glory in Italy's war against Austria, and the Greek wars against the Persians, and the war of modern Greece against Turkey—those people, who, if the working classes in England gained power and passed a law that all men with more than £300 a year should not vote, would advise their rising and fighting for their right—such have no justification for morally condemning the militant suffragettes. The freedom of women is yet more important than any question which humanity has yet fought out. If it was right for Garibaldi you a little thing, but nothing is small that is a step towards the large freedom.   I believe the whole future development of the race depends on woman's freeing *herself*—no one can do it for her.   If Con had died it seems to me she would have died so gloriously.   Good-bye, dear one.   I hope you can make out this scribble.

To HAVELOCK ELLIS.   DE AAR, *5th Sept.*

Yes, no one can write about things they are not interested in.   The most glorious books of travel in the world, Darwin's *Voyage in the Beagle* and Humboldt's travels, are so interesting because they did write about the scientific facts and the aspects of Nature with which *they* were interested.   Borrow writes about gypsies and tramps and scoundrels because they were the things he was interested in, and his book is wonderful.   All—I mean good— travels must be *a simple record* of what a person liked, disliked, and was interested in.   One musn't think of the writing—just say what one feels.   What I find is that people will not put down things simply enough.   I saw this so strongly after the war.   A squad of young un-educated Boers would sit in my room and recount to each other and me their doings and adventures.   Anything more thrilling, more wonderful, if their words could just have been taken down by a [? stenographer], has never been written.   The scenes, the facts, are imprinted on my mind for ever.   One of them, General Malan, was so wonderful [that] I got him to go to Cape Town and got a shorthand-writer to take down what he said, word for word.   I begged him to talk just as he had talked to me—but he tried to talk like a book, and the thing was less than worthless.   In telling me how they shot a man who had betrayed them and caused several of his men to be killed, he said just what he felt when he saw him and what the man said and looked—and he wound up by smiting his hand on his knee and saying " By God, I sent that devil to Hell ! "   Do you think he said that in his book ?   Oh no !   And he ended up with something about " I felt we were justified in shooting him " —nothing more !   As he *told* it me it was one of the most thrilling things I have ever heard.   All the tragedy, the

·HAVELOCK ELLIS·

HAVELOCK ELLIS, JULY, 1924.

From a Photograph by Em. Grevaux, Paris, of a Drawing done by Paul-Emile Bécat,
belonging to Miss Sylvia Beach.

To face p. 318.

anguish and passion, of war were in it.   Of course, if you're
not interested in anything you can't write interestingly
about it, but I always find you, when you will talk, one of
the most interesting of persons.   Your description of your
talk with your friend—I forget his name—when he would
say he was mad and put himself into an asylum [Ellis says :
" It was hardly like that ! "], was one of the most drily
funny things I ever heard !   I have numbers of pithy
wonderful little sayings and sentences of yours impressed
on my memory—but such never come into your books !
That's what I mean.   I'm very ill, old Havelock ; how long
is this to go on ?

To HAVELOCK ELLIS.   DE AAR, *Sept.*

Dear Havelock boy, you *are* unjust to me about sitting
on a hill and seeing the worms crawling below.   So far
from thinking I am the only person who understands the
woman question, whenever our Society has asked me to
make a speech or write them on paper I say it would be pure
waste of time when there are no end of splendid pamphlets
and books on the subject ;   why can't they read them
instead of getting stupid people to talk ?   In one case
I sent them Chumley's [not spelt right ?] pamphlets and
said all I wanted to say was expressed there better than I
could express it.   It is just because there *is* such an amount
of splendid writing on the woman question that it is so
unnecessary for fools to read other people's books, pick
other people's brains, and then vomit it forth mixed up
for the sake of writing a book.   Not only men like Zangwill
and Nevinson and many others write what I profoundly
admire, but women even more so.   Edith Wharton's
House of Mirth is one of the most wonderful expositions
of the degradation and evils of woman's present position
in modern civilisation that any pen could produce.   Women
like Elizabeth Robins, Evelyn Sharp and many others
are wonderful.   Old Mrs. Despard wrote two articles
many years ago called, " Why I became a Suffragette "
which go to one's heart.   I have heard a not at all clever or
highly educated woman make a little speech at a woman's
meeting that I'll never forget, it was so true, so sincere, so

simple, so at the point. We have, too, women of the Miss —— and Mrs. —— type, women who *will* gush into speech and writing, churn up other people's ideas and vomit them out. We have two women who will insist on speaking at every meeting—God himself can't stop them.

To HAVELOCK ELLIS.   DE AAR.

I ought to have been a mother with ten or twelve children growing up about me—that's really what I'm best fitted for, though it seems a conceited thing to say, because to be a real mother, intellectually and emotionally as well as physically, is the highest function in life, except to be a real father. There's such a beautiful sympathy between Will and his children. Oliver has something the same kind of sensitive sweetness you used to have when you were young. I wonder if you have it still.

To HAVELOCK ELLIS.   DE AAR (*Sunday morning*).

It is terribly painful to look through the *English Review*. All the failure of the English in the Boer War, all their decadence, is written here—it's terrible. I've just been re-reading Jane Austen's books—and then to turn to that ! It's like turning from Homer and Plato and Aristotle and Euripides and the great Roman historians like Tacitus to the dying classical world. You know three-fourths of it isn't even sense ! Words have ceased for these debilitated men and women to be the external form in which deep thoughts and intense feelings or clear calm perceptions were forced to clothe themselves that they might become tangible to other minds. They are an end in themselves, so many words so much pay, so much inversion of language, so much originality—where there is none in the writer's mind. It makes one feel sick and faint.

The only thing they seem to like to write about much is madness. Now madness is easy to write about—because most people who read are sane, so that they cannot prove what is written about madness is false. The verse is too loathsome for any words. There's one fine little story, full of nature and strength, though the subject is repulsive— *Second Best*, by D. H. Lawrence.

To Mrs. Francis Smith.   De Aar, *5th Nov.*

. . . I wonder what you would think of it if you could see this strange world of sand and heat, the clouds of dust towering up into the sky hundreds of feet with round, bulbous, drooping dark heads. The genii whom the Eastern stories always talk of must have been suggested by these vast dust clouds moving over the great plains.

1913

To Mrs. Stanley (Clifford Cawood).

? Muizenberg, *March.*

[The main homestead at Ganna Hoek was being very materially altered and improved.]   Have they finished the old house at Ganna Hoek, I wonder ?   Perhaps it would be less sad to me if the house were all changed, but my heart felt just breaking when I was there last time.   It was all so like it used to be—and the face one wanted was gone. We can never forget her, can we, dear ?

To S. C. C. S.   Cape Town, 1*3th March.*

I had a long argument with —— yesterday, about marriage.   She seems to think it ought to be a wild inebriation and excitement.   What it is at its best is a great peaceful calm and strength ; in a world of continual change and rupture, the one abiding fellowship and love ; it's that or nothing.   To expect continual excitement from it would be like building and furnishing a house for yourself with the idea it would yield you not a place where you could always be safe from the world and at rest but a continual variety.

To Miss E. Hobhouse.   Muizenberg, *Mar.*

. . . It isn't the pain and weakness one minds, it's the not being able to work.   My one novel especially I would have liked so to finish.   I feel that if only one lonely struggling woman read it and found strength and comfort from it one would not feel one had lived quite in vain.   I seem to have done so little with my life.   You have at least

22

that solid wonderful work you did here for the Boer women and children to look back to.

. . . I am much distressed about our dear, brave suffragettes in London. I feel such intense sympathy with them, but I cannot feel the letter-burning, &c., is wise or right. As long as they merely demanded to see the ministers and asked questions of ministers I was heart and soul with them : but it seems to me that the use of brute force and war in all its aspects are just the things we have to fight against. . . . My one hope and joy is in our dear beautiful young girls who are beginning to grow up, who will possess so much we only hoped for and dreamed of.

To Havelock Ellis.   Muizenberg, 23rd *Mar.*

I'll soon be going to De Aar. I'm so ill here that I look forward joyfully to escaping from the sea damp, though Cron says it's still very hot at De Aar. I often wonder if Nauheim, or some specialist treatment like that Edith has, could still do me any good. But unless I could get better during the winter and do some work I couldn't afford to come to England. I wouldn't mind the risk of dying on the voyage, that wouldn't matter. I'm so happy when I think of my sister Ettie lying so peacefully in her grave after all those awful years of anguish. To-morrow is my birthday ; I shall perhaps go and have dinner at my brother Will's. He's looking very ill too, just as Fred did those years before he died.

Death is just nothing ; but it's a gradual dying while you *seem* to live that's so ugly. There's just this, that when everything else is gone in life you can [be] still and endure—when there's nothing else to do. I don't know how people can endure unending physical anguish if they can't fall back on the thought that they've [not] caused any wilful physical or mental pain to human beings or animals. If all the world is permeated by injustice and suffering by sentient creatures on each other, one clings to the thought one hasn't willingly consented to it, or tried to increase it, as a drowning man clings to a straw. If I could be cured to-morrow by torturing animals I wouldn't have it.

The native question becomes darker and darker here, and one can do nothing. I've been wanting so long to write one little paper on it—but I can't.

To S. C. C. S.   ? MUIZENBERG, 27*th Mar.*

Dear loved one, I'm glad you like my writings. I wish I could more often shew you myself that which you could as well love. But you know I think one is driven to writing; the propelling force which makes all true artists write who do not write either for wealth or fame, is the feeling that so and so only can they express their inward self, the real self that lives always in loneliness. Art is the little crack in the iron wall of life which shuts one in awful isolation through which the spirit can force itself out and show itself to its own like-minded fellow spirits outside ; or rather can creep in through the cracks in their terrible walls that shut in the individual life and say, " You are not alone."

To MRS. RHYS DAVIDS.   DE AAR, 13*th April.*

Your P.S. about *Trojan Women* is most strange to me. If it is a sign of great minds to think alike then we must be very great ! because what you say is the exact expression of my thought on reading *Trojan Women* a few months ago. One of the most wonderful things in all literature to me is the appearance of the " Parasite " Helen on that scene of woman's suffering and anguish—" She comes through them gentle and unafraid : there is no disorder in her dress."

I value your P.S. on this matter so much I am going to fasten it into my copy of the *Trojan Women.* The reading of Gilbert Murray's translations of Euripides lately has been a revelation of joy to me. The wonderful thing to me is that any *man* could have written of women as he does. But genius has no limit of sex or race. It's curious to sit here in this little house in the karroo veld and feel that perhaps the thing nearest to you in the world is the brain of that old Greek dead now these two thousand years. We who can't read Greek should be so grateful

Gilbert Murray for giving him to us. I'm so glad I ln't die before I had him.

In a way my little book *Woman and Labour* is very sad to me. I shall never look at it or touch it again. Only that little verse of Tennyson's in my dedication to Constance Lytton is one to me always beautiful and fresh. The book is such a broken fragment. The first part of the whole book, which it seemed to me might have been of a little use, was the part dealing with the new moral code which must come into being if men and women are to associate freely together on equal terms. A " new chivalry," an unwritten code of honour more binding than any law, must grow, making many things, not deemed criminal now, as criminal as men and women in the past have deemed rape and sedition [? seduction], and, with the rising up of the new code, the present ethics of the ball-room and the music-hall must slowly fade away. Such works as Wells's *New Machiavelli* illustrate the ghastly condition which arises where the old laws of relation between the sexes are broken down and a high code of perfect Truth, openness and loyalty in all sex relations has not taken its place. But one need not grieve that one's own little world has been lost, because such a law is writing, and will and must write, itself in the hearts of the noblest men and women and spread slowly from them to others.

To EDWARD CARPENTER.   DE AAR, 29*th April.*

Every year my horror not only of war but of the argument of brute force all round grows stronger and stronger. If ever war and the exercise of force was justified it is in the case of millions of women fighting for freedom. But is it ever justified ? are not the evils greater than the good ? Cromwell, Washington, all the world's heroes who fought for freedom, were they justified ? I see so much to be said on both sides. Now I can only say *I* am for passive resistance, but I dare not condemn those who are not. Of course there's the narrow question of tactics— is it wise—even if right—at any given time to fight ? Things as far as the working-classes in England go seem advancing quickly. But the fight for freedom will have to go on through the centuries, because, as soon as one class or party or race becomes dominant, it oppresses the others. Look at our Dutch here ! But one day, far away, I guess we shall come to a full bloom.

To HAVELOCK ELLIS.   DE AAR, 12*th May.*

I think I shall try to come to England if Cron goes. I shall try to borrow some money from Will, giving him my " Prelude " in exchange. But it will be very sad to see you all, I'm so changed ; but perhaps the doctors will do me good. Don't mention to anyone, not even to Edith, I'm coming, unless you feel quite sure she'll remember not to mention it to anyone. I want, if I do come, to see no one but a couple of my dearest friends till I've undergone any cure I'm going to try. . . . Thanks for the copy of the *New Statesman.* I have just had a letter from Beatrice Webb asking me to write for it. I don't think it nearly equal to the *Nation.* There is too much attempt at fine writing in it. Fancy Bernard Shaw as a political guide ! He would give up any clear simple statement of fact for the sake of uttering a smart paradox ! Fancy Hubert Bland writing the literary criticisms ! Of course there is some tall writing in the *Nation* ; there is a terrible man writes articles on " nature " and the weather. What I can't make out is how people read such stuff. It's the same thing as affectation in dress or manner, doing a thing for the sake of doing it !

To HAVELOCK ELLIS.   DE AAR, 20*th May.*

Do you who know all about everything know of a good history of France, not too expensive, say, like Green's *Short History ?* Also do you know of a good history of French literature—I don't mean fine writing, but one which gives simply the facts of literary history ? I've had a very good history of German literature, giving you names of writers, dates, short biographies and descriptions of the different schools of thought. I want very much a good history of the Jesuits. . . . How ridiculous it is to teach children only the history of their own little countries. By the time a man or woman is fifteen or sixteen they should at least once or twice have read through the histories of the

leading European countries. We make so little effort
to make education *broad*. I think the teaching of languages
takes an altogether undue place in education. What a
farce to spend time gaining a little dry smattering of the
grammar of a foreign language and to know nothing of
its literature or the history of the nation ! Language
should not be taught through grammar, but through
reading and speaking and hearing it ; grammar should
be studied as a science apart, comparative grammar. The
structure of different languages should be compared :
Kaffir is a most fascinating study from that standpoint ; they
inflect the beginnings of their words, not the ends, and
they are inflected so as to make the words curiously
harmonious. . . . Good-bye, dear ; I wonder if I shall
go to England. It will be a ghost revisiting the earth where
it once lived.

To MRS. FRANCIS SMITH.   DE AAR, 30*th May.*

. . . When I was a tiny child I too was always making
stories and poems and I feel as if I knew just all he [a very
remarkable young nephew of hers] feels and thinks. But
I never showed anything I wrote to anyone. I used to
walk up and down in the bush or at the bottom of the
garden by the great willow tree making them aloud to
myself. Will and the little Kaffir boy used to hide themselves near by, and then suddenly burst out on me, saying,
" We've heard the whole story, we've heard every word ! "
And I used to feel I wanted to kill myself. I used to dance
with rage and bite my hand, and then they used to say,
" Look at the little scorpion, stinging itself ! " which of
course made me feel more than ever I wanted to die and
leave a world where I couldn't even makes stories in quiet !
They say this little boy [her nephew] is the gentlest and
most affectionate of children, but if anyone touches or
reads his MS. without his permission he is white with
rage. I would really like to go up to Pretoria to see the
child if I could. His mother told me that once (he was
then about 6) he was writing in a corner and his aunt came
and looked over his shoulder. He turned round on her
furious with rage ; it was *his* writing, his own, she had no

right to look at it ! Afterwards his mother came to him and asked him if he didn't think he was very unkind to be so angry with his poor aunt, &c. He said nothing at the time ; but when he wished his aunt good-night, he whispered to her that, when she went to her room, she must please look on her bed. There she found, pinned out on the coverlet, a long poem in blank verse, in reparation.

To Miss E. HOBHOUSE.   DE AAR, *4th June.*

. . . I don't know, dear, what I said to make you think I was opposed to the suffragettes. I think Mrs. Pankhurst one of the greatest and noblest women the English race has produced, one whose name will never be forgotten. *I* myself could not be a militant because I personally am opposed to the use of force ; I would never sue a person who injured or wronged me ; but I can admire people like Cromwell, and Washington, and Mrs. Pankhurst, who have felt it right to fight. What is so superb is their *courage.* My one fear with regard to women has always been that *perhaps* they were not as brave as men. After sincerity courage is to me the highest of all virtues. I always admired you so much for your courage. I believe they (the suffragettes) have done more to *rouse* the spirit of women, to make them free and fearless—and that is after all the thing that really matters !—than anything else in the world could have. Do you see what I mean ?

To HAVELOCK ELLIS.   DE AAR, *5th July.*

Adela Smith, to whom I wrote saying I shrank from seeing my friends again, being so changed, says, as you do, that people don't change, that the old heart is always there ; but I don't think it's true—some people do change— some people. Ettie changed so completely before she died that she was not Ettie at all. Both physically and mentally she didn't even recall herself to you. Two years before she died, when she had already begun to die, she was still *Ettie*, though she had to lie still and motionless in bed with a ghastly blue face. But a year later she was not Ettie, and by the time she died it was quite impossible to believe she had ever been Ettie. In face she became very like my mother whom she had never in the least resembled.   She had always had a little snub or round nose (the only one of the whole family who seemed to have it) ; during the last two years, as all the muscle fell away, you saw she had a sharp curved Roman beak underneath.   Her character changed entirely.   There was nothing left of her strong active nature—only a cry for air and to be lifted up.   Disease and unutterable anguish *does* change people. My mother suffered a great deal for years from her heart and she lived to be 82 [85], but she was still my mother to the end, old, broken, diseased, but just as you would have expected her to be at 82 ; she kept the old bright flashing eye, the keenness to the last ; a photograph taken of her three days before she dropped dead was the best ever taken of her.   She looks exactly like Cardinal Newman. I feel as if I were changing like Ettie.   I would give thousands if I had not seen her dying the last two years.

To Mrs. Stanley (Clifford Cawood).   De Aar, 18*th* Oct.

I am wondering how it is going with you all.   Write and give me all the family news, dear.   I am leaving for Europe on the 6th December, to go and try a heart cure at Florence in Italy.   I am now so bad I can't be worse, and the cure, which has wonderfully helped a friend of mine, may help me.   It is very hard to leave my dear husband for so long.   He seems to grow sweeter and finer as he grows older.

CHAPTER XII

LETTERS WRITTEN IN 1914 AND 1915

1914

To HAVELOCK ELLIS.

ST. MARY ABBOTT'S TERRACE, KENSINGTON, *5th Jan.*

We are just starting off. It *was* good to see you. Address : Poste Restante, Florence.

To HAVELOCK ELLIS.   GRAND HOTEL, ALASSIO, *15th Jan.*

I haven't written because I've been six days in bed. Those terrible internal pains came on suddenly as never before. I sent for an Italian doctor here ; he said it was stone in the kidneys. For two days nothing but blood, due to the edges of the stone, he said, tearing the walls. The lady visitors in this hotel were unspeakably kind to me. For six nights they took turns to sit up with me till the doctor said I was out of danger. He was afraid of the heart failing and so would not give me the large doses of opium the Cape Town doctors gave me. The kindness of everyone here has been astonishing when I think that a month ago I had never seen any of these people. . . . I shall not be leaving for Florence till the end of this month now. I feel weak and I shrink from the thought of Florence, and partly *afraid* of trying the treatment there. I'm walking on very thin ice, and I can't afford to be made any worse. Goodbye, dear.

To MRS. PETHICK LAWRENCE.   ALASSIO, *15th Jan.*

After many wanderings to Mentone, etc., I have settled down here at my beloved Alassio—which I find still the most restful and charming place on earth ; in spite absolutely I can't walk again for some hours. They say this passes off and several patients say they have been most marvellously helped by it. . . . Poor H. is feeling his wife's death dreadfully. I've written to Carpenter if he can't come and see him. The doctor thinks Carpenter is the only person who could help him, he's so depressed.

To HAVELOCK ELLIS.   FLORENCE, 16*th Mar.*

Dear Havelock Boy, don't come for my sake, I'm so sick and faint all the time it will be no pleasure to you to see me. Unless, indeed, the joy of seeing you makes me better. The weather here is awful to me, warm fog and mist all the time and the food at this hotel is very bad. I think the cure *does* relieve the chest, but it hardly seems worth all the other suffering. It seems I am not to get better anywhere. That little burst of betterness in England made me so hopeful ; but when I go back there in May it will be warm there too. I cling to the thought of Nauheim as my last hope. If I can't get better and work I would so much rather die. The terrible thing is that I may not, and may live on year after year to be a burden to others. I can't even read or write a letter without exhaustion any more. I'm sure you can't like Florence unless the weather gets clearer, but it won't affect you as it does me.

To MRS. HAVELOCK ELLIS.   FLORENCE, 6*th April.*

Dear Edith, I arrive in London by the 10.15 from Dover on next Saturday morning, the 11th. If Havelock is at home by that time, ask him to meet me, and tell me of any cheap quiet hotel you or he know of, *not* close to the river, but out towards the west or north. . . . I am so much better than when Havelock was here. That cure nearly made an end of me, but I'll soon be all right again, as well as I was before it began ! I shall be so glad to leave Florence, but it's much finer weather here now.

To HAVELOCK ELLIS.   FLORENCE, 7*th April.*

I wish I'd been better when you were here but it was *so* beautiful to see you. I'll go back to London as soon as

I feel strong enough.   Mrs. Pethick Lawrence wants me to go to Venice with her and her sister, and go home with them at the end of the month, but I don't see how I can wait so long.

To HAVELOCK ELLIS.
St. MARY ABBOTT'S TERRACE, KENSINGTON, 22*nd April.*

I've just got here.   I'm quite a different person from what I was in Florence.—I really am Olive Schreiner again ! . . . When can we meet ?   I don't want to trouble you, but I hope I'll soon see you.   I'd like to come to your rooms, we could talk better there. . . . I want to go to a couple of Beethoven Symphonies which are to be given each day this week—they are the only thing in the way of pleasure I am going to spend money on, but I've longed for twenty and more years to hear them.

To S. C. C. S.   LONDON, 24*th April.*

The Beethoven concert was heaven !   We had the 7th Symphony in A, perhaps the divinest thing the human spirit has ever produced except the 9th.   You feel yourself expanding and expanding with infinite joy.   I always seem to have those words of Pope's singing themselves in my mind : " I mount !   I fly !—Oh grave where is thy victory, Oh death where is thy sting ! "   You feel as if neither life nor death nor anything else matters—there is only infinite joy.   [She went later to Wagner's *Meistersingers.*   " If that is music," she says, she " doesn't like it.   Wagner is earthy."]

To HAVELOCK ELLIS.
St. MARY ABBOTT'S TERRACE, KENSINGTON, 28*th April.*

Friday would suit me well, dear.   I'll meet you at Charing Cross. . . . I do hope you'll get a wire from Edith and good news ; I'm anxious about you both.   The last Beethoven Concert was a dead failure.   That conductor is wretched.   He couldn't grasp the Ninth Symphony at all.   I'm not so fit as I was when in London before, but keeping about all right.   I feel as if something had gone out of me since Florence that can't come back.

To HAVELOCK ELLIS.   NAUHEIM, 30*th June.*

Have you read Sudermann's book of short stories, *Im Zweilicht*? They are wonderful. I like Mrs. Sawyer very much ; she is delightful. Miss Deane is bright and kind-hearted but does not attract me so much. I am going to tea with them this afternoon.

To HAVELOCK ELLIS.   OBERHOF, THURINGIA, 12*th July.*

We've been here two days. It's a little place on the top of the hills, with pine trees shutting us in everywhere. But it is beautiful in its way. My future movements are uncertain.

To HAVELOCK ELLIS.   OBERHOF, 21*st July.*

I am leaving Oberhof. Address care of the Countess von Moltke, Creisan, Schlesien. If it suits me I shall stay some time. [Daughter of Sir James Rose-Innes, Chief Justice of South Africa.]

To HAVELOCK ELLIS.   CREISAN, 26*th July.*

I have the *English Review.* The tone seems to me to get lower and lower from a literary point of view. The article on the militants is simple unmixed vulgarity. The vulgarity has nothing to do with the writer's view ; I regret the *later* militancy more than she does. I suppose the editor pays little to his contributors and so cannot command the best literary talent. I shall probably be returning to Holland in a few days.

To HAVELOCK ELLIS.   BERLIN, 29*th July.*

Am just leaving Berlin for Holland. Address care of Dr. Aletta Jacobs, Amsterdam.

To HAVELOCK ELLIS.   AMSTERDAM, 1*st Aug.*

I am, I think, leaving for London to-morrow, Sunday, if I can get through ; *perhaps* Monday, can't say. Have had striking experience during the last ten days. It seems as if it were six months since I left Oberhof ten days ago. Many interesting things to tell you. Address Alice Corthorn's care. I shall go there for a couple of days till I can find quiet quarters in or near London. Is Dulwich a nice place ? I want to settle down and write a little. . . . The military are using all the trains to-day but there may be more chance on Monday. . . . I am glad that low article was not by a woman.

To HAVELOCK ELLIS.   KENSINGTON, *3rd Aug.*

Arrived at midnight last night after a most awful journey of fifteen hours from Amsterdam. It was the last train taking foreigners, thousands of men, women and children on the boat fleeing—people just lay about on the deck in the wet when there was no more room in the cabins and saloons. The sea was wild and the spray poured over the deck. I shall never forget it. Then there was a wild fight for seats in the trains ! Goodbye, dear you and Edith. I long to see you.

Germany is determined to fight. It is *she* who is the cause of all. In Holland they are expecting the Prussians there to-morrow, to take the Hague and the ports. All the soldiers are mobilised, but of course they can do nothing. *War is Hell.* They will fight in Africa, too.

To S. C. C. S.   LONDON, 19*th Aug.*

At Weimar I got out as I wanted to see Goethe's house. It's a pretty little town. I walked about a mile and a half to reach it. The heat was intense and a great thunderstorm was just coming on. When I got to the house the man at the door told me it was closed till 3. I walked out my best German and told him I had come all the way from Africa, that I might never be able to come again and that since I was a girl of 16 I had dreamed of coming. At last his German heart was moved and he said I could go up with the little boy. It's a simple old house. I [can't] tell you how his study and death-room went to my heart. The tiny bedroom in which he died is not a *bit bigger* than our little spare room at De Aar ! Just room for a single bed—a *tiny* table and

To HAVELOCK ELLIS.   LONDON, 13*th Oct.*

I am going to-morrow to Durrants Hotel, Manchester Square. I hope I shall get better there as it's very dry. Do come and see me soon. I long to see you. How scared people are about the Zeppelins ? If you have lived through a war and had your house burnt and all you prized taken from you, you learn to take these things as all in the day's work. War *is* Hell. Though people like the English who have always made it in other peoples' countries have never realised [it]. It's when it comes to your own land that its full horror bursts on you. Did I tell you Oliver has joined his regiment and may be sent to the front any hour ? And the diplomatists who for ten years have been bringing things into this state will live on. Our beautiful innocent ones, of all nations, must die. Goodbye, dear.

To HAVELOCK ELLIS.

KENSINGTON PALACE MANSIONS, 16*th Oct.*

Yesterday at Durrants Hotel a boy brought a note. It ran : " Madam, When Mrs. Smith took the room for you she did not mention that your name was *Schreiner.* As we find that is either an Austrian or a German name you will please leave our Hotel at once." Of course I took a taxi and my things and left at once. I have fortunately found this place. It's much more expensive. I can't stay but I must rest here as I'm worn out. [She stayed for ten months.] The great use of not being very poor is that it helps one to health.

To EDWARD CARPENTER.   LONDON, *Oct.*

I think so much of your tired face as you went away. You know, Edward, we can live through all this, but it's simply crushing us, who had such hopes for the future 20 years ago. . . . I wish I could feel with you that this war is going to bring the Kingdom of Heaven. I feel it is the beginning of half a century of the most awful wars the world has seen. First this then another war probably of England and Germany against Russia, then as the years pass, with India, Japan and China and the Native Races of

Africa.   While the desire to dominate and rule and possess Empire is in the hearts of men, there will always be war.

To Miss E. HOBHOUSE.   MAVER LAKE, BUDE.

. . . Again and again when I tried to get rooms they wouldn't let me have them on account of my name. Just before I left I found very nice cheap rooms in Chelsea, there was a sweet refined looking little woman who let them ; I told her I would take them, and come the next day. When I told her my name she turned and *glared* at me. I enquired what was the matter. She asked me if my name was not German. I said it was, but I was a British subject born in South Africa, that my husband was a British subject of pure British descent, and my mother was English, that my father who left Germany 80 years ago, was a naturalised British subject, and had been dead nearly 50 years. She turned round and stormed at me, all her seemingly gentle face contorted with rage and hate. She said that if my ancestors came from Germany " three hundred years ago " it would make no difference, no one with a German name should come into her house, and poured forth a stream of abuse that was almost inconceivable. The worst was, that I was feeling so ill and worn out, that I dropped into a chair and burst out crying. It's the only time I've cried in two years. It seemed so contemptibly weak of me ; but you know how you feel when you are utterly worn out mentally and physically ! I could only say, " It isn't because you are so unkind to me, it's because all the world's so wicked."

Oh Emily the worst of war is not the death on the battle fields ; it is the meanness, the cowardice, the hatred it awakens. Where is the free England of our dreams, in which every British subject, whether Dutch, English, French or German in extraction, had an equal right and freedom ? I wouldn't have come here if I had not thought one would not be free here from these petty attacks. What this war has shown me is not so much the wickedness as the meanness of human nature. War draws out all that is basest in the human heart. Perhaps I shall be able to get up to London before you leave.

To S. C. C. S.   LONDON, *Thursday, October*.

My Cron, I have your long letter [dated De Aar, 18th Sept.]. I got it two days ago. When I got your letter I read the first page and then I came to the sentence about Ollie. I knew what had happened. For two days I carried it in my pocket till I finished reading it. It *was* beautiful that she went so, at the very feet she had always loved so [the little dog died suddenly and painlessly]. Oh, little Ollie! She had a happy life, dear one, was never struck, never hardly spoken to—had no suffering but that ear [which was cured before she died]. Oh, my poor Cron, my poor Cron! The little companion you had fed from your hand and carried in your bosom for 12 years. I can't, I can't bear to think of your loneliness. It has always comforted me that you had her. Oh, my little Ollie, my little Ollie! I knew I would never see her again. Thank you for writing me that beautiful letter. I value it, and know what it cost you. Oh, my husband, my darling husband, you are so lonely now! That dear little spot under my window!

To HAVELOCK ELLIS.   LONDON, 2*nd Nov*.

I wonder how you found your father. We are all in pretty deep waters! Affairs in South Africa seem crushing. Can you come on Tuesday? If it's fine we might go to Hampton Court. I hope you have good news of Edith. I met Norman Angell on Friday, a delightful man, something like John Stuart Mill in face. I am trying to read, determinately to take my thoughts from the ghastly realities, but often I only *seem* to read. There's a good war article in the *Fortnightly* for October, called "Armageddon and After."

To HAVELOCK ELLIS.   LONDON, 9*th Nov*.

I could come on Thursday. I wish you didn't live so far. We might, if you lived near here, often go out for half an hour to some gallery, etc. I have not been to the National Gallery or the British Museum since I came to London.

You see Bernard Shaw in his article in the *Nation* allows that England or France would have crossed Belgium, just as Germany did, " if necessary." Bernard Shaw can speak the truth sometimes. Have you read Norman Angell's *Patriotism under Three Flags*? It's very good. A splendid review of Maeterlinck in last Saturday's *Nation*; I am so glad to find someone who expresses exactly my view. We are never so solitary as we believe ourselves to be.

To HAVELOCK ELLIS.   LONDON, 16*th Nov.*

Dear, I found your letter here last night when I came home from Knebworth. It's beautiful your father kept so cheerful and bright to the last, and he'd had, I should think, a happy life. His own nature was bright. But there's a curious feeling when the last of one's parents goes. As the reaper comes, you know that now you *stand first in the next row*. I'll come on Friday if you don't write to say no. I've just seen a woman who comes from the Cape. We hear nothing of the awful things that go on there except by chance. I can't write about it. Goodbye dear. You seem having a dark time, dear, and I can't do anything to brighten you.

To S. C. C. S.   LONDON.
[Received at De Aar on 30*th Nov.]*

It is funny why I have always to be out of everything. The day will never come when I can be in the stream. Something in my nature prevents it I suppose. I have never before in my life been so lonely. Sometimes I don't seem to be alive at all, but only creeping about in a ghastly dream. No one wants me. I'm [in] no relation with the life or thought in England or Africa or anywhere else. What I do feel a little hard is that people should now turn on me—twenty-five years ago when I wrote " The Sunlight Lay Across My Bed " they all (my friends) approved and admired it. I am only holding the same views now ! Hell and Heaven are exactly to me what they were then. Rhodes understood it perhaps better than other people : he told a man he hated it more than anything he'd ever read ! You know, I feel paralysed. I can't write at a book or paper

—I feel there is no one left to write to. There is nothing left but blank space. . . .

Cron, you will laugh at me, but, when I said good-bye to you [at De Aar in Nov. 1913] near the door of the dining-room, I had a feeling I would never see *anything* of that which was dear to me again, that I would have nothing but that little bunch of carnations left ! [which I gave her]. Our beautiful Boy [a very large and extraordinarily handsome cat] with his big eyes sat looking at me from the pillar at the side : I knew I should never see him again, Ollie [my dog]. I felt as though, if ever I came back, all, all would be gone, the trees and the house and what is more precious than all [? myself] and only the red sand blowing about, as before we came to live there. [I saw her off at De Aar station.]

To HAVELOCK ELLIS.   LONDON, 7*th Dec.*

Please thank Edith for her book. I'm ill in bed, not able to write. I've seen a specialist. He says he can do nothing, that no doctors can ; that I need a nurse, not doctors. I love you, dear.

To HAVELOCK ELLIS.   LONDON, 14*th Dec.*

It was nice to get a word from you. Oh, how I wish we lived near that we could often see each other. Come any afternoon after 4. My kidney is getting worse and worse. The anguish is persistent. I am trying an electric treatment, which seemed to help me wonderfully the first day, but not since so much. I go every afternoon. My dear friend —— has just been found to have consumption of the left lung. Since I have been in London in all this terrible loneliness she has stood by me and helped me. No one is allowed to see her just now. I have never known such loneliness as during the past months. If one can work or think one is never lonely ; but I can't any more. I have lain here for three weeks now since I last went to see you, and have seen no one except once Isabella Ford, once my brother for a few moments, and once dear Dolly Radford. But it's not the loneliness of never seeing or speaking to anyone that matters, it's the sense of being entirely cut off from one's fellows. It isn't only because my name's German—though that may make the people in the hotel shrink from me—but it's all the people who know me and who know I contemn the war. One day things will change, but, oh, I hope I shall not be here to see it. I don't feel I can have very long to go on now. When the pay-day comes in three or four years time, then the English people will begin to howl. Now work is plentiful, and money, and women can feel themselves heroes when they knit second-rate socks. It's just the same in Africa : for the time being the war-fever is carrying everything before it, especially among women.

This afternoon I felt I couldn't stay alone in this room any more, I'd go mad, I've only once before felt such an agony of oppression, so in the pouring rain I went on the top of a bus to Barnes and back. I can't go to Africa, broken like this, and I can't get to Italy. Oh, Havelock, I do hope this is my last year.

I don't know why I am writing to you, life is sad enough for you. You know, I could bear all in my personal life, if it wasn't for this terrible exhibition of what humanity is. It isn't even the fighting and the hating, it's the lying. There is no truth on earth. I have always loved humanity and believed in it : now a great cry comes into my heart : Why doesn't God take up a sponge and sop us all up and squeeze us into space ?

The only thing that gives me any joy is the sparrows and pigeons that come to feed on a roof below mine every day. It's not only that. My heart quivers with love when I see them, but some person must be kind enough to throw crumbs out to them—though they are *not* of his nation. Nationality isn't everything ! Goodbye, dear.

To Mrs. PETHICK LAWRENCE.   LONDON, *Friday* (? 1914).

Oh, dear Friend, life is so grim now one cannot weep for our beloved dead as once we could. I do hope she did not suffer much. It is the remembrance of the suffering that crushes us. I am so glad you were able to be with her. While in a way, the terribleness of human life on earth to-day makes one cling less passionately to life, in another, it

makes suffering harder to bear. One seems already to have
as much to bear as one can. There is nothing to help, but,
if one is strong enough for it, to throw oneself into work
and strive to make evil less. Oh, dear friend, in a world
with all the suffering and death and disease which we humans
cannot escape, does it not seem inconceivable that we
torture and slaughter and crush each other ? If we did all
we could for one another on earth, life would still be tragic.
. . . If ever that League to *enforce* peace comes into existence, it will form the most awful *instrument of oppression*,
and lead to the most cataclysmic wars which earth has ever
known.

1915

To EDWARD CARPENTER.   LONDON, *Jan.*

Love begets love and war begets hate and war, as
surely as black men beget black children and white men
white.

To HAVELOCK ELLIS.   LONDON, 26*th Jan.*

Did I tell you I went to the National Gallery, but found
most of the pictures buried away ? Some of Rubens' pictures were left. Strange, I liked them much better than I
ever used to in the old days, just as I detest Wagner's music
much more than I used to. Frank straight sincerity is
what, in art and everything, my nature gets to demand more
and more. Isn't that tiger in " Peace Repairing the Ravages
of War " fine ? I don't mind the ugliness of the women,
they are true. . . . Yes, I liked Margaret Sanger.

To HAVELOCK ELLIS.   LONDON, 8*th Mar.*

At last I really am better. What I've had was measles
for the *third* time ! After some days of terrible headache
I came out the most extraordinary rash all over my face and
chest, etc. For a couple of days I lay nearly insensible,
not eating or drinking or moving, and in a dazed sort of
way I kept thinking : " It's just like I felt when I had
measles "—but of course I thought it couldn't be. Now I
find that the little boy in the room next mine, and whose

mother and sister (who've been nursing him) I sit next to,
has had a most terrible attack of measles ! He was in bed
a week before me. I've certainly had it three times now,
when I was a child, again at Matjesfontein, when I nearly
died with it, and now. I'm now quite well, only my head
still feels tired. I'm going out on the top of the bus to
Hampton Court to-morrow. It would be so nice if you
were near, perhaps you could go too.

To Miss E. HOBHOUSE.   LONDON (? 1915).

    . . . Yes, there is a change of tone—it is principally
caused by the rise of prices. This war will probably go
on for another year and a half or two years. France and
Germany would long ago have made peace, but England
and probably Russia won't let them. She wants German
traid [? trade] and colonies. If the Imperialists were severely
[? beaten] in German West and in Egypt peace would
probably come very soon, but as this is most unlikely to
happen, it won't. I don't think that feebly gushing over
the war does any good. To combine, as the labour party
under Keir Hardie and some Social Democrats are doing
in Germany, to protest against the action of *their own*
government, *is* immense good. If women could combine—
which they won't—in their millions to defeat the politicians
of their own country at the next elections, and to prevent
their husbands and sons from enlisting, that would do good,
and anything one individual ever does to diminish this
hideous nation-hatred does do good.

To Miss E. HOBHOUSE,
           KENSINGTON PALACE MANSIONS (? *Mar.*).

    I can imagine a " peace," quite as hideous and unjust,
taking place in Europe which would plunge us lower than
we have been into the depths of international hatred
and bloody strifes. I have studied European problems as
deeply as my ability has allowed me for many many years,
have read all I could on the Eastern question, I have done
little else for the last few months, and yet I am far from
feeling I can pour light and guidance out on the human race
by speaking my thoughts on a platform. If war is ever to

be stopped on earth it will be only by the passing away of the ideals of empire, national supremacy, and the search after national wealth as the first object in life.

To Miss E. HOBHOUSE.   LONDON (? *Mar.*).

. . . I would not go to that meeting even if I were well. I am so sick of English jingo-ism and self-glorification which ever, under the guise of a " peace " meeting, always comes out. I went to one peace meeting, and I and many of the audience hissed some of the speakers and called " Peace ! Peace ! We want *peace* ! " It was supposed to be a *peace* meeting ; and some of the women began to talk of how they could help the war ! ! ! It is much better I should stay away from such meetings.

To Mrs. FRANCIS SMITH.   LONDON (? 1915).

. . . No, the only feeling I have about my life is that I have thrown it all away, done nothing with it. I have only two excuses, that I started with everything against me, and that I have always done *at the time* what I felt to be the right thing. But I doubt me whether I have been right ; I have always felt, do the nearest duty first ; so one sacrifices all the larger ends. But it's no use weeping over the past—one must always live in the present and future while there is any—the past one cannot touch.

To HAVELOCK ELLIS.   LONDON, 9*th Mar.*

Could you lend me your copy of Gibbon, if you have one ? I need something to read so, and I can always read him. . . . I'm writing a few words to be read at our meeting of Democratic Control on the 11th, the first *public* meeting we've held. . . . The Lyttons and Lochs seem nearly the only ones of my old friends who stick to me.

To HAVELOCK ELLIS.   LONDON, 31*st Mar.*

I went to Dr. ——, whom I was strongly advised to go to ; he's a cad, not a gentleman. I'll tell you what I think of him when we meet. Nothing matters so much as that a man should be a gentleman. Of course you know the sense in which I mean it—now *you* are a perfect gentleman, with all your shy awkward manners ; so is Bob Muirhead ; so was my friend Major Marriott, that's why I put you three, in a way, above almost all men I've known well as friends. Oliver, my nephew, is *such* a gentleman too.

Have you heard that six of the generals have been re-called to England in disgrace ? In the big fight when so many were killed they muddled everything, so that they shot down their own men in masses. They are trying hard to keep it out of the papers, but everyone is talking about it, and perhaps very much exaggerating things. I wish I could see you, but I can't manage to come to you till I'm better because at the last moment I'm always too bad. Could you come and see me ?

To Mrs. FRANCIS SMITH.   LONDON, *April.*

 . . . . I must tell you about two such sweet little things that have happened. One is that I wrote to the Committee of Arrangement to say I was after all going to Holland ; about 50 of us [a Peace Delegation] are going in one ship on Saturday, and another 50 on Sunday. Of course we each pay our fare. But I asked the Committee to arrange that I should have a *deck* cabin, as I can't go below, and I would pay the extra £1 1s. They wrote back a sweet little letter saying, would I allow them to present me with cabin in token of their gratitude that I was going. Of course it isn't the money that matters, but wasn't it a sweet little thought ? Last night too a dear young officer belonging to a very " crack " regiment came to see me, and begged me to go with him to a theatre this evening. I think it was so sweet of him to want an uninteresting old person like me, when all the charming young girls would like to go with a handsome young Captain !

To HAVELOCK ELLIS.   LONDON, 16*th April.*

I did not send my application for a passport to Alice Corthorn to sign (she's away in the country) thinking you would be sure to be here and could sign it for me. *Now* if I send it her I shall not get it back in time and shall have to give up going to Holland. I don't know anyone but you or she who could sign it. Could you come to me to-morrow about 10 and sign it for me, or I can come to you. Then I've got to get the passport and then the permit at the War Office. One hundred of us women are going over. Some won't go because they are afraid of the submarines—but one couldn't die better. I'm so sick and lonely, dear. I long to see you so.

To HAVELOCK ELLIS.   LONDON, 2 3*rd April.*

Could I come on Monday to lunch? Yes, over one hundred of us were on the list to go. At first they absolutely refused to let any of us go. Two days after they said twenty could go. When the twenty got to the Docks they were told no ship could take them. I'll tell you more when we meet. God help the politicians!

To S. C. C. S.   LONDON, 2 3*rd April.*

After I'd finished writing to you to-day, I tried to lie down and read the papers, but I felt I was suffocating, I must go somewhere or do something—so I put my hat and jacket on quickly and took a bus to the Queen's Hall, where there was a big concert on this afternoon at 3. I got there just at 3, but there were still some seats empty, so I went in. The first thing, which lasted an hour and a half, was a horrible thing of Brahms', "A Requiem" like the most dreary church music—now, when one wants everything to cheer and comfort one! But I sat it through! Then came the beloved, glorious Beethoven, his 9th Symphony. The music was sad, the conductor was bad, all persons with German names have been turned out of the concerts and only Germans can handle Beethoven—but still it was Beethoven. I literally cried with joy all through the first and second movements. I felt as if I was in heaven. Surely there is nothing so ecstatic on earth as Beethoven's music, except seeing the face of one you have absolutely loved when you have hungered for it. They couldn't render the last two movements, they were beyond them—but I had the bliss of the first two. When I came out I felt quite like another person. My heart gushing over with love to every living thing I saw ! I thought as they sung the words of Shelley's glorious ode to Joy, to Beethoven's still more glorious music,

> O friends, no more these sounds continue,
> Let us raise a song of sympathy of gladness—
> All mankind are brothers plighted !

I send you a picture of Beethoven out of my programme ; so fine, isn't it ? And then I think of that and the beautiful cast of him when he lies dead—so peaceful and at *rest*. "After life's fitful fever . . ."   No man's face seems so gloriously to go with his art. I think he is in some ways the greatest of mortals—*is*, not *was*, because his music still lives.

When I was coming out, two fine-looking young men were walking beside me who had been to the Concert, and they were talking Cape Dutch. I turned to them and said in Cape Dutch, " I suppose you are students from the Cape ? I am from the Cape too." They said very politely " No, we are Belgians." I said in Dutch, " You must excuse me, but the language you were talking was exactly African Taal." They said, " Oh, yes, they are quite the same ! "

To HAVELOCK ELLIS.   LONDON, 30*th April*.

Things are getting just unbearable here, and yet I can't leave lest I find myself in a worse condition. . . . I feel as if this life must kill me soon. It's the atmosphere of hate and resentment from those to whom you have done nothing that blights your soul. I have never felt but once before that it would be quite possible to end one's own life. They won't even put me a clean table-cloth on my table or bring me up my milk or do anything they do for other people. Don't mention this in your letter to me.

To HAVELOCK ELLIS.   LONDON, 2*nd June*.

I wonder if you saw anything of the Zeppelins. I was so sorry I didn't. I was at the top of a bus coming from

Charing Cross where I go most evenings to get the air and buy my paper. I was astonished at the lot of searchlights working, but that was all I saw. Give my love to Edith; I hope she is better. Pethick Lawrence is coming to see me this afternoon.

To HAVELOCK ELLIS.   LONDON, 7*th June.*

. . . One can't end the business and yet it drags so, and if one's better for a couple of days one fancies one's always going to be better. The heat here was very terrible. I long so to go on the river, it's the only cool and always fresh place. The things I used to long to come to England for were to see the primroses growing on the railway banks in Kent and to pick may myself off the tree, and I've not been able to do either, but I will one day go up the river.

To Mrs. FRANCIS SMITH.   LONDON, 18*th June.*

. . . It's the thought of all these beautiful young lives cut down before they have even tasted of the cup of life that wrings my heart so. I have never met a human creature who hates war as I hate it; why I should have been destined, from my earliest years *always* to live where people are killing each other, I don't know. I can only fix my eyes on that far off time over thousands of years, when humanity will realise that all men are brothers; that it is finer to bring one noble human being into the world and rear it well for the broadest human ends, than to kill ten thousand. It's because men like Paul Methuen and my nephew Oliver do and might mean so much to the world that I feel the risk of losing them so much, and I can't bear to think they're killing anyone.

To HAVELOCK ELLIS.   LONDON, 2*nd July.*

If I could get [better] and work I should be so glad to live; but if I can't do anything, wouldn't it be better one had an escape? I'm striving so hard to write my little thing on war and peace. It's all complete in my mind, but it's sitting up to revise it is so hard.

To Miss E. Hobhouse.   Llandrindod Wells (? 1915).

. . . I am getting so mixed up. Sometimes I think this is England we are living in ; and then again I feel sure it is Russia.

To Havelock Ellis.   Llandrindod Wells, *August.*

I'm so glad Mrs. Montefiore is coming. I hear she always stays at the hotel just before my window. I'm very well. I am always hungry ! And during the whole year I was in London I never once felt I wanted food !

To Havelock Ellis.   Llandrindod Wells, 27*th Aug.*

I'm glad to hear you are working. One's always happy when one can work. One of the great drawbacks to living here is that there are no books. I have been actually driven to read *Oliver Twist* again.

I think one of the reasons why your views and mine are opposed about this war is the reason which makes my standpoint so different from most other people's in the affairs of personal life. I cannot base my opinion in any matter upon just what has happened at the last moment. If a man and woman quarrel, or any two human beings, I cannot [but] go back to the past where the *root of the present always is.* You may have strangely to invert your views if you do that. The attitude and condition of Germany cannot possibly be understood by one who forgets for a moment that only this time last century she was trampled under the feet of France, torn and desolated, her objects of art, even the sword and mementos of Frederick the Great, carried off from Berlin to Paris, the King and Queen of Prussia insulted, the whole land under the heel of France. If in the next century there is a war between Belgium and Germany, can anyone judge justly of it who does not continually remember the events of last year ?

The villainy of our proposal to dismember Turkey is something much deeper than merely the attempt of a big nation to crush a small one. Be she good or bad, we bathed the world in blood to keep Russia out of Constantinople ; we enabled her to keep her hold on the Balkan peoples.

24

keeping up a false relation or supposition. I believe that, in the *close* personal relations of life, this is as true as in the life and relations of nations.

To S. C. C. S.   LONDON, *April*

I have been reading *The Way of All Flesh* by Butler. I think the man Ernest is almost too weak and disgusting to be real, and all the characters in the book are so repulsive. God knows I have seen the shady side of life and looked it in the face ; but, mixed with the evil, the base, the disloyal, there is so much of infinite beauty and greatness and lovableness in human nature ; even in the wrong doing of those you love there come in elements that make your heart more tender over them ! But his characters repulse and disgust you all the time.

Oh Cron, one's never sorry for bearing little things from those one loves. The time comes when you are so grateful you have. Often when he hasn't spoken to me at all I went there, and when —— wouldn't speak to me, I felt " I'll give it up, I'll never come here again." But I'm so glad I didn't. The great silence comes all too soon, when they can never hear the words one would like to have spoken.

To MRS. FRANCIS SMITH.   LONDON, *late* 1916.

. . . I'm determined whatever this war does it shall never divide between me and anyone I love, from my side. The great thing, when you differ in abstract matters from anyone you love, is *never* to speak of that matter. *Great is silence.* I don't mind a bit being alone now. I did last year but now I don't. I don't even wish to see and talk to people. I love to see the dear folk walking in the streets, but I know how divided we are in thought and outlook in life ; I don't want to get off the top of my omnibus and talk to them and be among them as I did last year. It's not bodily contact or speaking that brings people together. The nearer you are in that way the more lonely you are, if your spirits are walking on different roads. I met a woman the other day whom I'd not seen for a long time and the first thing she said to me was, " Aren't you glad to hear the Kaiser's got cancer ? " Now what could I say ?   I've had much too much physical suffering to rejoice in the suffering of any sentient creature ; if a lion had torn my arm off I wouldn't want it to have cancer.   There would be *its* physical suffering added to *my* physical suffering, to make the terrible sum total of suffering bigger !   I think I can understand most things in human nature, but *delight* in human suffering (or animal) I *cannot* understand.

[I have no letters of special interest in the foregoing period except those already given.   Ellis seems to have destroyed (see previous note) such as he received in 1917. She wrote to me to South Africa by every mail, but the vast majority of such war-time letters contained but little of general interest.   Beyond personal matters between wife and husband, they dealt mainly in vague and general terms with the war and had frequent and very sad references to her ill-health and her apparently almost incessant sufferings, mental and physical.]

1918

To HAVELOCK ELLIS.   9, PORCHESTER PLACE, 26*th Mar.*

Dear old Havelock, I am sending to you a letter from my friend Dr. Green, a most beautiful and charming woman doctor.   I'm sure you'd like her.   Won't you come and see me here and we could go to the Zoo together ? Or we could go to the National Gallery and we could look at some of the old pictures that are left.   I hope you are getting enough to eat.   The remembrance of your thin neck quite haunts me.   We are all growing weak and ill with the want of proper nourishing food and this terrible war bread, on which I have to live almost entirely.   If one could get cheese one could do without meat and butter and all the other things one has to go without.   I hope the world is brightening up about you.   Good-bye.   " All of the best to you," as the old Boers say.

or my brother how bad I am as I don't want them to be troubled. I've told no one but Dot, because I had to give some directions as to what was to be done with my body, and I've told you because I fear you may misunderstand my not writing.

To S. C. C. S.   LONDON, *6th Dec.*

I have no news to give you ; have seen no one and heard nothing but what is in the papers. This morning I felt I *must* get out of my room or something would happen to me ; so, in fog and warm sweating misty rain, I went to Edgware Road, and from Orchard Street got a bus that goes to Hampstead. It was close and stuffy but at least I was out of my room. When I got out at Hampstead to change into the bus coming back, I saw a little hunch-back man with an old concertina, with the saddest most suffering blue eyes I have ever seen. He limped away and then my bus came. I was just feeling such a stick in my heart because I had not given him something (just to make him happy and feel someone cared for him) when in he climbed into the bus and sat opposite me. Such a pitiful little deformed figure with such clear sad eyes. I gave him a shilling and his whole face lit up, and then we talked. In addition to his deformity, he has chronic bronchitis. I said, " It takes so long dying, that's the worst of it." He lives in Islington by himself in a little room, he says. I wish now that I had asked him for his address. He's about 40 I should say. Well, that's not very interesting, but it's all I have.

Oh, I must tell you the one beautiful thing that has happened to me. A beautiful dream I had three nights ago. Perhaps you'll think it ridiculous, but it's made me happy ever since when I remember it. I was in a dark West English field with great elm trees growing about, and I was feeling very weak, and suddenly a little brown horse trotted up to me and rubbed his head against my shoulder and neighed with affection ; and when I'd walked a little I dropped down with a terrible attack of angina (I expect I *did* have a real attack in my sleep and that was what made the dream so vivid). As I lay on the grass a little yellow and black cow came towards me with her head down and her long horns, and I thought she was going to poke me or trample on me. But when she came up she knelt down beside me and licked me, and rubbed her face and horns against my left arm where I have the great pain. It seemed to me that for quite a long time she was kneeling there by me, and I felt her dear head against me. I was so happy when I woke, it seemed as if I had been in heaven. I have longed so during the last months just *once* to feel happy again, and now I am happy whenever I remember that dream. It was only a dream, but I had the *sensation* of happiness which I would have had if it were real. It comes to me every time I remember that dear head pressing against my arm.

1919

To S. C. C. S.   LONDON, 26*th Jan.*

When I sit here alone in the dark day after day, I know more and more certainly that nothing matters much in life but love and a great pity for all our fellows. We in this world full of agony and torture and wrong have to bring into being the only God we shall ever know, by love and pity. It is so terrible to be human creatures, the universe is so awful, *we* must make it beautiful. It's ten days ago since I've spoken to anyone except the girl who brings up my coals and water ; and, now I can't ride on the tops of omnibuses any more, my life is so walled in. One comes so dead face to face with the deep facts of existence.

To S. C. C. S.   LONDON, 16*th June.*

I also feel just as you do about Wordsworth. I did not like him at all when I was young—and now I read him with more pleasure than even my beloved Browning. I had a kind of feeling when I was young that I would like him some day, though I didn't then.

To S. C. C. S.   LONDON, 30*th Sept.*

There was a little deal box among the luggage Oliver brought to the station at Waterloo, a little larger than a *real* hard-shell old Tory. Just fancy, to-day I got an invitation to a dance ! The first invitation to a dance I have *ever had in my life*. I have never even seen a dance, or been in a ballroom. All the dancing I've seen has been that of naked Kaffirs, which was splendid though terrible, the real war dances, and Boers leaping about in their heavy boots. All the dancing I've done has been alone in the veld, when I've jumped in the air and thrown up my arms and shouted with the mere joy of living. Oh life is beautiful, while one has the strength to live it, isn't it, darling ?

To Mrs. FRANCIS SMITH.   LONDON, *late* 1919.

. . . I've been reading such a beautiful book, Karl Liebknecht's speeches during the war. It's called *The Future belongs to the People*. It's helped. What a brave great soul. If only one such soul existed one could not lose one's faith in human nature while one remembered them. I have such a wish some day to stand on the spot where he and Rosa Luxembourg were murdered—but I don't suppose it will ever be. Wonderful how that one man stood up in the Prussian Reichstag, against the whole power and of militarism and autocracy. His speeches remind me so of Jesus before the Scribes and Pharisees. Of course he had to die. I knew his father many years ago.

To Mrs. FRANCIS SMITH.

9, PORCHESTER PLACE, LONDON, *late* 1919.

All day I have sat here in this room, sometimes looking out at the wet and rain in the street, and I've thought of you so often and wondered what you were doing and how you are bearing this weather. I suppose it is in myself, but it seems I never knew such damp before. It penetrates into one's bones. There's an old man in the street, where they have taken up the pavement, just before my window. He's got a little shelter of canvas and wood like a gipsy tent, in which he sleeps; there's a brasier of coals burning in it, and all the afternoon his old woman has been there with him, reading to him out of the newspapers while he sat and smoked. I've envied them so, because they were two together. Now I think she's gone home, but I can still see the brasier burning and I suppose he's sitting by it. He has to watch the place all night. . . . Dear, one can't write about public matters. They are too sad, too heart breaking. I can't speak to anyone, and I hardly ever see anyone. People seem so much more *bitter* and hard than they were before the victory. And that surprises me. But there *are* rare and beautiful souls on the earth, the gods have always their own children of light who fear nothing and live for larger aims than self. . . . Do you remember once long ago our talking about what would happen after the war, and my saying there would I felt sure be an orgy of self-indulgence, dancing and dressing and going in for every kind of extravagance and dissipation, and *not* as some people expected a simpler more noble type of life ever after. The peace has not even really come yet, and our dead are not yet decomposed in their graves ; and there is an out-burst of extravagances and dissipation especially among women that stupefies one ; even though one expected it. Women gamble as they never gambled before. It seems to me they miss the excitement of the war so they are making up for it in other ways.

To HAVELOCK ELLIS.   LONDON, *Dec.*

It's just 12 o'clock. The middle of the night is the only time I can write because then the vibration of the traffic leaves off and my heart seems to rest. Do come and see me any time, but let me know beforehand. I could meet you in Soho if the weather is tolerable but it so seldom is. I am better than I was.

Have you read Keynes's new book, *The Economic Consequences of the Peace* ? It's worthy of John Stuart Mill in its large truth-loving spirit. . . . Christmas is rather a sad time to a quite lonely person. I like to think the little children are happy—but there is always the thought of the starving ones in Europe, men, women and children. We are a race of devils—shooting the Indians, starving the Russians and Germans, trying to crush the Irish—and so

I have lost all feeling of sorrow about ——. I love
to see him now. One has no right to form ideals of people,
and then, because they don't justify them, become bitter.
Life is so short there is no time for anything but love.

To Mrs. FRANCIS SMITH.

9, PORCHESTER PLACE, LONDON, *2nd Mar.*

. . . I don't think I shall get better in Africa, as I
might have in the Riviera ; the climate there has never
suited me, only England is worse—*but it's my own land.*
Here when Oliver is gone I would have no one to see about
my being embalmed and sent out to Africa to be buried
with my husband and my little girl and my dog Nita on the
top of the mountain where I bought four acres of ground
more than 20 years ago. [See p. 268 of the *Life.*] Cron
says he will give orders for his body to be buried there
wherever he may die. So we shall all be together at last.

To HAVELOCK ELLIS.   9, PORCHESTER PLACE, *July.*

We must arrange to meet somewhere for lunch. Cron
would so much like you to come. Could you come to
Evans' in Oxford Street where we generally go to get
our lunch? The room is so nice and airy and hot. . . .
Cron is so sweet, he is going to pay all my passage money
to the Cape, so I am quite at rest on business matters.

To HAVELOCK ELLIS.   LONDON, *4th Aug.*

I hope you will have a happy holiday in Ireland. It
will be so interesting. I am so sorry I shall not be here
when you return. [This was a mistake]. I am sailing,
as I told you, on the 13th August. I had hoped you might
have been able to come and see me before you left. I am
feeling worse than I have yet done and do not know how
I shall get through the Tropics, but perhaps I will get
better in the drier African air. It has been very beautiful
to have my darling husband here for this little time ; I
feel more willing to die now I've had this great happiness.
He's been so sweet and tender to me. I dread the going
to Africa but it may turn out better than I think. It is

such a bad climate for asthma and for the heart. It seems sad to be leaving Europe just when the day of Labour freedom is *beginning* to dawn after those long years of Capitalist darkness. Good-bye, dear.

To HAVELOCK ELLIS.   WYNBERG, CAPE TOWN, 15*th Oct.*

I'm so glad you have seen something of Cron. I hope you will see more of each other. I have been worse since I came here than ever in England ; but the last few days the rain and snow have left off and I am wonderfully better, and am staying with my sister-in-law for a time in a bright sunny little house. I hope you will stand the winter well.

To HAVELOCK ELLIS.   WYNBERG, 4*th Nov.*

Thanks for your letter. I hope you have seen more of Cron ; he was quite enthusiastic about you after his visit with you to the picture [National] Gallery. I am so glad he is going to Italy after Christmas ; he will enjoy the art so.

I have not more pain than I had in England, but I am much weaker. The heat here is very great, so oppressive— unlike the up-country heat. I have read only two interesting books since I came here. *The Rising Tide of Colour* by Stoddart is immensely interesting as showing how the white races have committed suicide in this war, but I don't agree with him in his view of life, nor as to the proved inferiority of the African races. Love from Olive.

[This was the last letter Ellis received from her.]

To S. C. C. S.   OAKHALL, WYNBERG, 18*th Nov.*

I am so glad you are going to Winnie's [near Porchester Place]. You will find that much the best part of London in winter. I know all parts, and that is the best. Give my love to dear little Winnie. [Winnie Smith. See p. 375 of the *Life.*] She's so sweet and good. I shall never find people I like so much to stay with as at 9, Porchester Place.

I go to Jessie Innes to-morrow for a few days. [Lady Rose-Innes.] How I look forward to it I can't tell you.

I am reading a *Life of Voltaire* in two volumes as I can get nothing else. [The *Life* was Tallantyre's.] What a great man he was in spite of all faults. His wonderful tender sympathy with all weakness and suffering—his hatred of injustice. How different from Beaconsfield whose life I have been looking at ; small, vain, shallow—not one bit of his work will stand. The more one knows of him, the smaller he becomes.

This thinking over business is so terrible ; this grappling with low mean business matters. [This refers to some business of her own.] In old days men hunted animals, now they hunt each other's labour, the labour of each other's brains and hands.

To S. C. C. S.   Oakhall, Wynberg (Cape), *7th Dec.*

Ireland will never be free till there is a Labour Government in England. I have said that for thirty years. The wealthy classes will never let her go. What a frightful picture of himself Lloyd George will send down to posterity!

Photo by

[S. C. C.-S.

OLIVE SCHREINER'S BODY NEARING THE VERY SUMMIT OF BUFFEL'S KOP
(5,000 FT.), 13TH AUGUST, 1921.

To face p. 370.

APPENDIXES

APPENDIX A.

Speech on the Boer War at a Public Meeting in Cape Town, 9th July, 1900.

This speech was delivered by Olive at a meeting held in the Metropolitan Hall, Cape Town, on the 9th July, 1900, called by South African Women to protest against the attack on the two South African Republics. The hall was crowded, even the sideways and passages being thronged. The effect of her oratory is described by H. W. Nevinson in his recent book, *Chances and Changes* (see extract therefrom on p. 316 of *The Life of Olive Schreiner*). She spoke publicly only twice in her life. The other occasion was at a Protest Meeting at Graaff Reinet in May 1900 (see pp. 315 and 316 of the *Life*).

After reading some letters which she had received, she spoke in Cape Town as follows, as reported at the time :—

Mrs. Cronwright Schreiner said these letters appeared to her most important, as they brought home to them the fact that, in addition to the sympathy of the whole continent of Europe, the intellect, and, before all, the conscience of the English-speaking race all over the world, was largely with them in the struggle to obtain justice for the Transvaal and the Free State. (Applause.) To those who, like herself, had English blood in their veins this was a matter of great importance. They had been proud of their English descent, and she knew she was speaking there, not only for herself, but for many South African women of English descent in the body of the hall and on the platform. They had been proud of their English descent—not because England was a great country, because the England they most loved and admired, the England of Shakespeare and Milton, of Pym and of Sir Harry Vane, was a very small England ; it was not because Englishmen were more numerous, for there were more Chinamen than Englishmen in the world— (laughter)—it was not because England was rich, because throughout the whole course of human history the accumulation of vast quantities of wealth in the hands of the upper classes of any nation had always preceded the downfall and decay of that people ; it was not because England was powerful, for the Roman and the Spanish pelling them to commit was suicide. South Africa to-day lay torn, wounded and bleeding at the feet of England. It was the hour of England's might; but the day would come when England would know that for her also the path of justice would have been the path of peace. (Loud and continued applause.)

APPENDIX B.

Letter on the Boer War, read at the Paarl Women's Meeting,
9th October, 1900.

I regret that it is impossible for me to be with you at the Paarl
to-day. My sympathy and my thoughts are with you.

I would have wished to add my personal protest to yours against
the attempt to break the spirit of the Republicans by the infliction
of suffering on women and children.

Further, I should like to propose that, as a large number of
South African women are gathered here, we should take this opportunity of passing a vote of thanks to and of sympathy with that
brave and large-hearted body of men and women in England who
have opposed this war, and who have laboured at immense loss to
themselves to obtain justice and peace for South Africa. They
did not succeed in preventing the war ; but these men and women
form the last strand in that cable of affection and sympathy which
bound England to the heart of South Africa.

The day will come when England herself, awakening from the
mesmeric sleep in which she now lies under the hands of speculators
and capitalists, will reverence the names of these men and women,
as now she reveres the names of Burke and Chatham, who fought
another hopeless fight for justice and peace a hundred years ago.

We in South Africa will never forget these men and women.

cised that primary right of the Englishman, the right to free speech, would do so with the vision of a manacle at his or her elbow, and that the very prayers of the people would be listened for by the spies of the Government—this I had not dreamed possible.

Now the bond of affection and confidence that bound England to South Africa has snapped.

For myself, I have loved England.

Ten years of my youth were passed there ; many of the men and women most bound to me by the ties of affection and sympathy are still on English soil. During those ten years I, in common with thousands of other young men and women, believed that the England we loved and laboured for was a power which made for justice and peace. That she who had wept over Poland, who had sent aid to Greece, who had backed Italy in her struggle against Austria, whose writers had chanted the praises of Marathon and Thermopylæ, of Tell and Arnold Winkelreid ; whose people had expressed shame and abhorrence at the crime and blunder of George III and his servile Ministers when they sought to crush by force the instinct for independence and self-government in the men and women of the American Colonies, and whose people have loudly professed to glory in their blood relationship with Washington, Adams and Franklin, the men who led the American nation in their resistance to England—that she who had done these things could ever in her old age fall into the hands of unscrupulous men, and under their guidance attempt to set her knee on the necks of two small, brave peoples, striving to force life from them, while with eager hands she grasped their gold and lands, this was a thing I, at least, had never believed possible.

Now England is dead to me.

I shall always think with love and honour of the great Englishmen of the past, who had made the name of England honoured by the liberals of all the world ; from Pym and Hampden, Milton and Sir Harry Vane, to Shelley and Gladstone ; I shall always feel it an honour (as I suppose every freedom-loving Englishman does) to remember that the same blood which ran in the veins of Washington and Adams and Jefferson I have the right to call mine ; I shall always regard with undying affection that heroic band of men and women who to-day in England are fighting, at infinite cost to themselves, for the honour of England and for justice.

But for me the England of my love is dead.

I know not how it is with you; but for me, though I should live to be a very old woman, never again while I live shall I hear the name of England spoken or see it written but I shall hear whispered two words, THE OPPRESSOR !

> Life's night begins ; let her never come back to us ;
> There would be doubt, hesitation, and pain ;
> Forced praise on our part, the glimmer of twilight ;
> Never glad, confident morning again.

If a little child lay in its bed and woke up suddenly, and saw bending over it the mother it had loved and trusted, with a knife in her hand with which she stabbed to death the little step-brother lying beside it : do you think, however long it lived, it could ever look at that hand again without seeing the knife and the blood ?

The England of our love is dead.

But England has lost yet more than the trust and confidence of the majority of Cape Colonists. The day is coming when she will realise that, great and irreparable as has been her loss in the death of her own bravest sons, her loss by the death of the Republicans has been yet heavier. Not a bullet has taken the life of a Republican, be he man or boy, but it has left an open breach in the defences of the Empire.

You have all read in your spelling-books as little children the story of the lion, who, having one day a mouse in his power, spared its life, and who, on another occasion, when caught in the hunter's snare, was saved by the mouse, who gnawed the cords for him.

But there is also a South African version of this story.

There was a lioness once into whose claws fell a red African mierkat. And the mierkat prayed her saying, " Let me go." But the lioness refused. And she tore it and mauled it, and the mierkat crept away to its hole in the red earth. And one day the lioness walked into a stone trap, such as we build in this country, and the door closed on it. And the lioness called : " Little step-son mierkat, come out of your hole and scratch a place that I may get my paw under the door and lift it ! " But the mierkat answered, deep from its hole : " Oh, good step-mother lioness, the marks of your claws are on my side, your tooth is in my brain ; I cannot come." And so the hunters came and found the lioness ; and the story ends.

The day is coming when England will know what was the price of the life of every South African she has taken.

Time was, when, had a foreign foe landed on the shores of Africa, the white men and women would have risen as one soul and body from the Limpopo to the southern coast and hurled the intruder back into the sea. How impregnable was South Africa is shown by the fact that a moiety of our people, in the two Republics alone, have been able for one full year to hold at bay the gigantic and well-equipped army of the mightiest Empire on earth. Had England maintained a close, friendly, and generous alliance with the two Republics, in her hour of need she would but have had to raise her hand, and the finest fighting race of the modern world mothers of the South African nation of the future, and the shaping of that future lies in your hands.   What South Africa has ultimately to fear is not the sword or the cannon or the rifle bullet or the match which sets alight the roof over the heads of women and children. These things but harden and anneal a brave people.   That which South Africa has to fear is the corrupting, corroding, enervating power of wealth in the hands of unscrupulous men.   While we, the people of South Africa, hold by the old, simple, brave ideals and manners of life of the first founders of the South African race, the future of South Africa is assured.   It is for you, the women of South Africa, to transmit these ideals to your children.   Freedom first, and wealth, ease, luxury last, if at all.   It has been said in South Africa that "Every man has his price."   But he lied who said this.   It is for you, the women of South Africa, to show that the heart of South Africa is unpurchasable by any gold from blood-stained hands.   The heart of the womanhood of a nation is the treasure-house where its freedom is stored—a fearless, indomitable, unpurchasable womanhood ; a fearless, indomitable, unpurchasable race.

Finally, there is but one word more I would say.

Bathed in blood and swathed in sorrow as South Africa is to-day, the time is yet coming when this land will be the home of a strong and independent nation.   It will take its place beside France and Russia and Germany and the United States of America, among the nations of the future.

I have a great ambition for that nation of ours.

I do not covet for it wealth, nor that it should stand first among the world's peoples in size or density of population.   I have a loftier ambition for it than this.   In one matter I would have it excel all peoples and be excelled by none.

When that day comes that we, a free and united people, dominate in these southern seas and on this southern continent, and other weaker nations and races are thrown into our hands, I would have it that we, who in the youth of our people have drunk to its dregs the cup of sorrow and groaned beneath the oppressor's heel, remembering what we have endured, should deal mercifully with all weaker and smaller peoples.   It is righteousness that exalteth a nation.

I would have it that the name of South Africa should stand first among all earth's nations for justice and generosity to small and wronged nations.

I have this lofty ambition for my people ; and, if so be that, in our years of anguish and darkness we have learnt this lesson, we shall not have wept and bled in vain.

Blessed are the merciful, for they shall obtain mercy ; no, more than this : Blessed are the merciful, for theirs is the infinite beatitude of extending mercy.

The future is ours. Let us, the women of South Africa, keep our eyes steadily fixed on it, and labour for it.

Though ten thousand shall fall on my right hand and ten thousand at my left, yet I will not be afraid.

APPENDIX D.

Letter read at a Johannesburg Shop Assistants' Demonstration, probably early in 1905.

Among all the reforms necessary to improve the life of modern civilised nations the first in importance in its bearing on human good is that a just return of the worth of his labour should be made to the worker who benefits the world by his work, whether it be of body or brain ; and that not all should go to the man who produces nothing of material use or of spiritual benefit or joy to his fellows, but who expends all his talent in collecting the fruits of others' labours for himself. If we are to reach this improvement three things are necessary :

Firstly, by means of writing and speaking and by all possible means, the general social conscience should be educated to see that the present condition is not healthy, either for the man who lives to accumulate for himself the result of others' ill-paid labours, or [for] the worker the profit of whose work is taken.

Secondly, that the man who lives and grows wealthy on underpaid human labour is as essentially a parasite, feeding on human brain and nerve and muscle, as the insect which fastens itself on another animal organism and saps its life.

Thirdly, there must be organised union among all workers—union among the workers in each branch of labour—a larger union among all the workers in different branches in the same society—and a yet larger union among the workers of all nations and countries, without which our labour problem can never be fully solved. For as long as there is an Italian girl willing to take the work for five shillings which a French girl did for ten, or a Chinaman who will take the miner's work for half that the Englishman or Kaffir demanded, there is always a hole in the bottom of the boat through which the water will ultimately creep in.

I am glad to hear of your meeting in Johannesburg for several reasons. I am glad because it shows that at last we in South Africa are, in part, waking up to take our place among other civilised nations in the great struggle for healthier and sounder conditions of labour. I am glad that in your meeting men and women are combined, because men and women are the right and left sides of humanity, capable of moving anywhere together and nowhere alone. I am especially glad that women workers are taking their place in this meeting, because, as the most poorly paid and heavily pressed section of workers—denied in all but a few enlightened societies such as Australia, New Zealand and some States in America, even that small means of making her wants felt which the exercise of the franchise gives to the other tax-paying workers in free countries— it is especially necessary that women workers should learn solidly to combine.

I hope your meeting will be large and successful.

I will no longer take up the time because I know that other speakers will be waiting to address you. Remember that it is not for yourself alone that you are working. It may seem a small thing for a little shop-girl in Johannesburg to be asking a few shillings more, or a room with decent air, but what you are each one doing is really a great thing. You are taking a part in the great movement that is going on in countries all over the world to benefit and make more large and healthful woman's condition of life, and in benefiting her to benefit all the race of which she is, as it were, the root and ground-work ; and, if you should personally have to live and suffer by the part you play, remember you are not playing it for yourself alone. It seems a small part ; remember it is really large.

APPENDIX E.

Letter on "The Taal" (Afrikaans) in the "Cape Times," Cape Town, 10th May, 1905.

SIR,—In a leading article in your paper some time back you dealt with a practical matter then before the House of Assembly— i.e. the desirability of Civil Servants in this country having a knowledge of the Taal. You quoted as an authority against this measure myself, and (I am sure in perfect good faith and under a misunderstanding) you gave certain quotations in inverted commas which were not mine, but taken from an article by Mr. Garrett, at one time Editor of the *Cape Times*, yet which were taken to be mine by many readers. Later you quoted other disconnected sentences from the same article by Mr. Garrett, in which, though the words were mine, the meaning was not.

I should not have supposed that my view on the matter could have been of interest to anyone, but, since your article has caused a good deal of correspondence and inconvenience, will you allow me to set right a misconception ? [1] . . .

In the year 1892 I wrote a series of cursory articles, speculative and descriptive [*Stray Thoughts on South Africa*], one of which appeared in the *Fortnightly Review* in 1896, and dealt with the Boer and his history. . . .

[1] The part of the above letter now omitted is of considerable length.
In it, in support of her attitude, she refers to "a series of cursory articles [written in 1892], speculative and descriptive, on South Africa, one of which appeared in the *Fortnightly Review* in 1896 and dealt with the Boer and his history," and, giving a *résumé* of such articles, adds a few comments thereon. The articles she refers to have been published by me in book form since her death under the title *Thoughts on South Africa*.
" The Taal " means simply " The Language." The word used by " Dutch "-speaking South Africans is not " Taal," but " Afrikaans " ; the word " Dutch " is unknown to them in any language except English. What is styled the " Dutch " language has now equal rights with the English language in the Union of South Africa, which is by law now bilingual. Afrikaans has already practically ousted all other forms of " Dutch " ; at the Stellenbosch University many (the majority, I am informed) of the lectures, both in Science and Literature, are delivered in Afrikaans, in which also a highly creditable literature, in prose and verse, is rapidly growing up.

Since these lines were written thirteen years ago, and published nine years ago, there has been a good deal of needle-prodding, of the kind referred to, in South Africa, and the results have not been happy to prodder or prodded.

But it is not only in regard to his [the Boer's] feeling for his birth-land and of what he is prepared to sacrifice for it, that brilliant and far-seeing persons may miscalculate with regard to the first-born white son of South Africa.

Hardly less dear to him than South Africa itself is his speech, the language his forefathers themselves shaped ; in which Boer mothers for generations have sung their children to sleep, and Boer youths spoken the first words of courtship to the women who were to be their wives ; in which the old fore-trekkers prayed over the dead whom they left in their solitary graves in the wilderness, and which is associated with every sacred and domestic emotion of their lives.

You cannot deal with Taal as though it were a commercial asset—a thing to be weighed and calculated over ! It has its roots deep in the hearts of thousands of our fellow-countrymen ; and it demands from us that respect and consideration which the wise head and the broad heart are always ready to give to that which has become an object of veneration and affection to the hearts of its fellow-men.

It is for this reason I should have been glad if the little practical measure we are discussing had been brought into the House of Parliament, not by a descendent of Taal-speaking South Africans, but by one of my fellow South Africans of English speech and blood who sit on the right side of the Speaker's chair. For it is by such seemingly small acts showing sympathy not merely with each other's material needs, but with each other's emotions and ideals, that we in this strangely complex little South African family of ours must ultimately be drawn close together.

It is a small thing to step aside to avoid treading on the grave of a man's father ; yet, if he sees you do it, he may remember that act when much larger benefits are forgotten.

It is such acts of sensitive consideration, seemingly so small, really so large, which help to bring nearer that time for which we so earnestly look when in South Africa it shall be as in America to-day, where no man deeply concerns himself because a Roosevelt, a Whitman, or a Bret Harte have Dutch blood in their veins, or a Garfield and a Lowell, English.

We shall all be South Africans then.

I regret that my letter has come to so great a length ; but the questions you have raised are of such profound interest that I have not felt able to deal with them more concisely.

There are just two things more I should like to say.

One is this : If there are any persons in South Africa to-day who believe that, by scheming or by legislative enactments or by force of any kind, they can suppress the Taal, they are mistaken. The Taal is watered by the affection of too many strong hearts in South Africa to allow of its destruction. Every time you try to nip off the tip of a shoot, it sends down a root six feet into the ground. Men and women have died before this for the sake of wearing a strip of green ribbon on their hat or their breast, not because the ribbon was anything, but the right to wear it everything ; it is a dangerous thing to allow any name to be inscribed on a banner of human freedom unless you mean to confer upon it immortality !

The other thing I would like to say is this : If there should be any persons so purblind as to believe that if they could forcibly suppress the Taal (which they never will do), and could substitute in its place from the Zambesi to the sea, as the only form of speech of every man, woman and child, English—English ! the language in which Milton wrote, in which Pym and Hampden protested, in which Vane spoke ; the language in which Cromwell's Ironsides prayed, in which the men of Concord bade good-bye to their wives when, taking their guns down from the wall, they went out to Concord Bridge to do they knew not what, and " fired the shot heard round the world," in which Washington cheered his men in their long and awful winter in Forges Valley, in which Jefferson spoke, in which John Brown, of Harper's Ferry, bade good-bye to life, in which Shelley's ode to Liberty is written, in which no Dutchman, but a great Englishman, on the floor of the English House of Commons, thundered forth his immortal words : " If I were to-day an American, as I am an Englishman, while a single foreign troop was landed upon my shores, I would never lay down my arms —never ! never ! never ! "—that they would of necessity produce a race servile to external dictation, submissive to internal over-centralisation and autocratic rule—they are mistaken !

It is not by teaching men to use this speech, nor by giving them the command of the traditions embedded in this language, that you will ever convert them into poltroons or submitters !

If, behind the Boer when he dies in his trenches or perishes in the person of women and children in camps, there stands the misty figure of William the Silent, grimly smiling, " Fall so, my fellows, true to the tradition of your blood. So we also died and watched our desolated lands when we broke the power of Spain ! " have we not also behind us great figures from the past and voices calling to us, " Hold the old flag up ! " Not the commercial asset, dyed yellow with gold and drabbled with blood, but the flag of freedom !

Liberalism and the love of freedom may die out in the little island home in which our speech took its birth, but in the new lands where nations are being built up there will always be found men and women of this race and speech who can and will whisper back : " We are holding it up with all the strength we have ! "

The day is coming, not in the far future, but the near, when Taal-speaking and English-speaking South Africans will stand shoulder to shoulder guarding the rights of the land which is theirs. And, when that day comes, the first step will have been taken towards the realisation of that for which we labour and for which we wait—a South Africa, not mighty in wealth nor in numbers, but great in freedom, not merely in the freedom from external control and interference, but in that deeper and much more important internal form of freedom which gives to every man and woman in the land, irrespective of race or sex or speech or colour, the largest amount of liberty and justice accorded to men and women anywhere.

It is a long row we have to hoe before we get there—but I believe we shall.

APPENDIX F.

"A Letter on the Jew" (extracts from), *read by S. C. C. S. at a Public Meeting of the Cape Town Branch of the Jewish Territorial Organisation, held in the Good Hope Hall, on Sunday, 1st July, 1906 (the Mayor, H. Liberman, a Jew, in the chair).*

Since first I gave any thought to impersonal matters, it has always been to me a subject of astonishment and pain—and yet most of astonishment—to observe the manner in which the so-called civilised nations of Europe have regarded, and in some cases still do regard, the members of the great Jewish race.

When I remember that all the religions and the ethical teaching which has dominated and shaped the European peoples since they emerged from barbarism has been that given them by the Jews ; that it is the national record of the Jew, rich with his marvellous history, enriched by the songs and the psalms of his poets, mighty with the spiritual weight of the teachings of his prophets and seers, which has embedded itself in the very substance of our spiritual life—so that to-day some are even found to cry " Take the Bible from our schools and religion and morality are dead " ; when I recall the fact that for centuries our churches, while their very steps might be reddened with the blood of slaughtered and tortured Jews, have borne the names of St. Peter and St. Paul ; that to-day it is the moral law as laid down by the great Jewish law-giver that is thundered from a million pulpits ; that for centuries it was the face of the young Jewish mother bending over her child that the artist of Europe with brush and with chisel strove to portray ; that the art and the poetry of Europe has been as much penetrated by the thought and teaching of the Jew as its ethical life ; and when I pass on to remember how, when in the dark ages Europe was still plunged in intellectual ignorance and sloth, it was the great Arabian and Spanish Jews who brought back to Europe the almost forgotten learning of the ancient world, and who were for centuries the intellectual beacon lights of Europe ; and when I pass on to modern times, and I note how, wherever he has been given a limited measure of protection and liberty, the Jew has blossomed out into the noblest forms, as poet, thinker, musician, ethical teacher, and social reformer ; when I recall the names of such men of the last centuries as Lessing,[1] Mendelssohn and Spinoza, men whose vast intellectual productions were overtowered by the lofty spiritual influence they exercised on the greatest of their contemporaries ; when I consider the mighty and almost inconceivable hiatus which the subtraction of the Jew and his intellectual and spiritual influence would leave in the life of the world, I am filled with astonishment that the entire civilised world is not dominated by the consciousness of the magnitude of the debt which it owes to the Jewish race !

And I am yet more astonished when I am told that the Jew should be kept out because he has nothing to-day to offer the world but unholy financial methods, and that he is incapable of any other aim than making wealth for himself.

For ages the Jew, persecuted and oppressed, allowed no social or political right, incapable in many countries of holding real property, and liable in all to have it torn from him, was driven to finance and the dealing in money as the one path open to him ; and he was bound to bend all his energies to the acquiring of wealth ; not only because no other paths for expending his intellectual powers were open to him, but because only by the possession of wealth could he hope to buy breathing space for himself or for his people. To-day the Jew excels in finance, as with his perseverance, concentration, and intellectual force he is bound to do in almost every line of life to which he devotes himself. But when it is asserted that the Jew should be excluded because he corrupts our exalted financial and commercial methods, I am astonished at the temerity of the assertion.

When I study those unhealthy, and sometimes deadly, results which in this country, or America, or Europe, have risen from ill-regulated financial methods and courses of action, I am myself surprised to find how small is the share that the Jew has played in these matters, whether in South Africa or elsewhere. When I turn to the list of names of the men who guide the Standard Oil or the Chicago Meat Trusts, or the great Life Insurance Companies which are to-day filling the world with their shame, I am myself surprised to find that the Jew is conspicuous only by his absence ; and when nearer home, or in Europe, or America, I study those financial influences which have corrupted public life or created war, I still find that the Jew's part has been subordinate to that of the non-Jew.

The cry "Keep out the Jew ; he corrupts finance and commerce !" is not raised by those seeking to save the community as a whole from degradation or loss, but often by those following those very financial and commercial methods themselves and who fear

[1] She was under the impression that Lessing was a Jew, but, when Ellis wrote it was not so, she acknowledged her error.

the superior ability of the Jew within their own fields. If any financial undertaking which is injurious to society be directed by fourteen men, two of whom are Jews, when the undertaking is exposed, the cry is at once raised, "Behold the Jew!" But nothing is said with regard to the race of those twelve who are not Jews. In their case it is supposed that their failure in right doing has been the result of the weakness of our common human nature, and it is not laid to the door of race.

In the Middle Ages, when a murdered body was found, the cry was continually at once raised, "It is the Jews who have done this!" and no inquiry into its truth was thought necessary; so to-day, when any financial evil is discussed, there is always sure to be the cry, "Ah! but it is the Jews!" and as in the Middle Ages men proceeded to stone the Jew physically, so we often, without inquiry, proceed to stone him in thought and word. It is not the voice of superior virtue we hear behind the cry, "Keep out the Jew; he corrupts finance!" it is oftenest the voice of racial envy and of greed. It is the survival in a slightly modified form of the saying which for centuries was universal in Europe wherever the Jews ventured beyond the limits of his Ghetto—"There goes a Jew! Are there no stones handy?"

And one is yet more astonished at the ignorance displayed when it is said that the Jew of to-day, whatever he may have been in the past, has now no power of grasping any higher ideal than the acquiring of wealth for himself.

In every country in Europe to-day, where the struggle for social and political reform is found going on, there also the Jew is found taking his part, and most often a leading part.

Among many others I need only mention the name of Karl Marx, the great German socialist and leader, who died only twenty-seven years ago—a man of such transcendent mental ability in financial directions that it has more than once been said of him by competent judges that, had he turned his efforts to the acquiring of wealth through finance, he might have been one of the greatest of the financiers of Europe. Yet this man chose to devote his entire life and his mighty gifts only to developing those lines of thought which he believed would result in benefit to mankind; and he chose poverty and exile—poverty so extreme that he, with his highly cultured wife and their young children, was often exposed to the extreme of physical want rather than resign the service of his great ideals.

And when I turn to consider the noblest of those Jewish men and women whom I have personally known, I find that the quality most distinguishing them has been a large idealism; the power of grasping great impersonal conceptions, of tenaciously clinging to them, and living for their practical realisation.   It is these qualities which have made the Jews in all ages the ethical leaders of the race, and which to-day find their expression in the fields of social and political reform.

Among that small body of men and women found in every age, who devote great intellectual gifts, not to their own service but to the service of greal ideals and the benefit of the whole race, the Jew holds to-day, as he has always held, his place in the front rank.

But it may be said that it is not the Jew of education, of wealth, whom it is desired to exclude ; that it is the poor Jew, the Russian exile, who comes to our shores with his clothes bound up in a handkerchief and a couple of pence in his pocket—or no pence at all ; that it is he who forms the undesirable element we desire to keep out.

Well, I do not deny his poverty—but at this moment a picture strikes me.   Far off across the centuries, in a long ago past, I see a stable from whose open door the light streams out, and in it I see a young Jewish mother, the wife of a carpenter, bending over the head of her newly-born child—a head which often in the years which were to come should find no place of refuge—" The foxes have holes, and the birds of the air have nests ; but the son of man hath not where to lay his head."   And I hear across the centuries a voice, which for nearly two thousand years the nations of Europe have professed to follow, accepting its teaching as their highest rule of life, cry : " Take heed and beware of riches, for a man's life consisteth not in the abundance of things which he possesseth ! "   And I marvel at the wonderful inversion which to-day makes the motto written over our national life read : " Take heed and beware of poverty, for a man's life (and by implication that of a nation also) consisteth entirely in the abundance of things which he possesseth ! " And I am driven to speculate as to whether the Jew, who is continually accused for his love of wealth and his worship of riches, is indeed the only people who has ever danced about a golden calf ; whether there may not perhaps be other races which still dance about their gilded idol, which the hand of no Moses has yet come to break.

APPENDIX G.

Letter on " Women's Suffrage," in connection with the then approaching " Union of South Africa," read at a Public Meeting in Cape Town in May 1908.

DE AAR, *May* 29*th,* 1908.

I regret that I cannot be with you on the second.

The time is a very important one ; because it is greatly to be desired, that (as in Australia) with the federation of the different South African States, should go the recognition of woman's citizenship, and her duty towards the nation.

The male members of our society, who have, in the past, alone, been intrusted with the duty of shaping laws and public institutions, have in South Africa often shown a sanity and breadth of insight not always shown by those of other societies.

In the non-sexual cases of our University Regulations we have the noblest example of this. This institution recognises that the benefits of the highest intellectual culture are unwisely denied on the score of sex as of race ; and that social health demands that these should depend entirely on the desire and ability of the individual citizen to make use of them.

In the splendid use which many of our younger women are now making of those advantages, we have as a society the reward of the breadth and foresight shown by certain of our men in the past ; and we have no need to fear that in the future South African men will be found falling behind those of other nations in the path of progressive and enlightened social development.

I have never regarded the desire (now as widespread as civilisation itself) that woman should take her share in the duties and labours of the national life, as in any sense a movement of the sexes against each other ; but, rather, as a great integrative movement of the sexes towards each other.

How deeply this movement is the expression of a great social need, felt equally by man and woman, is shown in our country by that large body of its most intelligent and advanced men, who not only stand shoulder to shoulder with woman in her struggle for this reform, but who have indeed often been leaders.

There have been within the last weeks councils held by certain of our men, seeking to forward what they hope will ultimately be a federation of our different States.

We here to-day are met in an endeavour to forward an even deeper and wider meaning of reform—the Federation of the Sexes.

I believe they will ultimately succeed—I know we shall.

APPENDIX H.

*On " Conscientious Objectors," contributed to the " Labour Leader,"
London, 16th March, 1916.*

(A Few Words to the Young Men of Britain who, being
Conscientious Objectors, are To-day called on to Fight.)

One thousand five hundred and twelve years ago at the Coliseum
in Rome a vast concourse of the most advanced and the most powerful Imperial people the earth has seen were gathered in their thousands
on tiers of seats to watch the gladiatorial games in the arena below,
and loud cries of triumph rose as men fell wounded, bleeding and
dying on the earth. Then, suddenly, there leapt down into the
arena one man, the monk Telemachus. He tried to divide the
fighting men. Wild cries of rage rose from the vast audience, wild
with the thirst for blood and excitement ; no doubt he was mad ;
and he was stoned to death.

The monk Telemachus died, and that one act is all we know
of him—but the Coliseum is to-day a pile of mouldering ruins ;
its arena is a great silent circle where only ghosts seem to whisper ;
nowhere on earth are the gladiatorial shows ; and that great Imperial people, the greatest the world has known, has vanished into
the past—and to-day men and women, looking backward, can hardly
believe such things ever were.

But it is only one thousand five hundred and twelve years since
the monk Telemachus died.

*   *   *   *   *

To-day, in the year one thousand nine hundred and sixteen, in
an arena greater than that of the whole Roman Empire, half the
nations of the world are engaged in a great fratricidal struggle, dyeing
the earth with the blood of their fellows, and the sky is darkened
with the smoke and the sea with the vast hulks of the engines of
death.

To-day those of you to whom I speak are called upon, not
merely to stand by and look on at what takes place in the arena,
but the demand has come, that whether that inner voice, which is
the only King to whom man owes allegiance through life to death,

has given you the command or not, you should step down into the arena and take your part in its action.

There are two things I feel I should wish to say to you.

One is—do not feel yourselves too much alone, though you may form only a small body. You stand to speak, not only for us, the men and women of your own nation, who, from the accident of sex or age, are not called upon to stand beside you, but who perhaps from early childhood, owing to some quality of mental structure and of some feeling with regard to the ultimate ends of human life, have been compelled to hold the faith you hold, and have never felt ourselves justified in taking or assisting in taking the lives of our fellow-men, but you stand also to represent, not only the men and women who may be in Siberian mines or continental prisons because they share our faith, but that still larger body of as yet voiceless souls scattered everywhere over the earth, from Canadian backwoods and American cities, from Australia to France, from Bulgaria to Italy, who share our faith. In the flesh we may never meet or know one another ; in the spirit we stand pressing up behind you.

The other word I should like to say is this : Let us allow no bitterness to enter our hearts and no misunderstanding of these our fellows, who, not having seen that which it is our joy to have seen, cannot therefore, of necessity, see their path of duty stretching where we see ours. Let us regard them in that broad human sympathy which is, indeed, the foundation of our faith, which desires always to discover and treasure that which is noblest in the action of our fellows, even when its direction is most widely opposed to our aim, as we would have them to regard us.

At a time when the beloved youth and the splendid manhood of all our nations, Turkish and English, Russian and Bulgarian, German and French, are pouring forth their life's blood for some Ruler, some Flag, some State, some thing which seems to them the highest good, shall we who believe that the beacon light which burns before us is the brightest and largest the soul of man has known— a light which is destined to shed itself over the whole earth till the petty competitions and hatreds and antagonism of races and States are melted in its brightness—shall we not follow it as faithfully ?

You are standing for the religion of the future.

In two thousand years' time the men and women of that day will find it hard to believe that those things ever were which are now.

APPENDIX I.

Letter to a Peace Meeting, held in London about March 1916, *under the Auspices of the " Union of Democratic Control."*

I regret that I cannot be at your meeting on the 11th.

On many sides there is rising to-day a cry for peace, for an immediate ending to this war among the so-called civilised nations of Europe, which, like a cancerous growth, is extending itself across the earth from Western Asia to Southern Africa.

But the question is—"What is to be the nature of the peace we are crying for ? "

Those of us who have lived through a long and desolating war know that it may end in a so-called " peace," more destructive than the war itself, which may continue to be the ground of war and of human antagonisms and conflicts, long after the men who framed it may have passed away.

A peace which is merely the cessation of hostilities, when the worn-out nations lie glaring at one another, each grasping between its paws as much of the dismembered prey as it can hold, is no peace. A peace not founded on broad principles of justice, and with a far-seeing regard to the welfare and wishes of the peoples of all the nations concerned, and which is not based on a desire to produce an attitude of amity between the nations, is but the preparation of a hotbed from which must inevitably spring up a luxuriant growth of those national resentments, consciousnesses of injustice and hatreds, which are bound to create wars—wars which may be immeasurably more destructive and widespread than the war which has been ended.

I take it that our Union of Democratic Control has two objects. The one is to draw together into an organised body those English men and women of whom, as in every other country engaged in this war, there are many hundreds of thousands, who have not desired war, and who are determined that when the peace comes it shall be a reality, and not a hotbed for the raising of future wars. We feel that the Governments have made the wars—the peoples themselves must make the peace ! We are organising ourselves, that, when the time comes, we may be able effectively to act.

Our second aim is to educate ourselves and others for this end.

The problem which we shall be called on to consider when the cessation of hostilities comes is probably the most complex and the most important which has ever faced the human intellect as a matter for immediate, practical solution, and is one which has to be grappled with by the human heart, as well as the human intellect. It stretches across the globe ; its roots go down into the deepest fibres of human nature.

If we are wisely to make our influence felt it is not enough that we should carefully study the immediate causes leading to this war during the last ten or fifteen years ; nor is it even enough that we should closely study those wars and international relations of a century and more ago, out of which the conditions of modern Europe have arisen (though without this we cannot judge justly of the present !) ; but we must deeply consider those elements in human nature and in national relationship which make universally for peace or war, for co-operation or antagonisms, between individuals or nations. We must firmly grasp the general principles on which we are determined to act, and hold by them as a guide through all the labyrinth of complex details.

We intend to educate ourselves to this end, while there is still time.

In that pathetic little peace which some of the soldiers on both sides framed for themselves on Christmas Day the Germans cried out from their trenches, " Englishmen, sing to us ! " and the Englishmen sang. By-and-by, one by one, they climbed out of their trenches, and, on the common ground between them, fraternised and exchanged little gifts.

On that day, when the slaughter of the battlefield ceases, when peace-desiring men and women of all other countries cry out to us, we, men and women of England, must be ready to answer back to them.

On all sides we must creep out of our wretched little trenches of national hatred and antagonism, dug for us by ignorance and the desire for vulgar dominance and empire, which has ensnared us all ; and we must meet on the ground of our common humanity ; each bearing in his hand something he is willing to give up, the strongest and greatest giving most.

So, and so only, can we attain to a peace which shall be in any sense a reality—a step forward, even if a small one, in the march of humanity towards nobler International Relations.

27

APPENDIX J.

Letter to a Women's Meeting, held in London in July 1918, in Commemoration of John Stuart Mill; sent to Miss Emily Hobhouse for the purpose and read by her at the Meeting.

We are meeting to-day to commemorate a man whom I believe to be noblest of those whom the English-speaking race has produced in the last hundred years.

John Stuart Mill laboured for the freedom of Woman. But he did more. He laboured for human freedom. Women can best show their gratitude to him by studying his writings especially his essay on Liberty.

Many women have now the vote, and are part of the governing power of their nation—all will have it soon.

If we wish to use our power to its noblest end, we shall have to learn the lesson Mill taught—that the freedom of all human creatures is essential to the full development of human life on earth.

We shall have to labour, not merely for a larger Freedom for ourselves, but for every subject race and class, and for all suppressed individuals. To do this is to lay the best tribute we can at the feet of John Stuart Mill.

INDEX

28

Printed in Great Britain by
UNWIN BROTHERS, LIMITED, LONDON AND WOKING